STRIVING TO BE THE BEST

✦

Brian
Enjoy reading
"our story"

Best wishes
Al Garber
11/12/2014

Striving
to Be the
Best

A MEMOIR

Allen Garber

Quinn Publishing

Minneapolis

This book is officially published on October 22, 2009, the 20th anniversary of the kidnapping of Jacob Wetterling.

Published by Quinn Publishing
www.quinnbooks.com

Book design by Dorie McClelland, Spring Book Design, www.springbookdesign.com

ISBN: 978-0-9759125-1-5

DEDICATION and ACKNOWLEDGMENTS

This book is dedicated to the people who have been dear to me. First is to my loving and caring wife, Kim. She is truly the light of my life. Kim cares for me every day of my life like no one else can and I love her with all of my heart.

Next is my son, Micah, who knows how much I love and cherish him. My greatest success has been raising my son. This is what my son wrote:

> I've never actually known exactly what my dad has done at his jobs. But somehow, even as a child, I've always known that there was something special about him. Probably people around me somehow have known it too. In fifth grade there was an assignment to write an essay about someone we admired, but that person couldn't be a family member. I asked the teacher if he could make an exception about the family member part, so he asked how close a family member. When I said my dad, he laughed. I told him that I didn't just want to write about my dad because he was my dad. The teacher, who was acquainted with my dad, replied "I understand why you'd want to write about him, but . . ." I don't remember who I ended up writing about but it probably wasn't someone I looked up to as much as my dad.
>
> When I was a child I always saw my dad exercising, either running or lifting weights. I saw him do it every day. Although I knew that not every adult exercised regularly, it didn't seem unusual to me that my dad exercised. It seemed a natural thing to do: exercise so that you can become healthy. As a child I didn't yet realize the need for discipline to motivate oneself to exercise, but watching my dad implanted the idea in my head that exercise was a good thing.
>
> I was an active child, but my dad never tried to force me into any physical activity, or make me do sports, or anything like that. Even though in my first season of the 5-year-old soccer league I doubt I

was the one who initiated my participation, I would guess my parents signed me up because most kids did a sport so they thought maybe I should too, not in order to get me on the road to being a sportsman. Throughout any of the various activities I did as a kid—whether it was soccer or hockey or track, or "working out" with my dad at the YMCA during our Christmas vacation, or my short-lived attempts at fitness as a high schooler—I was always the initiator, not my dad. But the reason I decided to do all these things is because I saw my dad doing variations of them. I saw that his activity had benefits for him, so I thought to try the same.

I remember my dad telling me that he started exercising when he was 19, and since I had in my head that, for my health, exercise was something I had to get going eventually, I had age 19 as a deadline for myself. I missed that deadline, but not by too much. After a number of mis-starts I finally started exercising regularly when I was 21 and I've continued that to this day. And my dad's example is directly responsible for that.

My dad was extremely accepting of decisions I made about my life, from trivial to not so trivial. During my school days the most notable thing for me was that he never balked (too loudly) at my appearance or my musical tastes. I'm sure he would have preferred that I would have had a flat top, listened to country music, and dressed more nicely, but I also knew that he didn't judge me negatively based on those things, and I always greatly appreciated that, and still appreciate that. From my dad I learned respect because he respected me.

During my first stint through college, I initially attempted a business major but soon into it realized I hated it. This was a dilemma for me: I wanted to get a degree that would allow me a good living, but other than business there wasn't anything I started out wanting to do, and now I didn't even want to do business. So I asked my dad for advice. And his advice: "Well, you seem to enjoy your art history classes; why don't you try that?" There was an answer I would never have expected. I was expecting something more practical than go with what you enjoy, with disregard to the good living part (which art historians are not particularly afforded).

I took him up on his advice, but actually, him saying that had been a head-scratcher for me for years until I recently realized the obviousness of it. He knew, and actually often told me, that my life was my life. As a parent he of course wanted his son to be happy, so what else was he going to suggest to me, to do something he wanted me to do? The only advice he could give was for me to try something that might make me happy.

I have a memory of asking my dad if he wanted me to become an FBI agent like him. He replied without hesitation, "No, I want you to be what you want."

Leadership is a big theme of this book; in striving to be the best, it's natural that one becomes an inspiration and leader to others.

A leader is someone who can show others paths that they can see have importance for their lives. A leader leads by example.

My dad's example has been my inspiration throughout my life.

A leader is someone who can show others a path that the others can see has importance for their lives. A leader is not someone who achieves a goal by getting others to do things they don't want to do. A sales manager can meet his target numbers by threatening his subordinates with being fired if they don't produce, but that strategy can hardly be called leadership.

A person can't be forced, cajoled or encouraged to believe something has importance for their lives. The belief has to come from the person himself. So all the leader can do is demonstrate how a certain path has importance for the leader's life, and from that point people will make their own judgments. A leader leads by example, and that is all a leader can do: give himself as an example.

A leader isn't leading someone towards a specific path because individuals decide their own paths.

My brother, Phil, has been the inspiration for my writing. This is my chance to tell him all about my life, the life that I have had and never had an opportunity to tell him about.

Thanks to my sister, Fran, for her enthusiasm for this effort.

Next there is my lifelong friend Pat Mahaney. Pat is a retired New York City Fire Department captain who served the people of NYC for over 40 years. He is my only lifelong friend. He has a heart of gold.

Finally, I thank Pat's dear wife Josephine who read my drafts and helped me.

My closest friend and partner for 20-plus years is retired FBI Agent Steve Gilkerson. Steve is as fine a man as I know. He is everything I wanted to be.

Finally this book is dedicated to retired FBI Agent Tom Lagatol. Tom was my partner when we were stationed in NYC. He is more like a brother than a partner. There were times when I believed I knew him better than his dear wife, Jan.

Thanks to all of you for caring about me and loving me.

CONTENTS

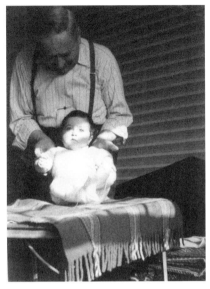

Allen with Grandpa

Allen

The Early Years

✦

I was born in Staten Island, New York, June 28, 1942. My mother, Sylvia, was a stay-at-home mom. (Was there any other kind of mom then?) My dad, Jerome, was a hard working, hard drinking, piano playing truck driver for Davidson Transfer and Storage Company.

We had the first TV in our Chester Place neighborhood and that made my home very popular. All the neighborhood kids came to our apartment and lay down on the floor to watch Howdy Doody and Superman.

Every summer we stayed at a small bungalow at New Dorp Beach, Staten Island. It had a hot water heater that had to be lit every time we wanted hot water. We had to be sure to turn it off because if it filled up with hot water there was no automatic shutoff. The shower was outside in the back in an old wooden mildewed, spider-ridden shack. It was no fun taking a shower.

The families who summered in New Dorp were diverse. Most were from Manhattan, Brooklyn, and the Bronx. The kids were tough and for me it was a new experience. Fighting to them was common and there were many skirmishes with other groups of kids.

The friends I made there have lasted a lifetime. Like Patty, who went on to a 41-year career as a NYC Firefighter and his wife, Bunny, who had career as a stockbroker. Another was John Shea, who had a heart transplant and is still with us, some 17 years later. Mike Marro, a rough-and-tumble guy, built a very successful trucking company business. He suffered some tough personal times.

New Dorp produced my first romance or at least something that I thought was a romance. I used to travel into Brooklyn during the winter to see the girl. It was pretty scary for a middle class teenager like me to be on the New York subway alone late at night. I did that a lot. So much is done for the young love of a woman.

My family moved to Paramus, New Jersey, in 1956, when I was 14. The family consisted of my parents, brother, Phil, and my sister, Fran. I was the oldest, then came Fran, who was four years younger and four years younger than her was Phil. Phil was just four when he suffered a burst appendix. I remember it was touch and go. I have a clear recollection of him saying to my mom and dad, "I just passed gas." Apparently that was a sign, crude as it was, that his body was working again.

There were good days in Paramus, like the many times when my dad played the piano for all of us. One night, he came home late with a badly cut eye and liquor breadth. I didn't understand what happened but later found out that he got in a bar fight.

There was no high school yet in Paramus, so we were bussed to Hackensack, New Jersey, High School. There were no after school activities or late busses so I really did not participate in much at Hackensack. I tried very hard to make the baseball and soccer teams and I succeeded, even if I was just a substitute and not a starter.

I have to believe I got much of my civic commitment from the examples set by my dad. He was a volunteer ambulance squad member. He would get a phone call and race out the door to our car, and then speed about a mile to the ambulance garage to get on board the ambulance. In those days, the ambulances were stretch Cadillacs that looked like hearses; hardly reassuring for those who were transported to the hospital. I don't think dad received much training but he was really into his work.

My dad was also a part time Paramus policeman. Things were sure different then. There was no training before he received his gun, badge, leather gear, and a uniform. His regular duty was directing traffic on Sundays at a local church. One day he was handling his gun and accidentally pulled the hammer back. The gun was loaded and he did not know how to lower the hammer without it discharging. Evidently, between him and my mom, they figured it out because nobody was hurt. I still proudly have his badge, number 95.

I met my first police officer when my dad was a part timer. One of his friends was police Lt. Herb Carlough. He was killed in a wreck during a high-speed chase. I met another officer who became a good friend of mine, Warren Koenig. Warren influenced my career choice later. He showed me that a good cop doesn't need to talk about his accomplishments. Actions always speak louder than words. It was a cliché that was true.

After high school I attended Rutgers University. We did not have the money to pay for my education, so it was up to me. But tuition was not that expensive so it was no big deal. I got scholarships and worked during the summers and at school. There wasn't much time for anything but studying, working, and travelling.

I had some interesting jobs. One summer, I was a mail carrier. I was so conscientious that I got the regulars angry. I would rush through the mail sorting and then rush to make my deliveries. By noon I was done so I returned to the post office. My boss asked what I was doing here and I told him that I had finished my route. He told me to "get out of here and come back at 4:00," and I got the message.

Another summer job was with the Paramus Public Works Department. I met some hard working old fellas. One guy, Les Zabriski used his hands to trap eels in the stream between three of his fingers. Then he ate the eels. Paramus hired many college students for the summer. Even if there wasn't really enough work for all of us, our wages were put to good use.

One summer my dad got me a job loading trucks. I found out later that getting me a job caused him a lot of grief with the union. To make matters worse I only worked there a short time and I dropped a box on my foot breaking a toe. The company had to pay for my treatment and I never worked there again.

While at Rutgers I got my first taste of the military. I joined the Army Reserve Officer Training Corps (ROTC). I was paid some scholarship money and it allowed me to work less and study more during the college years. I began to believe that the military was for me. I joined the ROTC Rangers and became their leader.

I also joined the Scarlet Rifles drill team. We had the honor to march in President Kennedy's inaugural parade. More about the president later.

In early 1960, I joined the Paramus Volunteer Fire Department. I was able to answer fire calls when I was home from college. This was another great experience. There was no training as we learned from others. The old timers were great teachers and kidders. We drank a lot of beer, but when the siren went off we were all business.

My friend, Police Lt. Warren Koenig, was also a volunteer fireman. He was well liked and was the object of many practical jokes. One time he stopped by the firehouse when he was on duty as a policeman. He parked his police car outside and came in to talk to his buddies. Someone (no one would ever confess) pushed his police car down the street and then called the police dispatcher, who was in on the prank. He called Warren on his portable radio saying he was needed. Of course, Warren ran outside to find his car gone. Everyone tried to keep a straight face but when Warren really started to panic everyone laughed. He got his police car back.

Like the other firemen, I was very much into it. I was at my house in Paramus one evening with my girlfriend. We were alone and things were going well, as they say, when the siren went off. Regardless of my girlfriend, I ran out of the house but found my car would not start. That didn't stop me. I got on my bike only to find out it had two flat tires. I still hopped on and pedaled the half mile to the firehouse, arriving just as the fire truck was leaving. I was so tired that when I jumped on the back of the truck I collapsed. One of the firemen grabbed me or I would have fallen off.

There was one particularly close call. We responded to a house fire and the door to the house was locked so we broke a window to get in. I climbed through the window with the fire hose. As I turned left to go to the flames, I ran smack into a wall. I was wearing a Scott Air Pack but as I fell down

Pat Maheney NYFD Engine 283

the air pack dislodged. I gulped in a big breath of smoke and nearly pan-icked. Luckily, I regained enough composure to reconnect the air pack and douse the flames with water. I don't think I ever told any of the firefighters what happened in that house.

Something else happened during the period of my college years that would stay with me for the rest of my life. My dad died on Aug. 4, 1960, at age 47 from a stroke. I had a summer job in a sewage treatment facility and every day I sat alone checking trucks in and out. The phone rang and it was my boss telling me my dad was in the hospital. He died later that day. I know that his early death made a lasting impression on me about the importance of being in shape and taking personal care. My dad worked hard, smoked, drank, enjoyed life, and never worked out.

I graduated from Rutgers University as Distinguished Military Graduate in June 1963. That meant I received a Regular Army Commission, the same type as West Point Graduates. I chose to serve in the infantry because I wanted to go where the action was. I was ready to go but fate changed things.

My mom came down with colon cancer. In those days the treatment was surgery. Because of my mom's condition, the army deferred my start to active duty until October 1, 1963. The army also agreed to keep me stateside at least for my first assignment.

Al and Sgt. Pike, 1966

CHAPTER 2

U.S. Army Service

Mom recovered and I went into the army. I reported to Ft. Benning, Georgia, for Infantry Officer Basic School (IOBC). We were all volunteers and we all thought we were indestructible. I don't remember a lot about IOBC but I do remember November 22, 1963. We were all summoned to the parade ground and were all shocked to learn that President Kennedy had been assassinated. We went into the day room to watch the events on TV where along with millions of other Americans. We watched as Jack Ruby shot Lee Harvey Oswald.

After graduating from infantry basic, I volunteered for airborne (paratrooper) training. It was a great experience. There was a lot of running and calisthenics always accompanied by lots of yelling in cadence. The instruction in paratrooping was excellent but there were some accidents. One poor guy forgot to bend his knees upon landing. He also forgot to watch where he was descending as he landed stiff legged on top of a Jeep. He broke his legs and he was finished with paratrooper training.

To qualify as a paratrooper you had to complete five jumps. We kidded each other saying that all were night jumps, because we had our eyes shut tight when we jumped out of the plane. It was the most exhilarating feeling to jump out of the plane and hear the engines roaring and the air blasting by. When your chute opens there is silence and a feeling that you can see forever. It is a feeling I can still vividly recall. Airborne was tough but nothing like what was to follow. After airborne I volunteered for Ranger school and it would be an experience that changed my life forever.

In Ranger school no one wears rank so that officers and enlisted are treated the same. A captain gets the same treatment as a sergeant. The first phase is three weeks of physical conditioning. The first night we were assigned bunks in a barracks. We unloaded our gear and went to sleep, but not for long. At 3 a.m. we were awakened for physical fitness training that started with a long run wearing heavy combat boots. One of the students fresh from airborne school yelled out a cadence but the Ranger instructor told him to shut up and run in silence. From then on we ran and exercised in silence. The idea was to make you suffer in silence and conquer your problems without the help of distractions. It worked for me.

After the 3 a.m. run we ate breakfast. They fed us well and a lot, and the instructors knew we needed a lot of calories.

There were no excuses. Each student had a Ranger buddy and we did everything together. My first Ranger buddy fell in a deep hole that was camouflaged by high grass. We were running in the grass and he fell in; and the next thing I knew he was no longer in Ranger school and I had a new buddy.

A portion of the first three weeks involved training in unarmed combat.

At one point, we learned how to defend against knife attacks. My Ranger buddy came at me with a bayonet and I blocked the attack but the knife flew up in the air and struck me point first on the top of the head. I was covered with blood and the instructor asked me if I wanted to quit. I said no and I was treated by a medic for the wound.

After three weeks we moved to the mountain phase of training in the north Georgia mountains. We learned mountain climbing and rappelling, worked very hard, and ate well. We began learning techniques of patrolling with small groups of Rangers looking for the enemy. The weather was brutal and sometimes cold with torrential rains. The worse the weather the better, for it meant the Ranger patrol could go undetected. We built rope bridges to ford streams that were swollen by rains. In one case I lost my balance and fell into a raging stream. I lost my rifle and almost lost my life before the other patrol members rescued me.

Upon returning to the base camp the instructor told me my rifle had been found. They gave the rust covered rifle back to me and I was told to have it cleaned and ready to go for the next patrol. It was a choice between sleep and cleaning my rifle but there really was no choice. Sleep finished second.

There were times when we were so tired that we had to choose between sleeping and eating and sleep usually won.

The north Georgia mountains had what we called "wait a minute bushes." They were so named because if you became entangled you whispered "wait a minute" to your Ranger buddy and other patrol members. The bushes had many sharp thorns and we wore gloves when operating in this environment. One day I lost my gloves in the bushes but didn't want to delay the patrol so I went on without my gloves. By the time the patrol was over my hand were so shredded by the thorns that I could not even eat. My Ranger buddy fed me.

The medics who treated us were part of the whole Ranger experience. I asked to see a medic for my hands and he tossed me a jar of cortisone. He told me that if it was not good enough he could summons a helicopter to take me to a hospital and Ranger school would be over for me. I accepted the cortisone and not the helicopter ride.

The instruction was excellent as the hardship had a purpose. You could learn and perform under the most trying conditions, provided you wanted to. Those who didn't want to subject themselves to the rigors left quietly.

We moved on to the Florida phase in the Okeephenokie swamps. The camp commander was Lt. Col Alphonso, a survivor of the infamous Bataan death march. Col. Alphonso had little time for excuses and the patrolling got tougher and longer. The cotton mouths, alligators, and other creatures were the least of our worries.

Army Rangers.
Al, second from right, Al Parrish, far right

As we trudged through the swamps exhausted, I could feel the snakes brushing up against my boots. One time I was so tired I did not realize that my boots became unlaced and came off in the water. I realized later that I had no boots.

We learned to plan well and trust our compasses. Everyone had their turn as patrol leader and everyone had to complete a number of patrols to graduate. When it was my turn to lead, I trusted my compass and it worked.

There were other problems. I awoke early one morning to begin a patrol and when the yelling to get us up started I realized my eyes were swollen shut and I could not see. The medics said I had conjunctivitis and one of them injected me with something and my eyes opened a little. I was again given a choice: I could be evacuated for more medical care or I could go on.

I went on and I hung on to my Ranger buddy's belt and completed the patrol as my eyes gradually opened.

Tempers wore thin as you can imagine. One Ranger student and I had a disagreement. He was the patrol leader and I was carrying an M-60 machine gun. He would tell me where to place the gun and I would do it. He changed his mind several times and I finally said if he wanted it moved again he could move it. I probably used other words.

The next thing I knew he punched me in the face. When I got up I hit him in the chest with the machine gun and the fight was on before it was broken up by the Ranger instructor. We both had to appear before Col. Alphonso to convince him why we shouldn't be booted out. It was the seventh week of training and Col. Alphonso decided to keep us after he told us why Rangers cannot fight each other but have to save it for the enemy.

On another occasion some students committed a relatively serious infraction. As a result we all had to run around the airfield at the base camp. No one dared drop out, but the heat and exhaustion took its toll on many of the students. There were no repeat infractions.

I met many great soldiers in Ranger school and I am sure some of these fine men died on the battlefield. One Ranger was Al Parrish. He was a special forces medic before coming to Ranger school and he saved more than a few students by wrapping injured ankles and treating other minor wounds.

Finally we graduated. All I can remember about graduation is how proud I was. We all really thought we were hot shit until a Ranger sergeant whispered in my ear that we had not seen anything yet. I was lean at 155 pounds and 6 feet tall. I still suffered some from the conjunctivitis, and still had very sore hands. But I made it.

The life lesson I took with me from the Rangers is that you can do almost anything if you want to badly enough.

The army kept its word and assigned me to Ft. Devens, Massachuesettes. There must have been a shortage of captains because I was assigned as

Lt. Allen Garber assuming command of C 2/2.
Major Graham D. Vernon passes the company guidon to Lt Garber.

company commander of an infantry rifle company. A rifle company had about 196 men assigned and was usually commanded by a captain.

I assumed command shortly after arriving. The former commander was 1st Lt. Rene J. Affordit. I don't know why I remember such full names.

I was a second lieutenant and my four platoon leaders were also new second lieutenants. The sergeants were far more experienced and right off the bat things did not go well. Soldiers always complain as it's just part of the job. My 1st sergeant (the highest ranking sergeant in the company) told me that it would be a good idea to meet with the members of the company to let them vent. He suggested that I tell the men that they could say whatever was on their minds without worrying about rank.

Lt. Garber leads the unit with Sgt. 1st class John Walker

I took his advice and it was a disaster. The men started cursing, yelling, and insulting me and all of my officers. That's when I stopped the meeting and took the 1st sergeant to my office where I told him if he ever tried to undermine my authority again I would see to it that he was "busted." I didn't know if I could do that but I was mad because I had been had.

There were some great soldiers in my company, C Company, 2nd Battalion, 2nd Infantry Regiment. Of course, none of us knew that some of these fine soldiers, possibly ourselves, would later die in Vietnam.

The company often gave demonstrations of rifle-company firepower. The demonstration included a "mad minute" when all of the company's guns were fired for one minute. That is a lot of bullets. One time we were giving such a demonstration after truckloads of ammunition were delivered to us.

The demo was conducted including the "mad minute" and at the conclusion there were many cases of unfired ammunition. The platoon leaders ordered that the ammunition be picked and hauled back to camp. We all made the fatal error of leaving the range before the ammo was all removed. That night I got a call from the base fire chief who told me that a fire had started on the range and that when his crew began to fight the fire ammunition began to explode, lots of it. His crews had to let the fire burn. Later he found many cases of live ammunition that been thrown into the ravine where the fire started. It seems that rather than return the unused ammunition to camp, the troops and their sergeants decided it was easier to throw it in the ravine.

I was later ordered to the regimental commander's office with my four platoon leaders. The colonel told us we had screwed up and it was our responsibility to have the range cleaned up. He said we could either face court-martial and take our chances with punishment or we could donate $100 each to the Red Cross. It was the beginning of our military careers and there really only one choice. The Red Cross got five $100 donations and we had learned another lesson.

From 1963–1966 the army assigned Ranger-trained personnel to regular infantry units to teach the Ranger skills to units. It worked well as Ranger officers and non-commissioned officers formed well-trained highly-motivated units out of the 2/2 Infantry.

I will never forget some of the men. There was Sgt. Quenga who was born in the Philippines or Guam. He was always sharp in appearance and performance. Specialist Roger Spradlin was a young free spirit, who was always getting into minor trouble. I talked to him a lot about being a Ranger and he finally completed Ranger school. Roger was killed in Vietnam and I will never forget him. Sgt. 1st Class John Walker was fearless, calm, and the soldier's soldier and his appearance was always impeccable.

2nd Lt. Michael Vincent Santo was a Brooklyn kid. He was a gentle man, quiet spoken, and not the typical infantry officer. He grew into an excellent platoon leader and one of my best friends. Santo probably wouldn't admit it but he learned a lot from my Ranger skills. He broke his back in Vietnam and recovered. We drifted apart and I often think of him.

Major Karol. P. Mijal, Jr. was my first battalion commander. He was an old soldier from World War II and Korea who always concluded his battalion meetings with the reminder "see you in church girls."

Lt. Col. George M. Schuffer, Jr., later assumed command of the battalion. He was another longtime veteran who took the battalion to Vietnam as part of the 1st Infantry Division, the "Big Red One." Col. Schuffer retired as a general and died in Texas in 1981. He was a tough boss who would not tolerate mistakes.

Then there was SFC Walter Penchikowsky, another old soldier from WW II and Korea. He said he was too old for another war but he went anyway. One time I became too familiar with him when I called him Walter. He looked at me and said, "OK Al," and I knew in an instant I had stepped over the line. Officers and sergeants do not address each other by first names.

We conducted winter maneuvers and during one training operation we were pitted against a Special Forces Unit (Green Berets). There was a lot of professional pride at stake for both sides. We knew we were every bit as good as the special forces unit. The exercise was conducted in the White Mountains of New Hampshire. We were walking down a road and one of the men yelled that there was a vehicle approaching. I jumped into a snow bank and realized we were on an overpass. I fell to the road below, shook up but otherwise uninjured. We outwitted the special forces unit and captured them. I joined with several of the lieutenants to volunteer for special forces. But Col. Schuffer would not approve and said he would not allow his fine officers to go to another unit. We were disappointed but proud.

I can't remember how I met Rachael Pursuitte. She lived in Ayer, Massachusettes, which was near Ft. Devens. We got to know each other quite well. The only problem was that her dad was a local policeman and he kept a close eye on his daughter. One rainy night Rachael and I were in my parked car when I was surprised to hear a rapping on the car window. It was her dad on duty checking on his daughter. My relationship with Rachael never really went anywhere.

Things were going well at Ft. Devens when I got orders to go to Vietnam.

I was excited to go and use the skills the army prepared me for—to fight. I read my orders further and saw that I was to be transferred to the Military Police Corps. I had expressed an interest in police work but the transfer came as a surprise.

I was ordered to go to Oakland, California, to board a troop ship for Vietnam. I reported to Oakland, California, and the only noteworthy thing I remember is leaving my friends of Co. 2 Paramus Fire Department. They gave me a beautiful Benrus watch and I still have it today. In July of 1965, I boarded the U.S. Navy ship *Patrick*. The trip took about 30 days as we stopped in Guam and the Philippines. Each day on the ship I practiced reading and speaking Vietnamese with a special forces captain. I cannot recall his name but I heard he was killed shortly after arriving in Vietnam.

We arrived off the coast of Vietnam and boarded smaller landing crafts for the trip up the Saigon River to Saigon. These boats were manned by MPs with M-60 machine guns. I had not been issued a weapon and I felt helpless. We arrived in Saigon and I was taken to the headquarters of the 716th MP Battalion. I was introduced to Lt. Little who was to break me in. Think of this. I had no MP training. I knew nothing abut MP duties in Saigon or anywhere. I was, however, a well-trained U.S. Army Ranger, Lt. Little did his best to scare the shit out of me as he drove me to deserted areas of Saigon at all hours of the night.

I became friends with Lt. Chet Lee, a good guy and a conscientious MP. Chet was later killed by Vietcong fire while on patrol in Saigon. A building was named after him at the MP school at Ft. Gordon, Georgia.

One evening we were on duty when an emergency call came from the U.S. ambassador's residence. It was an intrusion alarm and we raced to the residence only to find the ambassador peacefully asleep in his bed. I doubt he knew what was happening.

I had only been in Saigon for a month when I volunteered for the 1st Cavalry Division which was stationed in the central highlands of Vietnam. I wanted to be closer to where I thought the action was. I got orders to the 545th MP Company 1st Cavalry Division. The day I arrived at the An Khe Airport (which was near the cavalry base camp) I got off the plane into a

Allen and Guscott digging in at Oasis

stifling hot humid day. Just then I heard explosions from the other end of the runway. I didn't know what to do and some of the soldiers told me not to worry, that mortar attacks were common.

I reported to my company commander, Captain Lewis. He was a squared away soldier who I came to know as fair, honest, and competent. Many years later I came to understand Captain Lewis. When I worked for him, I could not understand why he wasn't out in the field more and why he spent most of his time in the base camp. Now I understand that he was doing his job. Captain Lewis understood his job. He had to be in the headquarters so that when MP services were needed he could get them. He knew that a leader or a manager cannot always be up front. He didn't try to do other peoples' jobs, just his own.

Allen at Highway 19 west of Pleiku

We spent time in the field providing security, guarding prisoners, and sweeping through villages near the field headquarters. We also spent a lot of time patrolling the highways. The highways were supply routes and the roads were used to move equipment too heavy for helicopter transport. We patrolled the roads in Jeeps with M-60 machine guns mounted on pods. The windshields were usually folded down to provide unobstructed views and, as a result, I came down with a serious face infection. My face swelled like a melon and I was sent to the base hospital and placed in an isolation tent. I was there for two weeks, alone and reading magazines, while the infection healed. I asked the doctor if he was going to send me home and he said "no way." Still today when my lip gets dry it cracks. It feels like the infection weakened my skin's ability to resist cracks.

The Republic of Korea (ROK) Tiger Division adjoined our area of responsibility. Their procedures were quite a bit different from ours. I witnessed a ROK soldier being reprimanded by his sergeant. It was not the way we did it. The sergeant punched the soldier in the mouth; and when the soldier hit the ground the sergeant said something and the soldier stood up only to be knocked down again. This happened a couple of times until the sergeant felt his point had gotten home.

One night my platoon took over a bridge security mission from the Koreans. I asked the ROK lieutenant how to tell if the people who approached the bridge in boats were Vietcong. He said anyone approaching the bridge was told to go back and if they disobeyed, they were shot. It sounded simple but we wouldn't do it. It was late at night and I was walking over this bridge to check on my troops. It was common knowledge that officers were prime targets for the enemy so most officers wore rank insignias that were dark in color. I was walking across the bridge when one of my troops called out, "Is that you Lieutenant?" Almost instantly a shot rang out and I heard a bullet whiz by me. Needless to say, I asked that soldier not to call out "lieutenant" in the dark again.

I became friends with one of the ROK lieutenants. He invited me to their regimental command post (CP). I saw that they had quad .50 caliber machine guns mounted on four sides of their CP. I asked him how often the CP was attacked and he said never. He explained that the people in the area were told to keep out of the valley surrounding the CP and that every day at various times the Koreans fired their .50-caliber machine guns randomly into the valley below. That made it very hard for the enemy to mount an assault or have observers to direct mortar or artillery fire into their CP.

The ROK lieutenant invited me to dinner as the guest of the ROK colonel. I accepted, and as we were sitting in the dining hall the colonel introduced me as his guest. The dinner that was served was *kimche*, which is fermented cabbage and ver-r-ry spicy. I didn't know this but out of respect I tried to eat. My eyes and nose were running and my throat was burning and I looked to see the Koreans laughing. The colonel said something and a waiter brought me a hamburger and fries. My lieutenant friend told me the kimche was a joke on me. We remained friends for the rest of my tour.

My platoon was assigned to recover the remains of a Huey helicopter and crew that had been shot down. When we arrived at the crash site, all that was left was a mound of ash and two flight helmets. You could not tell the debris was from a helicopter. I will always remember that the flight helmets survived intact and that one had a piece of tape across the front which read "Sizemore." Inside the helmet was a skull. It was another experience I will never forget.

Another time, we were sent to recover the remains of a C-123 aircraft which had carried a mortar platoon. The plane had crashed in a steep, heavily vegetated area, and as I climbed toward the wreckage I saw a foot and a boot hanging from a tree. No one had survived. The division commander General Harry W.O. Kinard came out to the area and, when he was out of his jeep, a sniper put one or two rounds through the windshield where he would have been sitting.

One of our duties was to patrol and inspect the perimeter of the division base camp. As we were walking, one of the men noticed that there were small stakes driven into a number of trees. The trees were in a line, and when you looked down the line of staked trees, you could see one of the division's fuel dumps. The VC probably intended to come back in the darkness and line their mortars up with the staked trees and fire into the fuel dump. We removed the stakes and carved very large holes in the trees.

On another occasion we were patrolling near the division trash dump when one of my men, SP4 Miner, stepped on a trip wire that was connected to two hand grenades. Fortunately for Miner and the rest of us, the grenades did not detonate.

There were also periodic mortar attacks on the base camp. With many incidents like this occurring, I asked the company commander if I could take a night patrol out into the nearby village to see who was moving around. My platoon was anxious to go and I was anxious to use my Ranger skills. We coordinated with units that were manning the perimeter, so that they knew we were going out and when we would be coming back. I didn't want any friendly fire incidents. The patrol was conducted without incident and without any helpful results. One of the troops on the patrol was Cpl. Dallas Mills—a tough no-nonsense soldier who went on to become a command sergeant major, the highest non-commissioned office rank in the army. We probably should have done more of these patrols but we didn't.

Our job often took us into villages where we tried to get along with the people hoping they would give us valuable information. I was shocked when we were given an order to shoot any cattle that came near our perimeter wire. The order said that it was necessary because the VC could get close to our perimeter and get through it using the cattle for cover. Of course we never carried out the order.

On one of the road security patrols I was with my driver inspecting the posts. We spoke to one of the soldiers and asked if he had seen anything. He said no so we drove on; but no sooner had we rounded the next curve when I heard a shot. We went back and found the soldier shot in the head. He did survive. You just never knew.

I was friends with a lieutenant who was an executive officer in one of the infantry companies. John always said that as exec he had to stay back, but that he wanted more action. Well, he got it. He told me he took out his first patrol and suffered 28 killed or wounded. John and I remained friends when we got back to the states but he was never the same.

The army did a good job of protecting us against malaria and insect bites. We were issued malaria prevention pills and platoon leaders were responsible to see that the troops took their pills. This responsibility was taken very seriously. Insect repellant was provided and it was effective. It was thick and gooey and while it repelled the bugs it also attracted dust, dirt, and all sorts of sticky objects.

My platoon was operating near the Plei M'Rong Special Forces Camp. We had a long day when I laid down to take a nap. I was jolted awake and my ears were ringing. A nearby battery of 155 mm Howitzer canons had fired without giving us warning. I don't remember if any of my soldiers were affected but to this day I have periodic ringing and I have moderate high-frequency hearing loss.

In the time I was in Vietnam, I saw relatively little violence compared to others who were in heavy combat. Everything is relative. I spent a lot of time with the sergeants but I always remembered my bitter experience as an infantry company commander at Ft. Devens. We never got too friendly. Some of my fondest memories are of my platoon sergeant Mack Sewell and SFC John Pike. They were both fine soldiers. I tried to keep my troops in good physical condition with fitness training. But there just was not enough action. I saw dead enemy soldiers and dead U.S. soldiers, but in all of the time there I only saw one live VC in combat. He popped out of a hole when he saw us and ran, and we never even got off a shot.

All things considered, we did our best to carry out each mission and to take care of each other. The people generally liked us. I never saw any atrocities by U.S. personnel or spoke to anyone who saw any. We treated the people with respect. And while the prisoners were treated with caution, they were not mistreated.

Then the time came to go home. We flew from the Division Base Camp to Pleiku in an army Caribou. I knew the pilot from other experiences. I don't know if he was telling the truth or trying to impress us, but he flew the big plane at tree-top level the entire trip. He told us it was necessary to avoid hostile fire but all I knew was that we were headed home. We were scared he would hit a tree but he didn't. From Pleiku we boarded a C-141 air force jet that stopped in Tokyo and then on to Oakland, California. I had a duffel bag with a civilian shirt and pants. Before I went to Vietnam, someone told us to bring one pair of civilian clothes and this one pair of clothes remained in my duffel bag for a year. At Oakland we were told to don civilian clothes if we had them so I put on the pants and shirt which had turned some shade of green.

There was an airline strike at the time and we flew to the east coast in a Flying Tiger cargo plane We sat in canvas cargo seats. It was not comfortable, but we were home.

I came home before public opinion was turned against us by the media. I was treated well and when I returned shortly before July 4, 1966, the City of Paramus made me Grand Marshal of the parade.

I was assigned to Ft. Totten in Queens, New York. The post provided housing and shopping for high-ranking officers who were assigned in the New York City area. For example, some were assigned to the United Nations and to the Brooklyn Navy Yard. My title was headquarters company commander and provost marshal (police chief). Almost immediately I knew the assignment was not for me. I wanted to get back in the infantry. I noticed that except for the MPs most of the soldiers never wore uniforms; I asked one of the sergeants why, and he told me they didn't have to. I scheduled a formation of all personnel one morning and ordered everyone to wear uniforms.

One of the sergeants complained that he hadn't worn a uniform in years and saw no need to wear one now. I asked him if he was ashamed of his uniform or of the fact that he was a member of the United States Army. He left angry. But we had the formation and I was later shocked when I saw how ill-fitting some of the uniforms were.

One night I came in unannounced at about 2 a.m. There was no MP at the gate as there was supposed to be. I entered the MP station and there was no desk sergeant as there was supposed to be. I also saw several New York City police cars parked on the side of the building.

Inside the station everyone was asleep in the cell block. There were gun belts everywhere. I woke up the desk sergeant and told everyone to get out. The desk sergeant said it was customary to allow the NYPD officers to take breaks in our station. I asked him if he really thought I would buy that, and he said that if we didn't allow them to take breaks, base personnel might get traffic tickets when they travelled outside the post. I hope you can imagine what my response was. I don't believe this ever happened again.

While stationed at Ft. Totten, I had my first experience of working with the FBI. One of my MPs discovered that the post exchange (post department store) had been burglarized. One of the suspects arrested by the MPs was a civilian so we notified the FBI. Special Agent Ken Sooker responded. Years later, when I joined the FBI, I was assigned to the same squad as Ken. He was a professional, smooth, and not a bit arrogant. He interviewed the suspect and got all the information he needed. Years later when I worked with Ken, he was just as professional.

One of the most meaningful and emotional duties I had was being assigned to be a survivor's assistance officer. My duty was to help surviving relatives of soldiers killed in Vietnam. I was assigned to assist the widow of Captain David Bujalski. I didn't know a lot about him other than that he was killed in a helicopter crash. I recall that his wife Barbara was pregnant with their child. I spent many hours helping her fill out the mountain of paperwork she needed to complete to claim her benefits. She was so courageous. Throughout the ordeal which culminated with Captain Bujalski's funeral, she showed unbelievable control of her emotions. I saw her courage as a means to insure the well being of her unborn baby. It was as if it were yesterday when I think about her and the day of the funeral. I attended the funeral and she shed the only tears I saw from her during the funeral. There were no outbursts, just quiet tears. Then the funeral was over. I did not keep in contact with her or the family.

On Memorial Day 2008, my wife and I were attending ceremonies in our town. For some reason Barbara and David Bujalski came to my mind. After all these years, I decided to find out more about David Bujalski. He was a graduate of the United States Military Academy, class of 1964. He was born on August 18, 1940, in Carrington, North Dakota, and was a captain in the U.S. Army Corps of Engineers when he was killed. He had arrived in Vietnam on August 5, 1967, and was flying a reconnaissance mission when his helicopter was shot down by sniper fire on August 15, 1967. He was in the country only ten days when he was killed. I don't know why it took me 41 years to find out more about this hero.

Soon I had enough of officers' club complaints, complaints from high-ranking officers' wives about parking tickets, and soldiers who didn't want to be soldiers. The MPs were another story. They were very professional and included good cops who responded to leadership.

The MP operations sergeant's name was Boroughs. The first time I heard the name "Micah" was from him. His son's name was Micah. Later I read about Micah in the bible. I saw the TV series *The Rifleman* in which the sheriff was Micah and that's what I named my son.

In 1967, I asked the army for a transfer to the infantry. My request was denied because the military police needed junior officers like me. I tried very hard for a transfer, with no success. I always had an interest in the FBI and meeting Ken Sooker brought back that interest.

So I applied to the FBI and was accepted after a series of interviews. At that time the FBI was looking for ex-military but a hitch developed. The army said they would discharge me only if I was finally accepted by the FBI. The FBI said they would not accept me until I was discharged from the army. So there was a stalemate for several months. I don't know who gave in but, on April 22, 1968, I became a special agent of the Federal Bureau of Investigation.

Allen, FBI photo

FBI Service

I reported to Washington, D.C. and was sworn in as a special agent. Training was in Washington, D.C. and at the FBI Training Academy in Quantico, Virginia. I had to find a place to live during the training and looked up John, the lieutenant I met in Vietnam. He is the lieutenant who was commanding 28 men who were either killed or wounded in his first combat operation.

John agreed to let me live with him and I soon found that so much had changed since Vietnam. He was not the man I knew in Vietnam. We argued and disagreed. Our friendship lasted until I moved to Quantico. To this day, I still feel badly for John.

The FBI training academy at Quantico was somewhat like army basic school. We lived in barracks, had curfews, and were inspected frequently. There were some real characters at the academy. One was Big George Zeiss who was in charge of firearms and defensive tactics training. His name fit; he was about 6´7˝. I don't remember anything in particular he taught, but I remember his size.

The class of FBI recruits was full of enthusiasm and raring to go. For one week, we were each assigned to work with a veteran agent in the Washington Field Office. I worked for an agent assigned to the squad who investigated interstate thefts of motor vehicles. I wanted to work all the time, a quality that stayed with me through my career, and I nearly drove the agent crazy. He kept telling me to slow down or we would run out of work.

Graduation from the academy was held at the Old Post Office Building in Washington. Director Hoover was to award us our credentials and the agent in charge told us all sorts of dos and don'ts regarding our meeting with Mr. Hoover. For instance, he told us to be sure to wipe our right hands with a handkerchief because the director hated sweaty hands. The graduation went off without a hitch and I saw that Mr. Hoover's assistants were more concerned than he was about our behavior. More about that later.

MINNEAPOLIS FBI

My first assignment was to the Minneapolis Field Office. I have no idea why I was assigned to Minneapolis as I had never been there. Evidently, it had to do with the needs of the bureau. I got an apartment in Plymouth, Minnesota, and reported for work.

I was assigned to work with Agent Tren Basford, an older, very experienced agent. He treated me kindly and tried to guide me; pretty soon I was on my own. Tren later died while piloting a small plane during an FBI operation. Tren died on August 25, 1977, at about 5 p.m. I was long gone from Minneapolis, but I found out he was the pilot of a Cessna 172 float plane. Special Agent Mark A. Kirkland, age 33, was his passenger. Tren was a 35-year veteran of the FBI. Their plane crashed on Dewey Lake near Hibbing, Minnesota. I don't know much about the mission he was on except that he was part of surveillance in a domestic security case. In fact there is a book entitled *The Secret Spy War Over Nerve Gas* written by David Wise that mentions Tren's mission.

Now back to my Minneapolis FBI experiences. My first case involved a Baltimore man who had been charged with interstate flight to avoid prosecution for bigamy. We arrested him in an apartment in Minneapolis and

I was thrilled with my first arrest. It was just a bigamist, but you have to begin somewhere.

I was in Minneapolis only a few months when I was transferred to Grand Forks, North Dakota. It was quite a change from New Jersey to North Dakota.

GRAND FORKS, NORTH DAKOTA, FBI

I arrived in Grand Forks, got a motel room, and knew nobody. The first night was memorable. I was a heavy smoker and tobacco chewer, habits I picked up in Vietnam where the army gave us free cigarettes. When I wasn't smoking, I chewed Red Man tobacco. So I was sitting in my motel room with nothing to do and I looked in the mirror and saw that my teeth were yellow. It really shook me up; I never smoked another cigarette. It was 1969.

I met the two agents assigned to the Grand Forks office. Merle Nelson was the senior agent and Bill McClain was the other agent. Both were fine men, full of enthusiasm, and a perfect fit for me. They taught me the ropes and soon I went out on my own.

My duties took me to the Indian Reservation near Devils Lake, North Dakota. I worked alone and got to know some very good cops who were there when I needed help. My closest working buddy was ND Crime Bureau Agent Milt Lennick. Like me, Milt also worked alone in the sparsely populated areas of North Dakota. He often went with me even though his duties were different than mine.

I also became friends with ND Highway Patrol Officer Gordon Engen. It was strictly against bureau policy for agents to help local or state officers, but on many nights I stayed over in Devils Lake. Since there was not a lot to do, I rode with Gordon when he was on duty at night.

One night Gordon stopped a drunk driver. I helped get the man under control, and Gordon said he was glad I was there because he was certain the drunk would later accuse him of mistreatment. All I could think of was that I would be fired if my bosses got word that I was with Gordon. Luckily, I never had to testify and no one found out I had been with Gordon.

Senior Agent Merle Nelson assigned me to work in the Bemidji and International Falls area, located many hours from Grand Forks. I willingly accepted the assignment.

For one case, I had to travel to International Falls which is at least five hours from Grand Forks. I was assigned to capture a military deserter and, before I left, I called the local sheriff and asked if he knew the fugitive. The sheriff did know the wanted man and said he would be happy to help in the arrest.

Some agents chose to ask local authorities to arrest their fugitives. The agents would then arrange to have the arrested person transported to court. I always believed that we all had our jobs to do and that was why there are different agencies enforcing the laws. That is why I would never ask someone else to do my job, though I would never hesitate to ask for help. I made the appointment to meet the sheriff and drove to Bemidji. I had some work there before I left for International Falls the next morning. It was winter but the roads were fairly clear. When I went to the sheriff's office, he asked me to wait while he went to the bathroom. While I was waiting, I heard a bell ringing and realized his teletype machine was receiving a message.

The message said there was a bank robbery in Grand Forks and the assistant special agent in charge (ASAC) of the FBI in Minneapolis wanted me to report there immediately. I called Minneapolis and spoke to ASAC Dick Ash, explained where I was, and asked if someone else could respond to the bank robbery. He told me the other agents, Merle and Bill, were in court in Fargo, and I had to go. So I followed my order, left the sheriff a note, and left. I never talked to the sheriff again and was transferred shortly after that. I wonder if he ever knew what happened to me while he was in the bathroom.

I drove back to Grand Forks at a very high rate of speed and when I got there the police had arrested a suspect. A detective and I interrogated him and he confessed. We gathered evidence at the crime scene and I think ASAC Ash was right to send me there even though it was a very long drive. It was okay to ask the police for help but the FBI had to be there too.

Since I didn't know anyone my age in Grand Forks, I drove to Minneapolis on most weekends. One late afternoon, I was driving on Interstate 94 towards Minneapolis and not paying attention to my speed. The speed limit was 75 m.p.h. and I looked in my rearview mirror to see a Minnesota state trooper car come over a crest with its red lights on. The trooper pulled next to me and activated a light on the side of his car which said STOP. I pulled over and the trooper asked me if I knew how fast I was going. He told me I was doing 115 m.p.h. and I kept quiet. I expected a ticket and then to be on my way but the trooper said he was issuing me a summons and I would have to immediately pay the local judge because I had an out-of-state license. I didn't argue and then he told me that since the judge was gone for the weekend, I would have to spend the weekend in jail.

I almost fainted. If the bureau found out I was in jail, I would be fired for sure. I told the trooper I was an FBI agent and explained my situation and where I was going. He looked at me, thought a while, and asked me why I didn't identify myself when I was stopped. I told him I was embarrassed and he gave me a warning to keep within the speed limit. He also told me my front headlight was out and I slinked back to my car and drove 65 m.p.h. the rest of the way.

Agent Bill McClain gave me reason to stay in Grand Forks on weekends and it changed my life. He introduced me to Marian, my future wife. Bill told Marian I was new in town and needed a bank. We were married in San Francisco in 1970. Marian died of cancer on June 10, 1999.

SAN FRANCISCO FBI

In May of 1969, I received orders transferring me to San Francisco where I was assigned to the selective service and military deserter squad. We chased draft dodgers and deserters and I couldn't imagine a worse place and time to be assigned such duties.

My partner was Dick Weaver, a great guy who as enthusiastic as I was. The problem was that outside of the FBI and the police we were very unpopular. But we did our job, working mostly in the Haight-Ashbury section of San Francisco looking for selective service violators. I have been in some pretty dirty places but none compared to the apartments we went to in Haight Ashbury. I learned a valuable lesson on one occasion when we were in an apartment and I was interviewing someone. They invited me to sit on the couch and later that day I developed a nasty red rash on my legs and butt. Lesson learned.

We worked very closely with the police. They helped us and we backed them up when asked. It conflicted with bureau policy which dictated that agents cannot help police if there is no federal violation, but you do what you have to.

The military deserter business was a dirty one. One of the agents developed an informant who would tell us where the deserter was, but not until he was ready to. He would get these guys to come to his apartment and, when they were not aware, he would look in their wallets and, if he saw a military ID, he would let the agent know. We arrested many deserters this way.

Having returned from Vietnam about three years ago, I had little sympathy for deserters and draft dodgers. After about a year the work started to wear me down and I began to feel that we were the odd balls.

The rumor was that the only place you get a transfer to was New York. But, before I made any decision, Marian and I had decided to get married. So on Feb. 14, 1970, we were married in San Francisco; our mothers and Marian's brother were there for the event.

NEW YORK FBI

We decided that I would ask for a transfer to New York City and the transfer was approved on June 26, 1970. We bought a house in Westwood, New Jersey, for $23,000 and no money down. I used my Veterans Benefits and obtained a VA loan; Marian got a job in a nearby bank.

The NYO was like no other office. It had the most agents, and I learned later it had more crime per square inch than any other city in the nation.

With so many agents there were bound to be many characters and it was also the best work in the bureau. I was assigned to the truck hijacking squad. We investigated armed robberies of trucks carrying everything from shrimp and lobsters to meat, clothing and electronics. These robberies occurred almost every day. The hijackers were mostly mafia wannabees but there were some exceptions. Usually the truck was hijacked, and left at a location where it was picked up by fences who sold the stolen goods. In most cases the drivers were not harmed, but not always.

Before I talk about the cases, I want to set the stage. My first supervisor was Toy Fuson, and you could not find a finer gentleman. He was a soft-spoken man from Tennessee who knew the business and liked his group of hard-working agents.

One of the first agents I met was Ken Sooker, the agent who responded to the break in at the Ft. Totten Post Exchange when I was stationed there in the army. I learned that he was one of the best agents I was to work with.

We worked with detectives from the NYPD's Safe, Loft, and Truck Squad. They were generally a good group and we got along well.

Working conditions were difficult. The garage where the bureau cars were parked was about a mile from the midtown New York office. There was very little parking at the office and many times we ran or took taxis to the garage to get a car and respond to a location where a stolen truck, hijacked driver, or stolen merchandise was reported to be. Most of the cars had no air conditioning and most had inoperative sirens and emergency lights. To make matters worse, the custodian of the garage was a civilian employee who decided who got which cars and when, regardless of need. During the gasoline shortage of the early 1970s, the bureau had not made arrangements for gas for the cars. We had to wait in long lines where gas was sold by license plate with plates designated for even or odd date sales. You had to wait for your scheduled day; there were times when we needed gas to respond to a crime and it wasn't our day. The gas station owners wouldn't make exceptions so we often siphoned gas from one bureau car to another. Despite all of this we were as highly motivated a group of law enforcement people as I have ever seen. Each one of us wanted to be in on the action.

My partner was Tom Lagatol who became one of my best friends. He was a big guy, about 6´4″ and about 220 pounds. He was an excellent shot with all types of firearms. Tom and I became inseparable; I was the thinker and he was the actor. Tom had a temper which he displayed one day when we were trying to park in front of the FBI office at 201 E. 69th Street in Manhattan. Tom pulled parallel to a parking spot, stopped, and signaled he was about to park. He then pulled forward and as he did the taxi behind us pulled right up on our bumper. Tom leaned out and yelled for the cabbie to back up and the cabbie yelled something back. The next thing I knew Tom was out of the car and had walked to the front of the taxi where he climbed on the hood and the roof of the cab and down the trunk. He walked to the driver's side, said something to the taxi driver, and got back in our car. The taxi driver backed up and we parked.

Jerry Jennings was another agent who became a friend. He was another real pro. One day Jerry said he wanted me to meet another agent and was sure we would become best friends. That agent was Steve Gilkerson who became a friend for life.

One of the first cases that Tom and I worked together was a particularly brutal hijacking case. Two men, James Kaylor and Willie Glen Hopkins, hijacked a man named Carl Wolverton at gunpoint. Wolverton's truck was hauling a load of meat for the CE England Company. Kaylor and Hopkins beat Wolverton, tied him up, urinated on him, and left him bound and gagged in a van. We worked the case with NYPD Detective John Flynn, another fine NYPD detective. We checked the van for fingerprints. Several days later, I was at home off duty when Supervisor Fuson called to tell me that prints from the van had been identified as Willie Glen Hopkins' prints. This was Fuson's way of telling us that he knew how much we cared about our cases and even on a day off would want to know this. He was right.

Tom, John, other agents and cops and I arrested Kaylor and Hopkins after kicking in the door of their Brooklyn apartment. Both were convicted. Kaylor got ten years and Hopkins got seven.

An interesting note is that John and I became good friends until an unfortunate event changed things. John retired from the NYPD, moved to Arizona, and applied for a job there. He asked to use me as a reference but bureau policy prohibits agents from allowing our names to be used as references. Unfortunately, I followed policy and lost a very good friend.

Another bureau policy was that we were not allowed to take bureau cars home. Often we worked so late that buses and trains to New Jersey stopped running. The parking garages where we parked our own cars were also closed. The dilemma was take a bureau car home and risk discipline or being fired, or find a place to stay in the city. Fortunately for guys on the hijacking squad, Steve Gilkerson lived just down the street from the FBI office. There were many nights when Steve had guests sleeping on his floor.

In June 1971, I attended FBI photography school in Washington, D.C. One day our instructor asked if any of us wanted to meet Director J. Edgar Hoover. I said I did and my classmates made fun of me. They said if Mr. Hoover didn't like something I said, I could find myself in Butte, Montana. Butte's reputation was that of a place where agents were exiled to. They asked me if I was trying to "brown nose" the director. I didn't say anything and the next day I reported to the FBI building. I was taken to an office outside of the director's office where an agent asked for my ID. He returned shortly and told me the director would see me soon. A few minutes later the agent ushered me into the director's office. There I saw large glass-topped desk that was spotless. Behind the desk was a large mirror and the agent told me to sit in an easy chair. The door opened and in walked the director.

I was thinking I was meeting U.S. history. The director gave me a firm handshake and thanked me for coming to see him. He told me he enjoyed seeing and talking with his agents. He asked me how I enjoyed my assignment in NYC and I told him living was difficult there. I told him I really enjoyed the work. He stood up and asked me if I'd like to have a picture taken. I said certainly, and a photographer immediately came in and photographed us shaking hands. Director Hoover told me I would have an autographed copy in two weeks and, sure enough, it came in two weeks.

It was signed by the director and addressed to me. I was thrilled. Director Hoover had a firm handshake. He was sharp and interesting to meet and when I got back to class the other agents asked how it went. I told them I wouldn't tell them anything.

Sometime later Supervisor Toy Fuson retired and Guy Berado took his place. That's when things really got interesting. Guy was a no-nonsense old-timer. He was smart and he knew NYC and its criminals. Guy had a remarkable style in terms of rewarding good work. He told us that what we did during the work hours was our business but when we were needed we'd better respond. Those agents who worked hardest and produced the most

FBI Hijack Squad.
Left to right: Bruce Brotman, unknown, Guy Berado, Sam Witchener, John Good,
Allen Garber, Assistant Director J. Wallace Laprade, Tom Lagatol, Tom Armstrong

results got the good cases and the new bureau cars. Tom, Steve, and I got the new cars and the good cases.

Guy demanded loyalty and that got me in trouble. The next rank above supervisor is assistant agent in charge (ASAC). Art Nehrbass was ASAC when I worked for Guy Berado. Nehrbass was a real go-getter who didn't have time to honor protocol. He summoned me and some other agents, and told us that intelligence had been received that an El Al airliner was to be attacked at JFK Airport in New York. He told me to take a specialty firearm up to the NYPD outdoor gun range to familiarize me with the rifle. I was friends with Lt. Frank McGee, the chief firearms and tactics instructor for the PD. He welcomed me to the range and I was firing away when I heard Lt. McGee on the loud speaker, telling me to come to his office ASAP. He told me my supervisor was looking for me and that my supervisor was not happy.

I called Guy and he said, "Where the ---- are you." I told him where I was and Guy asked me why I hadn't notified him. I said the ASAC told me to go to the range and Guy reminded me who I worked for. I apologized and he said to continue at the range.

After preparation, Steve Gilkerson, Tom Lagatol, and I, along with others, reported to ASAC Nehrbass at the airport. He had set up a trailer as his headquarters. Other agents had brought the sleek Cadillac limo that was maintained at the NYO for Director Hoover's use and we couldn't believe our eyes. Art Nehrbass removed a semiautomatic pistol from his holster and slammed it on the desk. Here is the plan, he said. I should note that the bureau had not yet converted from revolvers to semi-automatic pistols. Nehrbass told us that we would be in the director's Cadillac, and when the attackers crashed through the fence we would ram them with the director's limo. We all consented but hoped we would not have to do it. For days, 24 hours a day, we sat in the director's Cadillac eating sandwiches and drinking coffee and soda. If the director ever saw us we would have been history. The attack, fortunately, never came off. We all loved working for Nehrbass, who was affectionately known as "Crazy Otto."

Perhaps the most noteworthy case for our hijacking squad involved Henry Paul Caron, who was known as Buzzy. The case began in April 1972 when an agent on our squad, Pat Colgan, received information that a known hijacker, Billy Battista, had been frequently seen with a new face. The information was that Battista and his new friend were hijacking trucks for John Gotti. Pat had great sources, so the information was taken seriously.

We began a surveillance of Battista to identify the unknown person or to catch both of them in the act of hijacking. The surveillance continued and finally the new face was identified as Henry Paul Caron, aka Buzzy. It was quickly determined that Caron was wanted as a parole violator and that a warrant had been issued for his arrest.

Surveillances are not a good way to keep track of criminals because eventually they spot you, no matter how discreet you try to be. On April 24, 1972, most of the hijacking squad was looking for Buzzy Caron. Pat Colgan and his partner Tom D'Onofrio spotted Buzzy driving a dark Olds 98. Pat recognized one of the passengers as Mikey Castello, aka Little Mikey. There was another passenger that neither Pat nor Tom recognized. D'Onofrio radioed that they had spotted Buzzy and would try to stop him. Tom Lagatol and I were in another car some distance from Colgan and D'Onofrio. We tried our best to reach them but traffic was heavy as it always was. Moments later D'Onofrio radioed that he was chasing Buzzy. It was about 2:30 p.m. and school was just getting out in the vicinity of the chase. Caron showed no regard for the children as he sped through Queens at 50 to 60 m.p.h.

The chase was dangerous because Caron didn't care about innocent people. He blew through red lights and stop signs at crazy speeds. Our bureau cars were not well-equipped for a chase as some of the cars had sirens and some didn't. Our emergency red lights were also not the best. Despite all of this, we kept up as citizens were calling out directions to us as the chase continued.

At one point Lagatol and I were stopped in traffic and I got out and ran up the line of traffic telling people we had a police emergency and to get out of the way. Some did and some didn't.

During the chase Colgan burned the brakes out of the Bureau Rambler car. When Pat told D'Onofrio he would have to discontinue the chase, Tom told him to keep going because we were going to get the mother fucker. The chase continued.

As the FBI car rounded a corner the agents saw that Caron's car had T-boned another car at the intersection of Atlantic Avenue and 92nd Street. They approached Caron's car but the only way they could stop was to sideswipe parked cars because the brakes on the Rambler were shot. They stopped by colliding into Caron's car. Pat and Tom approached Caron's car on foot, very carefully. As Pat approached the passenger side, he heard a female voice

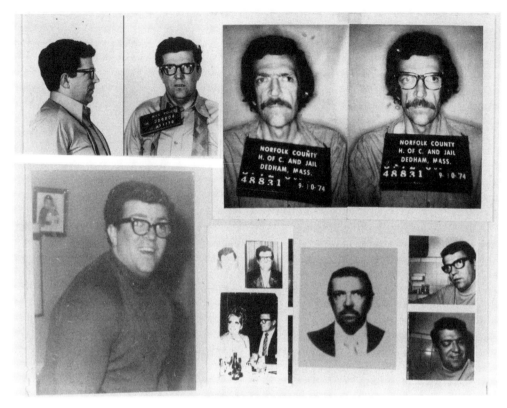

Buzzy Caron, before and after

tell him to look in the wrecked car. Pat looked up to see Buzzy rising up from the front seat of the wrecked car. Buzzy began to shoot at Colgan. Pat was returning fire and could hear the bullets whizzing by his head.

D'Onofrio also fired at the car and Caron calmly sat up and drove away. Little Mikey and the other passenger had gotten out somewhere along the chase route. Caron's bullet riddled getaway car was found sometime later. The woman who saved Pat's life by warning him was later identified as a Catholic Nun.

By the time Tom Lagatol and I and other agents got there Caron was long gone. Lagatol and I began a search for Caron that was unparalled. Tom

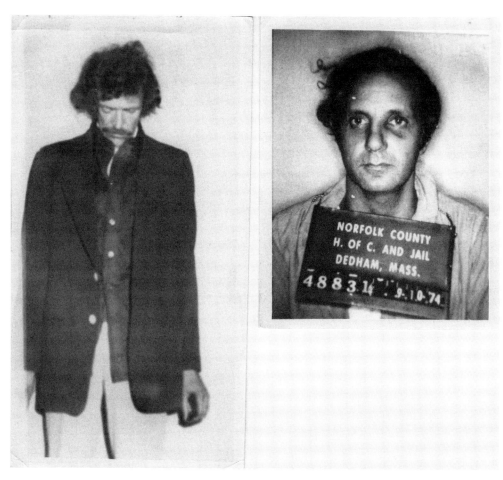

Buzzy Caron and Mike Castello

and I led the search but there were many other agents who participated. The word went out to all our sources that we wanted Caron at any price.

We kept up surveillances on known hangouts. One was the Bergen Hunt and Fish Club in South Ozone Park, Queens. We knew it was a major hangout for John Gotti, Gene Gotti, and others. Raid after raid was conducted there; each time we didn't find Caron we made it clear that the pressure would continue. We believed that, if we disrupted the crew's operation, at some point someone would give up Caron. That didn't happen.

Keeping up the pressure we learned that John Gotti was wanted for a murder that had occurred in Queens. He had reportedly fled to Connecticut and was recently seen at a social club hangout in Brooklyn. A large group of agents began to watch the club and, sure enough, John Gotti, Gene Gotti, and others showed up. We swooped in heavily armed and arrested both Gottis.

There were some very harsh words spoken but neither of them would tell us anything about Caron.

In another attempt to find Caron, Agent Steve Gilkerson and I went to conduct a surveillance of a hoodlum whom we were told was in contact with Caron. We went to the home in a rural area in upstate New York. It was evening and Steve and I were moving close to the house so we could see in. I was watching the front of the house and Steve was watching the back. Suddenly, the back door flew open and a woman said, "Out you go, Diablo." A big German Shepherd ran out the door toward me and all I could do was run. Some how I got away and I radioed, "Steve there's a dog."

The chase ended on September 10, 1974, with Caron's arrest by police in Westwood, Massachusetts. Caron was arrested with an accomplice, Michael Joseph Castello, also known as Little Mikey.

The two had robbed a bank and police gave chase. In the process all five of the Westwood police cars were damaged. The chase ended with Caron and Castello crashing into a tree.

When we got word of the arrest, Tom Lagatol and I were sent to interview Caron and Castello in the Norfolk County Jail, Dedham, Massachusetts. When Caron was brought into the interview room, Tom and I couldn't believe our eyes. I knew that Caron was blind in one eye and that that eye was off center. Had it not been for that fact, I never would never have recognized him. He was skinny, maybe 50 pounds lighter than his photos showed. We asked him where he had been hiding, but all he would tell us was that the reason we couldn't find him was that he didn't associate with any of his former friends.

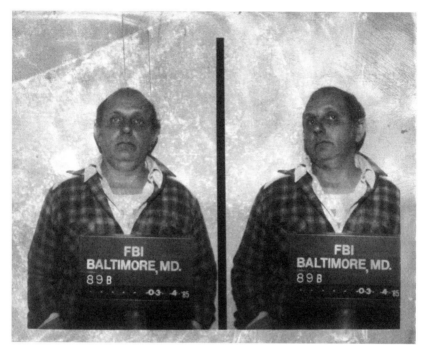

Little Mikey Castello in 1985

We interviewed Michael Castello. He was short, about 5´1˝. He told us that he would talk, but not at the Dedham jail, only in New York. The Westwood Police were not anxious for us or anyone else to take Castello from their jail. But we insisted and got a writ that ordered Castello to be taken to the Federal Metropolitan Corrections Center (MCC) in New York City. Tom Lagatol and I thought we were really going to get some good information. A few weeks later we went to the MCC to talk to Castello. He came into the interview room and said he had nothing to say to us.

"You guys treated me like a gentleman," Castello said. "I'm going to escape and on the street it's every man for himself." With that our interview ended. We went to officials of the MCC and told them what Castello told us and, believe it or not, Castello escaped from the MCC on December 6, 1974. But the story doesn't end here.

After Castello's escape, Caron was brought to the MCC in NYC to face Assaulting Federal Officer Charges for trying to kill Agent Pat Colgan. Someone tried to break Caron out of the MCC by driving a cement truck through the wall. The escape attempt was unsuccessful and, whose fingerprints were found in the cement truck? You guessed it, Mikey Castello's.

Caron later died of a heart attack and the search for Castello went on. On March 5, 1985, Agent Sam Wichner and other agents arrested Castello in Baltimore, Maryland. The rest of the story is almost too bizarre to believe. Sam was assigned to the New York Office truck hijacking squad at the time the Caron case began and Sam worked on the original Caron surveillance. Agent Wichner was transferred to Baltimore. Sam was assigned to determine the identity of a person who resembled Castello. After a violent fight and several attempts to deny his identity, Castello admitted who he was. Castello admitted robbing the bank with Caron and said he knew Caron tried to shoot an agent. He gave details of his escape from the MCC in New York City.

It took 11 years to find Castello and he was found by an agent who worked the original case in NYC.

There were some wonderful characters on the hijacking squad, like Agent Rick Redman. He was a hardworking guy who had no time for bullshit. One case we worked together involved William Kenneth Williams. We had gotten information that Williams had committed an armed hijacking of a truck filled with clothes from the garment center section of NYC. It was difficult to get evidence against Williams until finally we found a partial fingerprint on a hijacked truck. The FBI fingerprint examiner compared all available points on the fingerprint found in the hijacked truck with Williams' prints. They all matched, but the expert said there were not enough points on the print in the truck to positively identify fingerprints of Williams. We were able to get a warrant for Williams' arrest based on the print and the description given by the driver of the hijacked truck.

Redman and I went looking for Williams in a tenement in the East Harlem section of NYC. The neighborhood was not very nice and we went there at night. In hindsight, we should have brought along reinforcements.

The two of us we were in the hallway of the building and I found the "super" and asked if she knew Williams. The hallway was dark and and as we began talking to the super, we heard loud yelling and commotion coming from the street. Redman and I went outside and saw a man being chased by a screaming crowd. A few NYPD cars arrived and rescued the man from the crowd, which then turned their anger on the police. A brick was hurled through a window of one of the police cars and soon bricks, bottles, and garbage were coming down from the rooftops. I looked for Redman and saw him in the middle of the crowd yelling and screaming just like one of them. The police were able to escape the area. We later learned that the man was in his car trying to escape after a robbery when he ran over a child. The robber crashed his car and tried to get away on foot; the crowd was chasing him to administer some curbside justice.

I later asked my partner why he melted into the crowd without me, and he said it was the only thing he could do at the time.

We found out later that the person who gave us the original information on Williams was a friend of his. The source told us later that Williams was in the darkened hallway with a gun on the night we were there. Before he could shoot us, we went outside. We were very, very lucky.

Another agent was Bob Pecoraro, who died recently. Pecoraro was small and feisty. One day Pecoraro and Redman began arguing in the office over a parking space. I heard Redman tell Pecoraro that if he didn't shut up, he would punch him in the nose. Pecoraro couldn't keep his mouth closed and Redman flattened him. They made up later.

Some of the people I worked with went on to fame and fortune. One was Rudy Giuliani, who was an assistant U.S. attorney at the time. I had many cases with Guiliani who was an aggressive, smart prosecutor. Even more than most of us, Guiliani never wanted to lose a case.

There were times when we charged a person without the evidence we needed for a sure-fire conviction. One time, Guilani and I disagreed over a hijacking case that involved a hijacker and fence named Desi DeSimone. We had tried unsuccessfully for years to get evidence against DeSimone. We finally found an abandoned truck that had been hijacked. Empty boxes that contained the stolen cargo were processed for fingerprints and we found DeSimone's prints on some of the boxes. That was all the evidence we could get. We knew through sources that DeSimone was the hijacker, but that information could not be used in court. I presented the facts to Guiliani and asked him to authorize a warrant to arrest DeSimone. He agreed to the warrant but said he would dismiss the case if additional evidence was not found. We secured a warrant from a judge and arrested DeSimone. He was wearing a large diamond pinky ring and had a pocketful of big bills. Of course, he told us nothing. I tried to convince Guiliani to prosecute DeSimone but he refused. I appealed to Guiliani's boss but to no avail. In the end, there were no hard feelings, just an honest disagreement among law enforcement and prosecution.

Another assistant U.S. attorney at the time was Michael Mukasey, who was later named attorney general of the United States under President Bush. I remember Mukasey as an honest, hard-working, unusually competent prosecutor. We got along well, but lost track of each other. We had become good friends through our work. Mike invited my wife and me to dinner at the exclusive New York Athletic Club. When we got there, I saw how expensive it was and told Mike that I would split the bill with him. He was offended and told me that only members could pay the bill and we were his guests. He never invited us again. He is a good man.

Joe Pistone was another agent on the hijacking squad. Pistone went on to do a fantastic undercover job that was made into a movie called *Donnie Brasco* starring Al Pacino and Johnny Dep. I knew Pistone before he went undercover. He was a tough, hard-working guy who could easily pass for a mafia soldier.

To show his grit, Pistone and I disagreed over a case involving a hijacker who had escaped from police. During the escape, the hijacker pushed a detective down a flight of stairs causing serious injury to the detective.

When we arrested the hijacker, Pistone talked to him about helping us out with more information. Pistone wanted to give the hijacker a break and, since it was my case, he asked if I would request the U.S. attorney to be lenient. I refused and told Pistone I would have helped if the hijacker hadn't injured the detective. We argued but I wouldn't give in. Fortunately, we were still able to work together.

We had some big trouble one time, really big. Steve, Tom, and I arrested Carlton Boyd,who had played professional football for the Baltimore Colts and who was very big. We didn't have any trouble during the arrest but that changed when the shock wore off of being confronted by three armed agents who were obviously all business. When it came time to fingerprint and photograph Boyd, he would not cooperate. I told him one way or the other he would be photographed and fingerprinted. Steve held a large, black flashlight in his hand as he walked toward Boyd and was just about to convince Boyd to submit when the former football player changed his mind and submitted to the printing.

Since there are so many police agencies in NYC, there was always a danger that we would not be recognized as law enforcement officers. The rule we all followed was that when a police officer in uniform ordered you to freeze, you froze.

Tom and I often drove a red Volkswagen, which was a bureau car. One day we got word that a truck that had been hijacked had been found in Harlem. A company employee told us he happened to see the truck, but said he had not notified the police. Tom and I drove up and found the rear door of the truck open, and it appeared the truck was abandoned. We got out of our red Volkswagen and then we heard the sirens. Tom and I both looked up to see a NYPD car with two officers about 20 feet from us. Both officers stayed in the car and the driver told us not to move. I told him we were FBI agents as the officer told us to walk slowly towards him and keep our hands in front of us. As I got close to the police car I saw that the officer had his gun pointed toward me. He told me to slowly take out my ID, which I did to the satisfaction of the police. I am fairly sure that had I not followed instructions we would have been shot. We learned later that another company employee had notified police who were watching the truck from a rooftop. When we approached the truck, the police closed in us.

Tom Lagatol and I tried to be as careful as possible. In the early 1970s body armor or bullet proof vests were not commonly worn by law enforcement officers. The FBI did not issue its agents body armor, but Tom and I bought our own and wore them almost every day. We watched out for each other. We had an agreement that, if we were in a situation where a criminal got the drop on one of us and ordered the other to give up his gun, we wouldn't do it. We agreed there was no reason to trust that the criminal would not harm us if we gave up our guns.

Sometime in the mid-1970s Tom and I transferred to the bank robbery squad. The supervisor, Jim Murphy, was a former NYPD officer and one of the savviest cops I have ever met. He was a great boss who made us really want to work for him. The squad was composed of action-type guys; the more action the better. We worked daily with the NYPD Major Case Squad and I learned a lot from our friends on the Major Case Squad.

Jim Murphy had been the case agent in the Jo Anne Chesimard case. Chesimard was a black militant leader who was facing trial for bank robbery. Jim worked very hard putting the case together, but a long time passed between the time of the robbery and Chesimard's arrest. She was arrested about ten years after the robbery in a shoot-out in which a New Jersey state trooper was shot in the stomach. Since Chesimard had been a fugitive for about ten years, witnesses to the bank robbery probably had not thought about the incident in a decade. As expected, their memories were hazy. Shortly after the robbery, witnesses identified Chesimard from photos, but her appearance had changed dramatically in ten years.

Jim Murphy had been promoted to supervisor and he assigned the Chesimard case to me. It was my job to prepare the case for trial. The case was very important to a lot of people and I worked tirelessly with the prosecutor. The trial judge was Jack Weinstein, who seemed to be pro-Chesimard from the start. Weinstein forced us to have a lineup where witnesses from ten years ago were asked to identify her. Weinstein rejected the assistant U.S. attorney's objections that the witnesses would be unlikely to recognize Chesimard after so many years had passed.

Chesimard appeared in the lineup looking nothing like what had she looked like during the robbery, and none of the witnesses could ID her.

An FBI artist testified about his comparison of photos taken by the bank cameras and known photos of Chesimard. But, with Weinstein's support, the defense attorney was able to discredit our FBI artist. The case went to the jury and I decided not to go home until a verdict was reached. I was driving around alone when the FBI dispatcher told me to call the AUSA. I called and was given the news that she had been acquitted. I called Jim Murphy and told him. I don't know if I felt worse for Murphy because of all his hard work or because a guilty robber was acquitted.

We worked with partners and Tom and I were always together. It was very unusual to get information that would allow us to prevent a bank robbery and it was very dangerous to interrupt a robbery in progress. In three instances we did receive information that a robbery was planned but, in each case, we did not have enough evidence to arrest the robbers in advance. To safely arrest armed and dangerous individuals in the process of a bank robbery requires extensive planning, precise execution, and luck.

The first case involved a bank in the Bronx; our information included the bank location and a description of the getaway car. The robber's identities were not known to our source. We had concerns for the bank employees and customers as well as for bystanders. I won't discuss the tactics we used, but we practiced our plan over and over. Our team saw the getaway car approach and the incident ended with Tom and I arresting the robbers at gunpoint under circumstances where they had the choice to give up or die. The robbers had Scotch tape over their fingers, were wearing ski masks, and each had a gun.

Another time, we had information about the location and time of the planned bank robbery but not the identities of the robbers or a description of their vehicles. Again we planned and practiced, but this time things didn't go according to plan. The robbers spotted us and tried to escape in a car. I was driving and was able to force the car over, smashing into a cement wall. Tom was in the front passenger seat carrying a short shotgun and he leaned out and told the robbers to stop or be shot. He meant it and they stopped. They also had guns and wore masks and gloves.

The third case involved a bank in midtown Manhattan. Since midtown Manhattan is very crowded, it gave us an advantage because we could blend in. Our information described the getaway vehicle, the bank, and the robber's identity. The getaway driver was not described to us.

We were able to watch the area of the bank without being noticed. I watched the street in front of the bank while Tom and another agent, Mike Henehan, mixed in with the crowd near the bank entrance. Another team was to arrest the getaway driver. The plan worked to perfection.

I spotted the car and called it out by radio. The car parked right in front of the bank and the robber got out. Just as he approached the bank door he was thrown to the ground by Tom and Mike. The other team members simultaneously approached the getaway driver and arrested him. The bank robber was identified as William Patrick Hand.

There were times when the job got really crazy. On December 13, 1974, agents from the bank robbery squad went to arrest one of the men suspected of being part of a gang that robbed seven banks. In one case a robber had fired a shotgun and narrowly missed a bank guard. During each robbery the entire bank and occupants were taken over while the cash was collected. Our team of agents and detectives had worked for about six months to identify the robbers. The night started with one arrest. There was resistance but our teams were experienced and able to put down the resistance. The robber who was arrested first told us the identity of one of the other robbers and gave us a possible address.

We quickly deposited him in a nearby NYPD station house and sped to the next address where we arrested another robber. The same scenario was repeated and one arrest led to another until six robbers were arrested. We had prisoners scattered around different Queens police stations. In fact, we had to do some figuring when we began to collect our prisoners. This was the type of action all of us lived for.

In each of the cases and in almost every bank robbery case our partners from the NYPD major case squad were with us. The detectives took care to notify the uniformed police officers in the area so they didn't accidentally confront us. It worked great and to everyone's benefit. Tom and I responded to one bank robbery in Brooklyn and the report was that the bank guard had shot the robber. The robber had escaped and was soon discovered and arrested by an NYPD officer. I responded with Detective Eddie Zigo, a seasoned veteran who would be a key investigator in the Son of Sam murder investigation. The robber was bleeding heavily from a head wound. His nose appeared to be broken and he had been shot in the shoulder. He was moaning loudly as ambulance attendants loaded him up. Eddie and I got in for the ride to the hospital. Somewhere, probably in a movie, I had heard of a criminal giving a dying declaration so I told the robber that he was going to die and should confess. All the robber did was yell louder. He didn't say a thing.

We arrived at the hospital and the robber was taken to the emergency room. A doctor came out after a few minutes and he told me the robber would survive and that I could speak with him. The doctor said one shot had creased his scalp, causing the excessive bleeding. A second bullet hit the robber in the ankle and dropped into his shoe. The guard had apparently broken the robber's nose in the scuffle. The only real damage was caused by a third bullet in the suspect's shoulder.

Detective Zigo began to laugh and I asked him what was so funny. He said he knew the guy wasn't going to die because anyone who is shot and has enough energy to yell so loudly couldn't be seriously injured. I asked Eddie why he let me go through my routine about a dying declaration, and Eddie said he just got a real kick out of it. We did talk to the robber who admitted the robbery and gave us a lot more information. He also later recovered fully.

Tom Lagatol was a firearms expert. He mastered every weapon he carried. He had very large hands and could handle handguns that I couldn't control. One of his favorites was a Smith and Wesson .44 magnum revolver with an 6-inch barrel. Now, someone who doesn't know or hasn't worked with him might call him a cowboy or showoff. But I know better. He practiced with any weapon he carried. I'd seen him shoot his .44 magnum and I knew how proficient he was. If I'd had any doubts about his competency, I wouldn't have been on the street with him.

We had been chasing a bank robber who we nicknamed "the rabbit" because he wore a rabbit fur coat when he robbed banks. We cornered him in an apartment and he wouldn't give up. We forced our way into the

Bill Carbone, S.A. Staedler, Al
© *New York News, December 14, 1976, photographer unknown*

apartment. We confronted him. Tom drew his .44 magnum from his holster and stuck it in the rabbit's face. End of story.

Good work was rewarded with things like being assigned new cars. I had
just been assigned a new car. Major Case Squad Detective Bill Carbone,
Agent Dick Staedtler, and I were in the new bucar. I was driving. We were
following up on some leads. Bill knew the area very well. We were on Hollis
Court Blvd. near the corner of Jamaica Ave. when we saw two guys running
toward a yellow Cadillac. One guy got in the front passenger seat and the

other dove into the rear seat through an open window. Bill said there is a bank around the corner.

These guys spotted us and started to drive away. Bill yelled, "Ram them. They robbed the bank." I thought of my new car, but just for a moment. We pursued them a short distance until I was able to force them off the road onto some grass, where they stopped. Bill and Dick ran to the front of the Cadillac yelling for the occupants to freeze. I ran to the back window and saw the guy on the floor pulling a gun out of a zippered case. I yelled, "Freeze," but he continued to draw the gun. I pulled the trigger but my gun malfunctioned; well it was more like operator error. The gun I was carrying was a semi-automatic pistol. It carried more rounds than the bureau authorized revolvers. But several of us carried these guns even though they were not approved by the bureau. The reason was that there had been a recent shootout where a bureau agent was carrying a semi-automatic and, because it contained many rounds, he was able to shoot a criminal who had a detective pinned down under fire. The downside to carrying the semi-automatic was that during firearms training we could not practice with it because it was not authorized. Any practice with the semi-automatic was done on our own time. The end result was that my actions on that day were not automatic; even though I don't remember doing it, I must have placed the weapon in a safe (nonfiring) position instead of a firing position.

Anyway the robber looked up at me and surrendered.

As we were handcuffing the three, Bill's police radio announced the holdup of the Hanover Bank, 211-31 Jamaica Blvd. Bill answered we had them in custody. The dispatcher couldn't believe it and asked Bill to repeat. We recovered the loot and three guns. One of the guns had been taken from the bank guard. When I was transferred from NYC, my friends on the major case squad gave me a plaque with a NYPD detectives shield (badge). Under the shield is a ribbon with an NYPD award for bravery and excellent police work. This is the same award that Bill Carbone got. I don't know if the ribbon is the one Bill got, but that plaque is one of my most treasured possessions.

The most prolific bank robbers were Michael Thomas Savich and Michael

Savich and Ferrara

Patrick Ferrara. Together they robbed 23 banks and got over $1 million. At the time of the robberies Ferrara was 31 and Savich was 42. At least eleven of these robberies were committed between noon and 3 p.m. All of the robberies were in Queens, Nassau County, or Suffolk County. The robberies were take-over jobs as opposed to note jobs. In other words, the robbers took control of the entire bank. In note jobs the bank employee would be handed a note demanding money. They were very brazen. They didn't wear gloves so they didn't care about leaving prints. They were always armed. Often they would walk into the bank unmasked. Once in the bank, they would disguise themselves in some very unique ways. They would sometimes simply hold pieces of paper in front of their faces. Other times they would put masking tape over parts of their faces. I had never seen these methods of disguise before or since. On other occasions they wore wigs, fake mustaches, ban-danas, and glasses. They called each other by fictitious names.

*Savich and Ferrara,
another robbery*

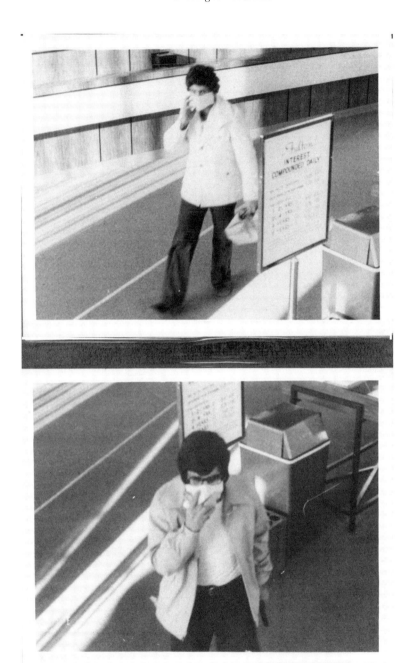

Ferrara and Savich after their appearance

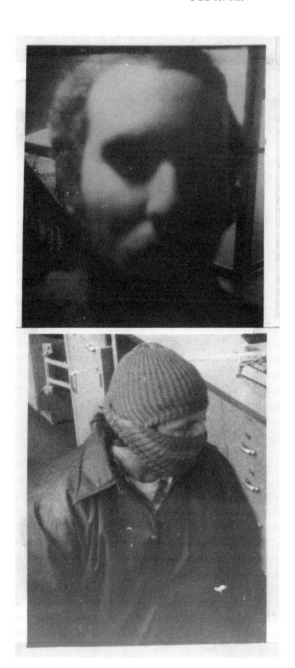

Ferrara, above, and Savich, masked, robbing a bank

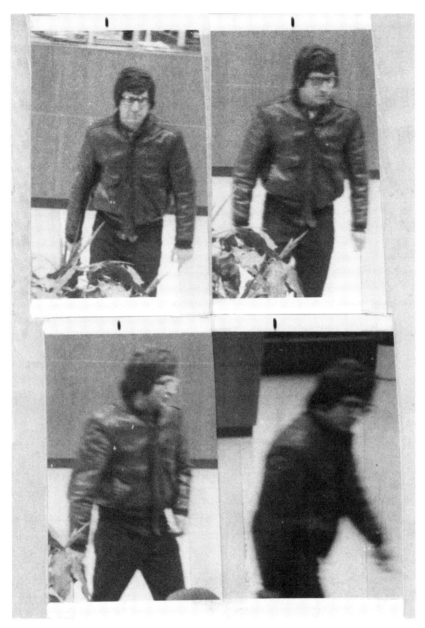

Savich, robbing by himself

Michael Thomas Savich

Michael Ferrara

They were always armed with either pistols or shotguns. It was clear from witness descriptions of what they said, and their speech tone, that they meant business. They used stolen cars for getaways. In one case, their stolen car wouldn't start so they commandeered a citizen's car.

Their largest haul was $202,000 from the Long Island Savings Bank on January 8, 1975. On February 20, 1976, they robbed the Dry Dock savings Bank of $178,400. These were unusually large amounts to be taken in a bank robbery.

Since they didn't wear gloves or masks we had plenty of partial prints and good eye witnesses. Partial fingerprints today can be electronically searched through millions of fingerprints. However, in the mid 70s, this technology did not exist. At that time, in order to identify fingerprints left at a crime scene, the print had to be complete or you had to have a specific suspect. If you had a suspect or suspects, the partial print from the crime scene could be compared with the known fingerprints of the suspect(s).

Unfortunately, in the Ferrara, Savich cases there were no complete fingerprints left at the scene and we had no suspects. We were not getting any information from our sources. So it was up to Tom Lagatol and me to do a lot of legwork. The bank robbery squad and the major case squad surveilled many banks. We tried to figure out a pattern to their robberies. Many hours were spent with no results.

We prepared a collage containing bank surveillance photos, police artist drawings, and descriptions. We personally delivered a copy of the collage to each of 79 NYPD precincts. Then we would return to each precinct during each roll call to ask the officers if they could help us.

One night, we were in a Queens's precinct following up. One of the cops looked at the collage and said, "What do you want Mike Ferrara for?" I couldn't believe it. I asked the officer if he was sure it was Ferrara. He said, "Yes," he had arrested him several times.

I phoned the NYPD latent fingerprint unit and asked them to compare prints from the banks with Ferrara's. One of the detectives with whom we worked the case looked up Ferrara's criminal history and found he had been arrested with Michael Thomas Savich. The detective had Savich's prints compared too. Within about thirty minutes we had solved 23 bank robberies. Both of their prints were identified with latent prints left in the banks.

We arrested Ferrara in Queens. The Suffolk County Police arrested Savich. Both pled guilty and were sentenced to 25 years in federal prison. As of April 2, 2008, Savich was still in prison with an expected release date of October 6, 2015.

During our time on the bank robbery squad, the record for robberies in one day was fifteen including three shootings. We worked all the time. Sometime during this period, the City of New York was facing a financial crisis. The order to eliminate as much police overtime as possible came down. The detectives had to ask for permission to work overtime. It got so bad that they were ordered to go home when we were in the middle of surveillances. Most of the time they worked anyway, not reporting their overtime. They were as dedicated as we were.

Often, when a major crime occurred, many agents and cops from different squads were assigned. One such case involved the son of an owner of a major liquor company. The son was kidnapped. A ransom demand for $46 million was received. I saw 16 large black garbage bags filled with cash. The father was reluctant to let us follow him as he delivered the ransom. He said the money meant nothing compared to the safety of his son.

We convinced him that kidnappers were not trustworthy. There is no reason to believe that people like this will keep their word and release their hostage. So the dad agreed to let us follow him. There were many teams of agents involved in the surveillance. Dad loaded all of the money into an old junker car and left to follow the kidnappers instructions.

One of the teams was a husband and wife. As it turned out they were the closest to Dad. All of a sudden I heard on the radio "honey we lost him." Then there were all sorts of screaming and cursing. Luckily Agent Pat Colgan (the victim in the Buzzy Caron case) was able to spot Dad and the surveillance continued.

The surveillance was successful. The kidnappers were followed to an apartment in Brooklyn where the son was found tied up. Later we found

News photo by **Keith Torrie**
Police sharpshooters keep watch on bank from rooftop.

Overlooking Bankers Trust, 6th Avenue, New York City
© *New York Daily News, Monday, October 6, 1975*

out that the kidnappers didn't wear masks around the victim. This tells me they probably were not going to release him since he could identify them. I still have the wonderful card that Dad sent to each of us thanking us for rescuing his son. All the hard work was worth it.

We all worked hard. When something was happening everybody wanted to be involved. There were times when we were gone from our families for days. I tried to check with my wife to see if she had any reason why I couldn't work. Usually she said, fine, go ahead. I always will remember that Tom Lagatol used to tell me he didn't have to ask his wife because he made the decisions, until one day I caught him in a phone booth saying, "Honey is it okay if I work tonight?" I never let him live that down. On a serious note, all that time away took its toll on my marriage.

In fact, my decision to ask for a transfer out of New York was made because I could see that the job was becoming the only important thing for me. So, in 1977, I asked for a transfer. The FBI made assignments based on needs of the bureau and also based on an office of preference. Agents would put down their preferred office. They would then wait for an opening. There were certain offices that were not considered desirable; therefore any agent who wanted to go there was pretty much assured of a transfer. That's how I was able to transfer from San Francisco to New York. And finally, like any bureaucracy, it sometimes paid to know the right person.

I told my former supervisor, Guy Berado, that I wanted a transfer. I asked for his advice about possible spots. He told me he had a friend who was the assistant agent in charge (ASAC) of the Rapid City, South Dakota, FBI office. The ASAC was Norm Zigrossi. Norm was looking for an agent for Rapid City. I knew that the Rapid City office agents often worked at the Pine Ridge Indian Reservation. Every FBI agent knew about Pine Ridge. On June 26, 1975, FBI agents Jack Koler and Ron Williams were murdered by Leonard Pelletier, Dino Butler, and others. The agents were trying to arrest James Theodore Eagle when they were ambushed and murdered.

I also knew that Rapid City was as complete a change from New York City as I could get. So Guy Berado spoke to Norm Zigrossi on my behalf and my transfer came through.

RAPID CITY FBI

I packed up my family and we left for Rapid City. The very first day we were in Rapid, we were walking down the main street and almost everyone said hello. I thought this was odd because no one in NYC says hello to strangers. I asked my wife if she knew the people who said hello, because I didn't.

Rapid City was the friendliest place I've ever lived. We were able to buy a very nice home that was next to a golf course and the Black Hills. We sat on our deck many times looking into the beautiful pines of the Black Hills. To make it even better, there were no bugs, and we hardly ever had to use our air conditioner.

The Rapid City office had about 13 agents. We had two helicopters and one small fixed-wing aircraft. Two of the agents were ex-military pilots with lots of experience. Two other agents were civilian-trained pilots. I had a rule I followed, which was that I would not fly with a pilot unless he had been shot at in combat or had landed on an aircraft carrier. I believed that if a pilot had been subjected to these stressful conditions and lived through it he would be better able to handle emergencies. I was able to keep this promise to myself throughout my assignment. The two ex-military pilots in Rapid City were Joe Goss and Wade Jackson, both of whom qualified under my rule. The aircraft were often used to transport us to remote areas at Pine Ridge and to transport prisoners.

The majority of our time was spent at the reservation investigating crimes of violence. I found Pine Ridge to be a high-crime area. Given the fact that two agents had been murdered two years before I got there, there was every reason to be careful.

We travelled with at least two agents per vehicle. We always carried rifles as well as our handguns. Our radio coverage was spotty at best, so often you were on your own. The Indian police would help us occasionally. They were in a tough spot. At the end of the day, we would leave Pine Ridge. The police lived and worked there. If the criminals knew the police helped us, there was retribution against them and their families. I also learned that, if the criminal was related to the officer, there was a chance the officer wouldn't help us.

We were often away from our families two or three days at a time. Serious crimes would occur and we would have to go to Pine Ridge immediately. So many family plans were ruined. Not much difference from NYC.

My first partner was Gene Crouch. Gene was a real southern gentleman from Arkansas. I have never met a nicer guy. We worked well together. On one occasion, Gene and I were in a house in Pine Ridge investigating a crime. In those days, FBI agents were general investigators. We did all of our own crime scene investigation. There was no CSI like you see on TV. So Gene and I had spread out our crime scene gear out on the floor. We had fingerprint powder, cameras, gloves, tape measure, note pads, etc. I was intently working when someone came into the house and started whispering to Gene. Gene calmly told me he thought we should leave. I said I wasn't done. He whispered in my ear lets go out of here now. That guy told us there are carloads of unhappy Indians headed here. We just scooped up our gear, ran to the car, and were gone. I never heard what the people in the house thought was going on.

James Theodore Eagle was the first person arrested in the murder of agents Koler and Williams. He was later acquitted, but there was little doubt he participated in the murder. Gene and I, along with other agents, were again looking for him. This time he was charged with shooting his cousin in the chest with a rifle. The Indian police located and arrested him. They put him in the Pine Ridge jail. So Gene and I went to the hospital to talk to the victim. The victim gave us a good statement identifying Eagle as the person who shot him.

We then radioed two other agents, George Hafner and Ed Diem, who were in Pine Ridge, telling them the results, and that we were headed back to Pine Ridge to transport Eagle to Rapid City. On the way back, George radioed that someone was trying to break Eagle out of jail and there was shooting. I was driving. We raced to help our fellow agents. Gene tried to contact them on the radio. There was no response. All I could think of was, not again. I looked at the speedometer once and it read over 100 m.p.h.

As we approached the town of Pine Ridge, we heard shooting. We drove to the jail to find Ed and George okay. They didn't hear our radio call. Eagle had successfully escaped.

Before I go on with the Eagle story, I want to tell you of another incident Gene and I were involved in. We were in the town of Oglala on the reservation. I was driving. We had stopped to discuss which house to go to when Gene looked over his shoulder and saw Dino Butler sneaking up next to our car. Gene yelled, "Watch out!" and Butler ran. Butler had also been charged in the murders of the agents. He was acquitted and was on the street. Again we knew that he participated in the murders and we could only guess what he was trying to do to us.

Now back to James Theodore Eagle. We looked for him for months. Gene transferred from Rapid City. My new partner was Don Dealing. Don looked like a college professor, wire-rimmed glasses and all. He is a great friend and I was about to find out courageous he was. We got a tip that Eagle was hiding in the home of Gladys Bissonnette. She was an elderly resident of Pine Ridge who was not particularly fond of FBI agents.

Don, other agents, and I, and some Indian police went to her home. She came out and said Eagle was not there. However, she allowed us to search her house. This was a dangerous situation. We carefully searched. The house contained a dirt basement with a cutout that led under the house. The opening into the cutout was wide enough for one person. Don said he would go in. Flashlight in hand, he entered. It was dark and scary. Eagle was not there.

We continued to search. The only place left was an attic. Access to the attic was through a narrow space in the ceiling. I asked Bissonnette if Eagle was there. She said no. So it was my turn to look in the attic. I climbed on a chair, opened the panel, and climbed through to the attic. The opening was so small that I had to holster my gun to fit through. I pulled myself to a sitting position, took out my gun and flashlight. I looked it over without success. I was going to come down when something just told me he was there. I saw a pile of insulation move and I yelled for Eagle to give up. He came out of the insulation pleading with me not to shoot him. I didn't shoot him. We got him down and handcuffed him. When he saw he was safe, he really got belligerent. He said for everyone to hear that the only reason he didn't shoot me was that he knew the other agents would shoot through the ceiling.

We also arrested Bissonnette for harboring a fugitive. Both she and Eagle were convicted in federal court. I learned a lesson that day about attics. For the rest of my career, I never did that again. We figured other ways to get criminals out of attics.

Don Dealing and Agent Dave Price began a case that was to have nationwide impact. On February 26, 1976, they were summoned by police to a remote area on the eastern edge of the reservation. A rancher had discovered the decomposed body of a female. The body was so decomposed that neither Dave nor Don recognized her. An autopsy was performed and the cause of death was given as exposure. Since, according to the medical examiner, there was no reason to believe a crime was committed, she was buried as an unknown.

Shortly thereafter, a lawyer for the American Indian Movement (AIM) said that the body was Anna Mae Aquash and that she had been murdered. He claimed the FBI covered up her murder because they had been responsible for it. At the time of her death she was wanted by the FBI after she failed to appear after being charged with weapons and explosives charges. The FBI had arrested her but a judge let her go with her promise to return.

Based on information from the lawyer and other information an order to exhume her body was obtained. A second medical examiner performed a second autopsy. He determined she had died of a gunshot wound. A .32 caliber bullet had entered her head behind her right ear and come to rest behind her eye. Thus there was a small entrance wound and no exit wound. When the first medical examiner was asked how he could have missed the bullet, he simply said, "We all make mistakes."

Since the body contained no identification, the hands were cut off and sent to the FBI Identification Division. The fingerprints were identified as Aquash's. AIM and their sympathizers screamed that the FBI killed her and tried to cover it up.

Aquash was a Canadian citizen. The Canadian government joined in the investigation. The case had been investigated for almost two years when I was assigned to investigate it. When I received the case there had already been a tremendous amount of work done, without finding out who did it.

The Royal Canadian Mounted Police introduced me to a cultural anthropologist, Ted Van Dyke. They suggested I work with him. He had worked with Indian people for many years and had a unique understanding of their culture. Ted and I travelled all over the U.S. and Canada.

We travelled to Nova Scotia to talk to her family. I can recall that the family had no interest in talking to me, but Ted convinced them otherwise. We sat around a table and eventually they told us a lot about Anna Mae. I promised that as long as I had the case I would not stop my efforts to find her killer.

A picture started to take shape. AIM had been suspicious of her because she had been released twice by a judge after the FBI arrested her. AIM thought she was cooperating with the FBI who obtained her release. This conjecture was in fact as far from the truth as possible. A suspect was developed. His name is John Patton also known as John Boy. He was located in a remote area about 90 miles from Whitehorse in the Northwest Territories of Canada.

Arrangements were made with the Royal Canadian Mounted Police for me to travel with them to talk to this suspect. This was in February. When I arrived in Whitehorse, it was about -25°. It was so cold that the police kept their cars running all the time. The officers treated me with respect and admiration for the effort the FBI was putting in to solve the case.

We drove the 90 miles to the man's cabin. The local officer knew him and took us to the cabin. We all went into the cabin after the man agreed to talk to us. There was a fire burning in the fireplace as we sat face to face with the murderer of Anna Mae Aquash. I asked if he killed her and he did not answer. We left.

Several days later, we flew to his cabin to try again. We were unsuccessful. The flight back to Whitehorse was terrifying. The wind was blowing fiercely and it was snowing hard. We came too close to a mountain. We landed at Whitehorse and the wind blew the plane sideways down the runway.

I boarded a plane for home. It was still -25° and the wind was blowing at 40 m.p.h. I was glad to leave. I had a layover in Vancouver, British Columbia. Sitting in my room, I began to notice a rash. I developed the worst case of poison ivy you can imagine. It seems that the fire in the cabin was made with wood that contained poison ivy residue. What a trip.

Other agents took over for me when I transferred. Eventually after a ton of work by FBI agents, the Denver Police, and Bob Eccoffey of the Bureau of Indian Affairs, Arlo Frtiz Looking Cloud and John Graham, who is also known as John Boy Patton, were indicted on March 20, 2003, for the murder of Anna Mae Aquash. Looking Cloud was convicted on February 8, 2004, and sentenced to life. Graham was extradited from Canada on December 6, 2007. His trail was scheduled for June 2008, but has been delayed several times.

We kept our promise to her family. The murderers were caught. I guess it does not surprise me, but after all the nationwide media attention when she was killed, and after all the fingerpointing at the FBI, there was almost nothing said when Looking Cloud was convicted and Graham was brought to the U.S. to stand trail.

There are only two roads that we travelled from Rapid City to Pine Ridge and back. One of the roads took us through Scenic, South Dakota. Scenic consisted of a bar owned by Halley Merrill and his daughter Twila. It was the wild west in the 20th century. Halley had a long, grey beard and wild-looking grey hair. Twila was a tough cowgirl. It probably doesn't do Twila justice to call her a cowgirl. She tended bar and could fight with anyone. One day, I stopped at the bar and saw she had two black eyes. She said she'd been in a fight with a cowboy and she won.

I enjoyed stopping at the bar to talk to them. On more than one occasion, we found persons we were looking for at the bar. Halley kept a sawed-off shotgun behind the bar. I can't say if he ever used it but it wouldn't surprise me if he had. I often wonder if the bar is still there and if they are still alive.

There were some Indian police officers we could work with. One of them was Billy Jumping Eagle. One day my partner and I went to see

Billy because we needed some help locating someone. We found Billy at his house working on a car. His head was swollen and his eyes were black. He told us he quit the police department. When I asked why, he told me he was on duty a few days ago when he was dispatched to a domestic disturbance in a housing area. There were no other officers available. While trying to quell the disturbance he was hit with a baseball bat. After getting treated at the hospital, he went to complain to the Tribal Police Chief, Fred Two Bulls. Billy said officers should not have to answer calls like this alone. Fred threw a helmet at Billy and said stop complaining. Billy quit on the spot.

Then there were officers we learned we could not trust. One of them was Lt. Pat Mills. We all thought that Mills was a friend of ours; we had worked with him often. One evening we were at the Pine Ridge police station making a plan to arrest a dangerous person. We asked Mills for his help. He refused, saying the person we were seeking was his cousin. As we talked Mills became angry, and finally said the agents who were killed (Jack Coler and Ron Williams) got what they deserved. I never spoke to Mills again. This was in 1979.

Years later, when I was the United States Marshal in Minnesota, I was at the Red lake Indian Reservation. Deputy Marshal Butch Visger and I went to the police station and guess who was police chief. It was Pat Mills. He didn't remember me but I remembered him. Our conversation was short. I can't say I was sorry when he lost his job shortly thereafter.

Now to get back to Pine Ridge. Another very sad case was the murder of Sandra Ellen Wounded Foot. Sandra was 15 when her body was found on August 16, 1976. She had been shot in the head. When I was assigned the case, Bureau of Indian Affairs (BIA) Investigator Paul Duane Herman Jr. was suspected of the crime. I worked closely with BIA investigator Nate Merrick. We finally got enough evidence to indict Herman for murder.

On August 24, 1978, Nate and I travelled to Ft. McDowell, Arizona. It was a brutally hot day. Someone said it was a dry heat. I guess at 110 degrees dry doesn't mean much. When Herman saw us he said, "I knew you were coming." He confessed and later pled guilty. This was another case where the FBI and the police worked very hard to see that justice was done. I know the family of Sandra appreciated our efforts.

I generally got along well with the residents of the reservation. I enjoyed talking with them. However, since conditions then were dangerous, we had to be careful when we were interacting with the people. I was the proud winner of a third place certificate for running in the first annual Chris Bald Eagle run. Chris was a youngster killed there.

I also taught schools for the tribal police. The officers were respectful but really didn't seem to have the same safety and tactical concerns that I had. After a week-long school about safe practices when confronting suspects, I held a series of practical exercises. I had become friendly with a young officer who had recently gotten out of the military. When it came his turn to participate, he did very poorly in my opinion. So I asked him why he did these unsafe actions. He looked me straight in the eye and said we don't want to be white cops. I tried.

Another close call I had occurred after someone stole two M-16 rifles from an FBI car. Pennington County Deputy Sheriff Ken Bradford told me he had an informant who knew where the stolen rifles were. Rapid City is located in Pennington County. I knew Ken and trusted him. So he told me to pick him up and we would meet his informant outside of town.

I picked him up in the afternoon and we drove about ten miles outside of town. We spotted the informant in his car. My mind was thinking, the informant is trying to help us in a very important matter. The stolen rifles could very well be used against us. So we pulled up and I got out with Ken. We approached the informant's car. He got out with a shotgun in his hand. He racked it and stuck it into my stomach saying, "I'm going to kill you." I started to back up trying to get my car between him and me. Ken was able to sneak up behind him and hit him on the head with his gun. We jumped on him and handcuffed him. It turned out that the informant was drunk and had no information about the rifles. I learned a lesson that I would take with me the rest of my career. Informants are important, but they should always be viewed with caution.

As you can tell, most of the FBI work for agents in Rapid City was at

Athletic Award

This is to Certify that

Al Garber "Superstar" 1st Place 1 Mile Run (Group D) 5 min. 54 sec.

HAS PARTICIPATED IN THE ATHLETIC PROGRAM
of

Oglala Community High School

GIVEN FOR

"Superstars"

this ____ 19th ____ day of ____ May ____ 19 __ 77

Donald O. Boynton
Bryan L. Brewer
Director of Athletics

Stewart Swallen
Principal

Al, SA Mick Sherer, and Det. Al Scherr

Pine Ridge. However, once in awhile, something interesting would occur in Rapid. Twenty-four to twenty-six bars of gold were stolen from Black Hills Gold Creations from January to March 1979. The gold bars were valued at over $200,000. I worked this case with Agent Mick Scherer and Rapid City Detective Al Scherr. Our investigation was probably the biggest property theft criminal investigation ever conducted in Rapid City.

We determined that the theft was committed by an employee of Black Hills Gold creations. The gold eventually found its way to a local pawn-shop owner Mark Lee Blote. Blote then sold some of them to a gold dealer in New York. We were able to trace the shipments through the U.S. Mail. Blote shipped nine bars to NYC. He kept the other 16 in a safety deposit box. After we arrested Blote, he tried to return the bars to Black Hills Gold Creations.

At trial he contended that he didn't know the bars were stolen and that, once he found out they were, he returned them. The only problem for Blote was that, before he was arrested, Detective Scherr interviewed him and asked him if he had purchased any gold bars. Blote said no. That statement really sunk him at trial.

Wade Jackson was a pilot assigned to the FBI office. He was an agent with the added duty of flying. Wade had gained my respect by his thoroughness and knowledge. I flew with him often. I watched him go through his pre-flight checklist and it was obvious to me that he was a true professional. Three convicted killers escaped from the South Dakota State Prison near Sioux Falls. We were sent there to assist in the search. Agent, pilot, Joe Goss was in the left seat of one of our Huey helicopters. Wade was in the right seat and was the co-pilot. I was in the back along with agent Don Dealing. The doors of the helicopter were open so that Don and I could look down at the cornfields. Joe flew the chopper low so that the rotor wash parted the corn fields where we suspected the escapees were hiding. This was very dangerous business because of the criminals, who between them had been convicted for seven murders and, because of the low flying we were doing.

All of us had headsets so we could communicate with each other. I heard Wade say to Joe to watch out for the power lines we were approaching. There was no response. Wade repeated his warning—still no response. I looked out and saw we were flying straight towards the power lines. I heard Wade say he was taking control and we veered away from the wires. I know Wade saved our lives. He later told me that in two or three seconds we would have hit the power lines. How this could have happened with Joe at the controls is a mystery. Joe was a very experienced U.S. Army helicopter and fixed- wing pilot with about 8000 hours of flight time and combat experience. I can only guess that he was so intent on the mission that he was not looking at the general area. Thank goodness for Wade.

We continued the search. We hovered over a tree line where one of the escapees was hiding. Our presence made him move so that officers on the ground saw his movement and captured him. A second escapee surrendered after not moving for three days fearing we would see him from the air. One of the officers said the only part of his body not covered by bug bites was his lips.

We were at the command post and saw a camouflaged dune buggy come roaring up. It skidded to a stop and a young guy with dental braces jumped out. One of the officers told us that was the South Dakota Attorney General Bill Janklow. Janklow went on the become governor and U.S. congressman. He was carrying a submachine gun of some type. We got to talking and he said, "Watch this." He aimed the gun at one of the officers. The gun had a red dot sight. He yelled to the officer to look at his chest. The officer did this and Janklow said something like that's where the shot would go. I didn't think that was funny. But Attorney General Janklow was a strong supporter of law enforcement and thanked us for our help. I had several more occasions to work with him over the years and I came to respect his enthusiasm and candor.

Wade Jackson deserves our thanks for saving our lives and for his service to our country. Wade was a Chinook helicopter pilot who served two tours in Vietnam. In 1967–68, he served with an experimental helicopter unit nicknamed "Guns-A-Go-Go." These were unusually heavily armed CH-47 Chinooks. He was assigned to the 1st Air Cavalry Division. He returned to Vietnam in 1970 to again fly Chinooks. He received many commendations.

I considered finishing out my FBI career in Rapid City. It is a great place to live. The cost of living is comparatively low. South Dakota has no income tax. The people are very nice. There is no hustle and bustle. However, there is very limited opportunity. Tourism and cattle ranching are the major economic draws. I knew that when I retired from the FBI I would get another job. Law enforcement jobs in South Dakota are few. After we considered all of the facts, my family and I decided to try to move to Minneapolis. I applied for the position of training coordinator. The coordinator directs and conducts training for agents and police. The coordinator is also responsible for selection and screening of police applicants for the prestigious FBI National Academy.

MINNEAPOLIS FBI

I was selected and, in October of 1980, I was transferred to Minneapolis. I was assigned to Minneapolis until I retired from the FBI in 1993. From the time I moved to Minneapolis, I had my sights set on a career as a police chief. I also knew that, as much as I had worked with the police, I had never been a police officer. I needed an edge, so I enrolled at Mankato State University in the masters of public administration program. It took six years of night school, but I got my masters. More about that later.

I really enjoyed training and I dove headlong into the assignment. I was also appointed to be the leader of the Minneapolis FBI Special Weapons and Tactics (SWAT) Team. Another very important event occurred shortly after I arrived in Minneapolis. My close friend Agent Steve Gilkerson transferred from NYC to Minneapolis. We were back together again.

Our SWAT team developed in a manner unique in the U.S. We formed a partnership with the Minneapolis Police (MPD) SWAT team. We knew that our FBI members were highly motivated, well trained, but lacked practical street experience. On the other hand, the MPD SWAT members had a lot of experience but didn't have the training opportunities we had. So with the blessing of the FBI agent in charge Dick Blay, and the chief of police Tony Bouza, we formed a joint team. The police officers were sworn as special deputy U.S. marshals so that they could enforce federal law when they operated with us.

The key to our success as a joint team was that all members were treated equally. All training was done together. The mutual respect that developed among the police and agents was just wonderful. It was reminiscent of the my days in NYC working with the detectives of the NYPD Major Case Squad.

Minnesota has the well deserved reputation for being extremely cold in the winter. One of the most difficult schools I have ever attended was the Minnesota National Guard Winter Operations Instructor. I attended the school in January 1981. It was consistently $-20°$ and colder. We were outside most of the time. My face stayed raw and red for the entire eight

Minnesota cold weather ops training

Minnesota cold weather ops training

days of the school. We slept in large tents heated with stoves. If we got the stoves too hot, we would sweat, and then when we went outside the sweat froze. But we learned how to control the heat in the tents.

There was very little snow that year. The skis that the military provided were heavy and made of wood. The effort needed to break a trail through the woods almost brought me to exhaustion. Again you had to be very aware of the heat your body generated when you were skiing. If you didn't unzip some layers of clothing, your body would sweat. And, once again, being wet was the kiss of death in that kind of environment.

There was also training in shooting in cold weather. You can imagine how difficult it was to handle weapons and ammunition. We learned a lot and successfully completed the school. My reason for attending the school was to learn skills that I could bring to our SWAT team. We used these skills many times over the years.

There was a police shooting that occurred in Winona, Minnesota, not long after I got to Minneapolis. Officers were called to a disturbance at a trailer park. They went to the trailer and tried to get the man to come out. They entered the trailer and one of the officers was shot with a rifle by the man inside the trailer.

The sheriff called me and asked if we would work with his department to devise tactics for confronting barricaded, armed suspects. It is fairly common for law enforcement officers to find themselves in situations where they believe or know that a person with a gun is in an area and won't surrender.

So Steve Gilkerson and I, using our experience and drawing on the experiences of our many police friends, devised the "Barricaded Suspect School." The school lasted three days and was designed for law enforcement officers at all levels who were not SWAT members. We eventually taught that school to hundreds of officers in Minnesota, South Dakota, North Dakota, and Manitoba. I recall getting a call from Eagan, Minnesota, Police Sgt. Pat Geagan who said he had heard about the school. Pat asked how the school was designed. He quizzed me thoroughly about my experience. When he was satisfied that our school was based on actual experience, he asked us to

Al, Steve Gilkerson, Brian Compton

conduct it for his police department. Pat became a great friend. He went on to be chief of police and mayor of Eagan. A footnote to our relationship is that his son babysat for my son. Later his son went on to become a U.S. Army Ranger.

The Winnipeg, Manitoba, police asked Steve Gilkerson and I to conduct the barricaded suspect school for them. We made arrangements to go there. Getting across the U.S.-Canadian border was quite an adventure. Canada expressly prohibits anyone who is not a Canadian citizen from bringing guns into Canada. In our school we used blank firing guns. Winnipeg police made arrangements with Canadian customs to allow us to bring in the blank firing guns, or so we thought. We arrived at the border, told the customs officials who we were. They said no matter who we were they had to search our van for illegal items. They tore our van apart. I believe that, when we told them we were FBI agents, I saw them smile to each other. After a delay of hours we were allowed to pass.

We conducted the school. It proved to be one of the most rewarding schools we had ever done. We were teaching tactics for police to search for armed suspects inside buildings. About two months after the school, one of the officers called. He said that he and his partner were searching a food store for a suspect who had robbed the store at gunpoint. They were able to locate him and, by using the tactics we taught, they were able to conceal their location. The gunman shot where he thought the officers were. They were able to return fire and kill the gunman.

It was rewarding to know that our efforts saved police lives.

As more law enforcement agencies heard about our training, requests grew. The Minneapolis Police training officer asked if I would work with his trainers to devise a handcuffing class that emphasized officer safety. Sgt. Jerry Larson and I worked out the course. It was to be taught to every MPD officer. This was a monumental task because of the number of officers and the varying hours they worked. The training was all to be done when the officer was not on normal duty.

The first class was held at the 5th Precinct MPD. Just before the class was to begin, Lt. Hugh Rohrbacker came up to me and said that, before I taught his officers, he had to be sure the techniques were sound. I thought this was a reasonable request so I gave him the class alone while the officers waited. He liked it and the class went on.

It took Jerry Larson and me ten weeks to complete the instruction to all officers. That was a great experience. Jerry and I became friends. He was a colorful character. His nickname was "Lurch." That should give you some idea of what he looked like. I will tell you more about Jerry later.

On Tuesday, August 31, 1982, Wayzata, Minnesota, Police Sgt. James Anderson was shot and killed. He responded to a domestic dispute between Gladys Johnson and her son, George, who had recently returned from Alaska. Wayzata is a small town and Jim was the only officer on duty. He requested backup from neighboring communities. When he got to the apartment, Gladys Johnson told him her son was breaking up furniture and insisted that the officer stop him. We were told that Sgt. Anderson asked Gladys if there were any weapons in the apartment; when she said no, he decided to try to stop George Johnson. Sgt. Anderson was shot three times by George Johnson.

Sometime in the early afternoon the Hennepin County Sheriff asked for the assistance of the FBI. Dick Blay was the agent in charge. He had recently arrived in Minneapolis and had never seen our SWAT team in action. He sent us to Wayzata. When we got there, I was directed to the command post and spoke to Sheriff Omodt and Inspector Mike Postle.

On the way to Wayzata, we were told that the suspect had fled to the post office and taken hostages. He had also wounded another officer who had responded to the post office.

Shortly after arriving on the scene, I asked the sheriff where the Post Office was in relation to the command post. He pointed directly down the street. I told him the command post should be in a safer location. He agreed. We then learned that all of the hostages had either been released or escaped. So the only one left in the post office was the killer.

The sheriff was in charge. I recommended that we deliver tear gas to the post office to try to drive the killer outside. I told him it was just too dangerous to enter the post office. The sheriff was a veteran officer and was a reasonable person. I came to become friends with him. That friendship remains today.

Anyway, it was only recently that a new type of tear gas was developed. This gas was delivered in a liquid form. So there was no heat and no chance of starting a fire. This was the wrong time to try to convince the sheriff that our tear gas would not burn the post office down. In fact, as a result of this problem convincing the sheriff, my partner Steve Gilkerson and I began giving classes to chiefs and sheriffs about what tools are available to SWAT teams. We knew that educating the commanders in the heat of battle was not going to work.

Sheriff Omodt was adamant that tear gas could not be used. Law enforcement emergencies are much the same as military operations, the commander is in charge. Other officers maintained a perimeter around the post office to prevent the killer's escape. We began interviewing the freed hostages. One of them told me she was the last hostage out and, when she was leaving, she heard what she thought was a shot. She said she looked back and thought she saw the killer seated in the postmaster's chair with his head slumped. Based on this information I agreed to enter the building without delivering gas.

We had been considering integrating police dogs and handlers with our team for situations just like this. But we had not trained with them yet. A police officer volunteered to use his dog. This was risky because we had to protect the officer while he watched his dog. No one knew how the dog would react to the SWAT team. We decided to try it.

Another footnote to this situation concerned the FBI Supervisor Dag Sohlberg. He was the ranking FBI agent on the scene. He was dressed in a suit and tie. We were dressed in our SWAT uniforms and had all of our equipment. We were well trained as a team. Dag was a former SWAT member. He insisted on accompanying the team into the post office. I tried to talk him out of it. I told him he was not suitably dressed or equipped. He insisted, and he was the ranking agent, so he went with us.

We approached the back door. Team members opened the door and the K-9 officer told his dog to go in and "find him." The dog took two steps inside and stopped, sat down, and looked for his handler. The handler tried to get the dog to search, but the dog would not move. Once again, we learned that new tactics are likely to be unsuccessful if they are not practiced.

We then began a careful search. As soon as we entered the postmaster's office, I saw the killer seated in the chair with his arms hanging down. He had a .357 magnum revolver in his right hand. We carefully approached and determined he had a gunshot to the head. Still not sure that he was dead, I grabbed the gun from his hand. He was dead. Later, the crime lab guys chewed me out for grabbing the gun. They preferred that we would have left everything as it was. Of course, from a safety standpoint, we did the right thing.

Sometime as we were entering the post office, our agent in charge Dick Blay arrived. This was the first time he had seen us in action. He congratulated us and became a strong supporter of our team. Having the boss in our corner made all the difference in terms of getting equipment and training time.

Steve Gilkerson and I worked very closely with many good Minneapolis cops. Two of the most active were Sgts. Jerry "Lurch" Larson and Dennis Xersa. They were both aggressive and experienced. When Steve and I started to work with them, I think they liked us but thought we were inexperienced feds. An arrest occurred in the summer of 1982 that changed their opinion dramatically. The case involved two bank robbers, Clarence Fox, Jr. and William Givens. They had been robbing banks and other businesses. They carried guns and were violent.

Finally, we got information that Fox was hiding in an apartment in north Minneapolis. Steve, Jerry Larson, and Dennis Yerxa, and I went to make the arrest. I started to make a plan which emphasized our safety and stealth. Jerry and Dennis disagreed and said there was only one way— to break in the door and quickly move in. I would not give in so they agreed to do it our way. We approached the apartment door. We heard a person who we thought was Fox talking. We had other officers surround the apartment building. I banged on the door and told Fox he had to surrender. There was a long pause followed by the sounds of movement in the apartment. Finally, Fox surrendered by coming out into the hallway. Shortly thereafter, when Fox got his confidence back, he told us he was waiting for us to crash in. He bragged that he had a shotgun and would have killed us. We did find a shotgun in the apartment. Jerry and Dennis were sure glad we didn't crash in.

Givens was later arrested. He and Fox were sentenced to long terms in federal prison. Fox died in prison. He was found stabbed over 70 times and tied in a laundry bag. Somebody said sarcastically: "Damdest case of suicide I ever saw!"

On February 13, 1983, I was sitting in my living room in Apple valley, Minnesota, at about 6 p.m., when FBI Supervisor Dag Sohlberg called. He said that the United States marshal and a deputy U.S. marshal had been shot and killed. He told me to head for Medina, North Dakota, with six members of my SWAT team to meet one of the FBI agents stationed in North Dakota. I asked him why I could take only six of the twelve members of my team. He told me I only needed six because ND authorities would probably have the murderer in custody by the time we got there. He couldn't have been more wrong.

So, Steve Gilkerson and I and four others headed for Medina. We arrived in Medina late that night. We met an FBI agent and Medina Police Chief Darrell Graf at Graf's house.

We learned that Gordon Kahl and others had committed the murders. The U.S. marshals and police attempted to arrest Kahl, A shoot-out occurred near Medina. The marshal, Ken Muir, and a deputy U.S. marshal (DUSM) Bob Cheshire had been killed. DUSM James Hopson was wounded critically by asphalt which ricocheted into his ear after a bullet hit the ground near him. Stutsman County, ND, Deputy Sheriff Brad Kapp had his trigger finger shot off. Brad had a bullet fragment lodged in the center of his body armor. Medina police officer Steve Schnabel was shot in the leg. Yori Kahl, Gordon's son, was wounded in the stomach.

Brad Kapp and Darrell Graf told me that they knew that federal warrants had been issued charging Gordon Kahl with violating the conditions of his probation. Kahl had been convicted of tax evasion. They knew that Kahl was a member of a violent group called Posse Comitatus. Kapp had spotted Kahl and others at the Medina medical clinic. The U.S. Marshals were notified and requested Kahl be kept under surveillance until they could get there.

Gordon Kahl

DUSM Cheshire knew how dangerous Kahl and his comrades were. He asked for help from other agencies. However, the U.S. Marshal Ken Muir said he had enough help. When the marshals got to Medina, they asked Darrell Graf for help. He tried to talk them out of attempting to arrest Kahl there. Graf knew Kahl had spotted the police and feared there were not enough law enforcement personnel there.

The marshal said they would go ahead. Medina Police Officer Steve Schnabel and Deputy Sheriff Brad Kapp said they would help. Chief Graf said he would have an ambulance and medical personnel standing by.

During the arrest attempt, the shootout occurred. After it was all over, Kahl brought his son Yuri to the Medina clinic. Brad Kapp was also being treated there. When Brad saw Kahl he asked him if this was all worth it. Kahl responded that it was to him.

I asked Chief Graf and FBI Agent Ken Aldrich, the local agent, if Kahl had been arrested. They said, no, and they believed he was at his farm near Heaton, ND. Ken took us to the scene of the shooting. I will always remember seeing Bob Cheshire's grey Dodge SUV. The driver's door was open and on the ground were Bob's glasses and some bone fragments.

I met up with ND Bureau of Criminal Investigation (BCI) Agent Dick Hickman. We knew Dick from SWAT training. Dick was in charge of the ND statewide tactical team. Dick has become a great friend over the years.

He and his men were examples of how competent rural law enforcement officers can become.

We formulated a plan to form a perimeter around Kahl's farm. I realized that our six team members and Dick's team were not enough to form an effective perimeter. It was dark and I felt uncomfortable. Kahl was as dangerous a criminal as I had ever faced. It was clear that he would shoot any of us who got in his way. But we all did the best we could. Sometime during the night my boss Dick Blay called and asked for a status report. I told him the details. He asked if we needed anything. I told him we needed the rest of the SWAT team urgently. He said he'd get them on their way from Minneapolis. It is about five hours from Minneapolis to Heaton, North Dakota.

The next morning the other members arrived. The Bismarck, North Dakota, police department offered to send two police canine teams to help us. I spoke to officers Doug Ketterling and Duane Houghton, who told me they had been training with other officers in building searches. I asked them to come immediately. They arrived with their dogs, Beau and Silver.

The plan was to form a close perimeter around the farmhouse. We were to make announcements calling on the occupants to surrender. If there was no response, then tear gas was to be delivered. If there was till no response, then we would open the side door to the house and let one of the dogs search while the SWAT team covered the handler.

The perimeter was made up of our SWAT team and the North Dakota State Tactical team. The first problem was that Hickman's team had no gas guns. We lent them two of ours. I asked Dick if his men had trained with these types of guns. He assured me they had. When the perimeter teams were in position someone at our command post telephoned into the place. There was no answer. We then announced on a loud speaker. Again no response.

I gave the order to deliver tear gas. All of a sudden we saw gas rounds coming over the house towards us. They were coming from the direction of the ND team. I called Hickman on the radio and asked what was going on. He told me his gunner had shot too high. I said I guess so. After the tear gas was delivered, we waited, called upon the occupants to surrender. When

Bismark ND PD Duane Houghton and Doug Ketterling

there was no response, we delivered a second volley of gas. Still there was no response.

Steve Gilkerson and I made our way to the side door. We thought we would break open the door and call up the K-9 team. However, once we opened the door, we found that it led to a small foyer and then there was another door. So here we were, trapped in a small foyer. We tried to open the inner door but the floor was slippery and we couldn't get any leverage. We both slipped on the floor. We were sitting ducks. So we made a hasty retreat.

Now for plan B. We borrowed an armored personnel carrier from the ND National Guard. We mounted a telephone pole on the front of it. The armored personnel carrier drove the pole through the front door of the house. We were then able to get the K-9 in to search. We went with the dog and handler as they searched the entire house. The dogs did an outstanding job. We would use K-9 teams regularly in the future.

So Kahl had escaped. We searched the house for anything that might help us find him. We found 53 loaded guns in that house. There were guns everywhere, in the freezer, in the piano, in the stove, in the toilets, just everywhere. We found a huge cache of ammunition. I don't know how many millions of rounds we recovered. But it took 12 of us four hours to load all the ammo into trucks. We found gas masks, crossbows, and explosives. Kahl and his followers were ready for anything.

The next day officials from the U.S. marshals service arrived. It had been their men who were killed and the FBI investigated killing of any federal officers. So we got a chance to work closely with them. I never really knew much about the marshals. But I gained a new respect for them. Their ranking person was Howard Safir. Howard went on to become the NYC Police Commissioner under Mayor Guiliani. Howard and I worked from positions of mutual respect. Other marshal service people who we worked with were Chuck Kupfer and Roger Arechiga. Chuck was old school and had no particular love for the FBI. But, through our joint efforts, new bonds were formed. Roger was a very competent planner. He got the needed resources to continue the search. I certainly had no idea then that some 19 years later I would become the U.S. marshal for Minnesota.

We conducted a raid on a house in Ashby, ND, hoping to find Kahl. We selected a staging area near Ashby where we would get ready to approach. The media got wind of our staging area. They really tried to interfere. But they all promised not to interfere. Well, we finally got in the house and we were carefully searching with our K-9 partners when the phone rang. Steve picked up the phone. The caller said he was a reporter for the *Chicago Sun Times*. He said the FBI would be raiding this house and he wanted to call back after the raid. He wanted to do a story on our conduct. If he had called before we got there and tipped off the occupants, he might have cost us our lives. This was my first experience with media integrity in cases of national significance.

I drew on what Minneapolis Police Sgt. Jerry Larson, aka Lurch, told me about controlling your emotions. When it came time for action, I was in a high state of emotion. But, right after it was over, I came back down the emotional ladder. In this way, I was able to stay sharp when I needed to be.

I felt some embarrassment when working with the marshals. It was their men who were killed and we were doing the raids. So I went to Howard Safir and told him we would be happy to support his men if they wanted to conduct some of the raids. I gained so much respect for Howard when he told me that he appreciated my offer, but our SWAT was equipped and trained for these missions and his men were not. So we established a routine where the U.S. marshals would establish a perimeter around the target and we would conduct the raid. It worked well.

Many of the places we raided contained large stocks of food, water, guns, and ammunition. These residents were members or sympathizers of the Posse Commitatus. Their general belief was that the only legitimate law officer was the county sheriff. They had no duty to obey police or federal agents. Furthermore, they told us that if the sheriff did not act like they wanted, they would remove the sheriff. We conducted a raid and, afterwards, I was talking to a woman who lived there. She was middle aged, well-dressed, and articulate. She very matter-of-factly told us that she knew how to solve the whole problem in our country. I asked how, and she responded, "Just kill all the Jews and niggers." It is impossible to reason with people like this.

There was intense stress on all of us. Every raid carried the distinct possibility that Kahl and his followers would be there. Every raid was dangerous. Some of our team handled the pressure better than others. The only way to approach one of these farmhouses was across open ground. We were very vulnerable as we approached. So the plan was to have our marksmen or snipers watch the windows as we approached. If they saw anyone with a weapon and pointing it towards us, they were to shoot. This was the best plan we could devise, so we executed it. It went well. After the raid, one of the team members came to me and said I was unnecessarily endangering his life by ordering us across open ground. I asked if he had another idea and he did not.

He said he was going to Agent in Charge Blay to get me replaced. Dick

Blay convened a meeting of our team and asked each member if I was performing my duties as leader appropriately. They all said yes, and the issue was laid to rest. That team member left the team. I never had any bad toward feelings toward him. The pressure was too much.

Kahl was eventually killed in a raid in Arkansas. The other participants either surrendered or were captured. Deputy Sheriff Brad Kapp and I kept in contact for many years. He returned to his duties and learned to shoot with his left hand. Chief Darrell Graf was accused by many as sympathizing with Kahl and alerting him to the marshals' presence. I don't believe that. Graf tried to convince the marshals that Medina was not the place or time to try to arrest Kahl. When the marshal would not change his plans, Graf had emergency medical personnel standing by. I had known Deputy U.S. Marshal Bob Cheshire before this incident. He had attended a tactical school that Steve and I conducted about two weeks before. There was a lot of bravery and tragedy in Medina, Heaton, and the surrounding areas.

Our SWAT team returned to Minneapolis after spending about two months in North Dakota. We had a unique group. As I look back on those days, I believe that Steve Gilkerson was the real brains behind our successes. I was the leader but he had most of the good ideas. He had courage and technical skills. Our team worked hard to stay in good physical condition. An agent, Ben Canny, came to me and asked if he could join the team. I told him if he lost 40 pounds and quit smoking he could try out. I never really expected him to accomplish this. Don't you know it, but about six months later he came to me again. He said, "I lost 50 pounds and I quit smoking." He joined us and became our tear gas man. Ben was a hell of a guy. Some of the guys really didn't fit the mold of the macho SWAT agent. But they were skilled and courageous as any. Don Dealing, my old partner from Rapid City, joined the team. Bobby Erwin was a quiet, low-key guy. Physical fitness did not come easy to Bobby, but he did it all. He became an excellent shot with the MP-5 submachine gun. I trusted every one of them with my life.

Shortly after returning to Minneapolis, I asked Minneapolis Police Chief Tony Bouza if he would allow some of his K-9 teams to train and operate with us. The trade-off was that we had been providing no-cost training for his officers. He agreed. MPD Officers Ron Johnson, Luke Koerner, Bill Lundquist, and Dave Dobrotka were the first ones. They were just great cops and friends.

These officers were criticized by other K-9 officers who said we would send their dogs on suicide missions. We established criteria for using the dogs. We would never send the dog if we were certain an armed suspect was in a house. We would use them after we exhausted all means to locate the suspect. We trained very hard providing protection for the dog and handler as they searched. The dogs actually learned to differentiate good guys from bad guys. I believe the dogs did this by learning that the bad guys hid in closets, under beds, and behind doors. The SWAT team didn't do this.

Officer Ron Johnson was our strongest supporter. He was the trainer for the MPD K-9 unit. He was very experienced. He was open-minded and willing to try new techniques. On top of that he became one of my closest friends. This is the type of cop he was. I met him one day and he was covered with sweat. I asked him what happened. He explained that he answered a call to assist an obese man who had fallen out of bed. No other officers were available so he went alone. It took him an hour to get the man back to bed. The wife was so thankful to Ron. I asked him if anyone else, like his boss, knew this and he said no.

On another occasion, Ron was going home after working. He saw a man on the interstate highway. Ron stopped his car and tried to get the man to safety. The man was incoherent and he was big. After a great effort Ron got the man to the side of the road. This guy turned out to be a football player for the Minnesota Vikings. No one knew what Ron had done.

And, finally, one more Ron Johnson story. His dog Bravo was tied on his porch at their home in Farmington, Minnesota. The dog slipped or jumped off the porch and choked. Ron gave him mouth to mouth resuscitation and revived him.

While it may appear that work was the only thing in my life during this time, that is not entirely true. Sometimes work and life outside work got intermixed. My son Micah began playing hockey at about 10 years old.

Every kid in Minnesota plays hockey. So I wanted to be part of my son's hockey experience. I bought a used set of skates from a neighbor. They didn't fit right and they were way too expensive. But I strapped them on and went out on the ice with Micah and other dads and kids. I had never skated before and it showed. Pretty soon Micah skated over to me and said, "Dad, get off the ice. You're embarrassing me."

Instead of being discouraged, I found an adult skating school. For three years I attended skating school. When I thought I was ready for hockey, I called on my good buddy MPD K-9 officer Ron Johnson. Ron was an outstanding hockey player in high school and college. So every Sunday I met Ron and Sgt. Doug Smith, who was then head of the MPD SWAT team, at the Farmington ice arena. They both taught me how to play hockey. I am forever indebted to them.

After three years of preparation, I got on the ice with Micah. He said, "Dad you're not too bad." I've been playing hockey ever since. That's almost 25 years of hockey. I have made some great friends and stayed in pretty good physical condition.

In July 1984, Agent in Charge Dick Blay told me the go to Rapid City where a major drug investigation was underway. I arrived there and I was briefed by agents of the U.S. Drug Enforcement Agency (DEA). The investigation was being led by DEA with help from the FBI, the SD Division of Criminal Investigation (DCI), the U.S. Marshals Service, and the Custer County, SD, Sheriffs Office.

My SWAT team's assignment was to conduct the raid on the drug lab. Right from the get-go there were disagreements between the DEA agents and me. DEA told me how dangerous the suspects were, that they had many guns, and they were producing large quantities of meth. Then the DEA agent told me there was only one way to conduct the raid. That was to rush in and storm the lab. I told him that was crazy and I was not about to get any of my men hurt. He told me that there were expected losses in any raid.

Planning is what gives SWAT teams the edge over other officers and agents. If a SWAT does not plan and rehearse, its chance of success is no better than any other group of good officers. So I was firm and Dick Blay backed me. Reluctantly, the DEA agreed to let us do it our way.

Steve Gilkerson joined me. We asked to work with someone who knew the country well. The lab was located in a remote section of the Black Hills near the town of Pringle. We were introduced to Special Deputy Sheriff Paul Meuhl and Deputy Sheriff Matt Peters of the Custer County Sheriffs Office. Paul was a very unusual person. He had been a staff sergeant in the U.S. Army Special Forces. He served in Vietnam. Paul knew the Black Hills like no one else. We gave him the map coordinates of the lab and asked him to take us to the area so we could make our plans.

To get to the area of the lab we had to travel through rugged mountainous, heavily-wooded terrain. Paul led us at a pace that was exhausting. Steve and I were in excellent physical condition. But Paul pushed us to our limits. He had stashed food and water along the route. We would be running through the woods when Paul would stop, reach into a hollow log and pull out a package of food and water. It took several hours to reach our objective. This was great. I felt like an Army Ranger again.

We finally reached our destination. We were on a heavily wooded hilltop that overlooked the Wahle ranch. The ranch was the site of the lab. In addition to the lab which was in a barn, there was a main house, and large metal lean-tos. We watched the ranch from our perch for several hours. We made several of these recons.

On one occasion I decided I needed a closer look. So I began to crawl closer. I got in some high grass and heard a rattle close by. I carefully retreated. This was rattle snake country. When I rejoined Paul and Steve, they asked me how come I came back so soon. I told them and they said I made a wise move.

Finally, on August 13, 1984, I was told that the raid had to be conducted on August 17. My SWAT team arrived on August 15. Sheriff DeWayne Glasgow allowed us to use his ranch near Custer. The team assembled there to be briefed.

I used the available time to our best advantage. Steve and I prepared a detailed plan. We always used the U.S. army's five-paragraph operations order to plan. The army's op order outline is contained in a pocket-size card. I always carried the card with me. The method is called SMEAC. S is for situation where the facts that we know are listed. M is for mission. The mission is stated clearly and concisely. E is for execution. Details of how we will accomplish the mission are here. Every detail is planned for. A is for administration, including caring for any injured, handling prisoners, weapons to be carried. C is for command. Leadership assignments are made here.

It was my practice to write the operations order. I would then brief my boss. When he approved it, I read it to the troops. I answered any questions and made any modifications necessary. Then we practiced the execution portion. The process worked well. Nothing ever goes exactly as planned. But when you have a good plan and practice it, you can easily adjust.

The plan called for Deputy Meuhl and Deputy Matt Peters to lead us through the night to a jump-off point near the ranch. We then planned to quietly approach on foot. Each building was the responsibility of an element of our group. When we were in position, any suspects in the open were to be arrested. Then any buildings containing suspects was to be surrounded. They were to be ordered to surrender. Tear gas and K-9s were available if necessary. We practiced and were ready.

The lab was under surveillance. We all went to sleep early anticipating jump-off time to be 5 a.m. At about 9 p.m. we got word that the suspects changed their plans and decided to move everything that night. The result for us was we had to act now or they would get away.

We modified our plan. We would travel by vehicle to the ranch. We had surveillance on the ranch from nearby. When all of the suspects were out of the main house loading lab equipment, we would drive straight towards them. The house would be surrounded. The lean-tos would be secured. Since we had a detailed plan we were able to adjust quickly.

We arrived at the ranch. The surveillance team counted all suspects loading a trailer with lab equipment. We swooped in. Paul Meuhl and I, agent Phil Sena, and others got to high ground overlooking the trailer. The suspects had no chance and surrendered.

The main house was surrounded. There were some women and children inside. We had anticipated this so we didn't act until all the suspects left the house. The women and children were cared for. We also knew there were two dogs on the property. We were prepared to shoot them if they attacked us. I'm glad that they ran when we arrived.

We recovered about 30 pounds of meth and about 15 guns. The operation was a success in every respect. Paul Meuhl was a demolitions technician. He worked for many years blasting at the Crazy Horse monument near Custer. Sadly, Paul died of cancer in 1996.

Deputy Matt Peters went on to become chief of police in St. Peter, Minnesota. He is still a friend.

Our SWAT team continued to train with the K-9 teams of the MPD. On October 31, 1984, we got a chance to prove that our K-9 and SWAT partnership was a life-saver. The IRS and the FBI were investigating a group of tax protesters. The group was lead by Wilhelm Ernst Schmitt and included Roger Roy Luther, Harry Leroy Mott, and Ernest Willard Faust. They were all members of a tax protest group in northern Minnesota. They were plotting to kill an IRS employee. Schmidt was a skilled engineer with extensive knowledge of explosives. Mott was an appliance salesman from Rochester, Minnesota. He and his friends bragged that if the FBI ever tried to arrest them, they would kill the agents.

We took this talk very seriously as we prepared for the eventual arrest of Schmitt. We devised a plan using Ron Johnson and Bravo as a diversion, with Steve and I as the takedown team. We did extensive surveillance of Schmitt and his associate Roger Roy Luther. We did night surveillance using night-vision equipment. We noted that Schmitt always used the same door to enter and leave his house. That meant that door was not booby trapped. We learned that almost every day he would travel to the Perkins restaurant in Bemidji, Minnesota, to meet his friends. They used two-way radios to communicate. We heard them threaten us often.

On the day of the arrest we surveilled Schmitt from his house to the Perkins. He got out of his van and began to walk toward the restaurant. Steve, Ron and Bravo, SWAT member Phil Sena and I approached him in a van. We got out and ordered him to freeze. We told him he was under arrest.

FBI/MPD SWAT
Top row: Phil Sena, Al Garber, Gary Samuel
Middle row: Dave Bolles, Mike Kelly, Grant Geise, Len Matthys, Bob Erwin, Steve Gilkerson
Front row: Don Dealing, Ron Johnson, Bravo, Bill Lunquist, Louie, Ben Canny

Steve got behind him as Bravo growled. Schmitt held his hands in front of him and said we had the wrong man. He started to back towards his van. At the command of Ron, Bravo growled fiercely. Steve tackled Schmitt from the rear while Ron and I grabbed his arms. The result was that he fell flat on his face without the benefit of his arms to break his fall. We handcuffed him and got him to his feet. So this killer threatened to kill us and all he could accomplish was to fall on his face in the Perkins parking lot. Then to add to his embarrassment, when agent Sena got him to his feet, his pants fell down.

But this was serious business. We found a derringer pistol concealed in his wallet. He had a loaded 9 mm pistol and a hand grenade between the front seats of his van. In the back of his van he had a machine gun mounted on a tripod. We went to his house to execute a search warrant. Two MPD explosive ordinance demolition officers, Dave Indrehus and Dave Estenson, were with us. They had trained with our team for operations just like this one. We entered through the door that Schmitt used. The other door was booby trapped. We found quantities of black powder and the base plate for an 81 mm mortar. We never found the rest of the mortar. We also found notes that outlined their plan to rob a bank in Rolla, North Dakota. The notes included a sketch of the bank and a list of items they needed like tape, gloves, and masks. The list was later determined to have been written by Schmitt.

Other weapons we found were hand grenades, a grenade launcher, several MAC-10 submachine guns that had been altered to fire fully automatic, and silencers.

Then we went to the home of Schmidt's associate, Roger Roy Luther. We had a search warrant. It was a very cold day with sleet. As we were getting ready to approach my rifle jammed. I later learned that the lubricant the FBI was using would gum up at certain cold temperatures. Can you imagine how I felt when I attempted to load my rifle only to find it would not work? We never used that lubricant again. The raid on Luther's place went well. He was not there so we waited for him in his home. The home was dug into a hill and had shooting portals throughout. As we waited we began to hear the sounds of our team members talking from outside the house. Upon further inspection we found that Luther had installed motion sensors and listening devices outside his house.

He eventually came home and we arrested him without incident. We recovered many other illegal guns and silencers.

Sometimes members of SWAT teams and other highly-trained, well-equipped teams think they are elite. They believe that doing the routine tasks that are part of every case are beneath them. One of my team almost brought down the entire group by exhibiting this attitude. After the raid on Luther's place, a search for evidence was conducted. A lot of evidence was found. The agents who conducted the evidentiary search asked this SWAT guy for help. His response was that SWAT doesn't do stuff like that. They only do the action. The agent complained to agent in charge Blay. Dick came to me and he was mad. He told me if he ever heard that kind of attitude coming from a SWAT member that would be the end of SWAT. I made sure it never happened again.

We were concerned that someone would attempt to help Schmitt escape from our custody. So instead of putting him the jail in Bemidji, we chartered a plane. Steve and I were told to transport Schmitt to Minneapolis. We boarded the small chartered plane. Schmitt was so fat that the seat belt wouldn't reach around him. The seats in this plane faced the door. Thus Schmitt was seated facing the door with no seat belt. He made some comment like what would you do if I tried to jump out. I think I said, "Nothing." He did not try to jump and we arrived in Minneapolis.

The chief prosecutor was U.S. Attorney Jim Rosenbaum. Jim went on to be a federal judge and later chief judge. We became good friends during and after the case.

The actual prosecution was handled by Assistant U.S. Attorneys Janice Symchych and Jon M. Hopeman. Both were outstanding prosecutors. Jon was of significant help to me in writing about this case. There were two trials. In the first trial Schmitt acted as his own attorney. When he cross examined me, he asked me how old I was. He told me he was 20 years older. He asked me how much I weighed. He told me he weighed 50 pounds more. He asked me if I exercised regularly. He said he never exercised. Then finally he asked why it took four younger, better-conditioned officers, and a police dog to arrest a man like me. My response was that we knew he was dangerous and we were determined to overwhelm him, and we did. He didn't ask me any further questions.

It's never a good idea to represent yourself in court. But Schmitt was doing pretty well until he told the jury that he had intelligence that the Russians had landed on the east coast of Mexico and were headed north. Things went downhill for him from that point.

The prosecution had a minor problem. The Bureau of Alcohol, Tobacco, and Firearms (ATF) had prepared a video showing them detonating one of the grenades we found in Schmitt's home. The video was supposed to show the jury just how powerful the grenade was. Unfortunately, no one on the prosecution team previewed the video. It was played in court and was very graphic. However, a voice of one of the ATF agents was heard on the tape saying, "That cocksucker really went off." That mistake caused a minor furor in court.

All defendants were tried by U.S. District Court Judge Edward J. Devitt. Schmitt, Luther, and Foust were convicted of conspiring to injure and impede an agent of the IRS. Schmitt was also found guilty of assaulting an agent of the FBI; carrying a firearm in the course of the assault on the FBI agent; possession of an unloaded firearm, a loaded wallet derringer; possessing an unregistered .308-caliber machine gun; possessing two unregistered M-61 hand grenades in his vehicle; and possession of a loaded 9 mm pistol by a convicted felon.

Luther was also convicted of manufacturing three machine guns without permission of the secretary of the treasury and possession of unregistered machine guns.

Foust was also convicted of possession of an unregistered wallet derringer and an unregistered machine gun.

All of them got long prison terms.

Then the second trial concerning the plot to rob the Rolla, North Dakota, bank began. The sketches, notes, and equipment lists we found in Schmitt's house were key pieces of evidence. But there was more. Mott was identified by witnesses as casing the bank. The bank had windows that were above eye level from the street. An employee looked up one day and saw Mott who had pulled himself up, peering through the window. He was also identified as being in the small town of Rolla wearing a wig to disguise himself as an Indian. If you saw Mott you'd know how funny that would have looked. To make matters worse, the bank manager identified Mott saying he looked just like his brother. They were convicted on all counts.

Judge Devitt was again the sentencing judge. Things didn't go well for them. They got more prison time.

I was always looking for innovative ways to make our SWAT team more effective and safer. I met Dr. Pat Lillja who was the director of emergency services at North Memorial Hospital in Robbinsdale, Minnesota. Pat had the reputation of caring a lot about police in the performance of their duties. I had been concerned that if one of us got shot it would take valuable time for a paramedic to reach us. Pat and I decided to experiment with the concept of SWAT paramedics. The medics would accompany us to a position close to the objective but safe enough so that they could deliver their services without being shot.

Dr Lillja asked for volunteers. The first ones to volunteer were Mike Murphy, Mike Peach, and Nancy Larson. They were all very experienced medics. We began training with them. The agents were just thrilled to have these life-savers so close. As the concept took shape, specific protocols were included. The medics were responsible for planning for medical emergencies for upcoming operations. They did things like contact local ambulance services where we would be operating. They contacted local hospitals to determine if they had adequate supplies of such things as snake bite anti-venom or areas of the hospital which could be isolated to treat wounded members who had been in tear-gassed areas. They put together a list of emergency medical equipment that they could carry on operations. These included MAST trousers, back packs, four 500cc IV bags, two trauma sets, dressings, airways, and many other items. Each medic carried a backpack weighing 42 pounds. The FBI purchased the equipment.

In every operation some team members were designated as the paramedic security element. Their job was to protect the medics and to get them to a place where they could safely deliver emergency medical services. The medics dressed in dark uniforms which were different than the other SWAT members. This was done so that we could easily recognize the medics in the heat of battle. They did not carry weapons because their job was to treat not fight. However, they trained with all of our weapons so that in an emergency they could use the weapons.

The medics became great friends and remain so today. They really cared about us. When the weather was hot, and because we wore a lot of equipment, the medics made sure we took in the proper amount of liquids. I know that they prevented many cases of dehydration. In one case they removed a bullet fragment from one guy's head. They were great for morale. The members felt confident that if they were injured they would get the best medical care available right now. Their presence made the team know how much their well being meant to me as leader.

This concept spread all over the country. Many SWAT teams have medics. Some teams arm their medics, but we firmly believed that paramedics should not be in a position where they have to fight. That is not their job.

The objective in developing our SWAT team was to have a self- contained unit that could deal with any situation. The next step was to add explosives experts. Again we looked to Minneapolis. And again Chief Bouza made his bomb squad available. We selected two members. They were enthusiastic. Again, they were not intended to be fighters. They were experts in their field and that is how they trained with us.

The final element was to add SWAT members from the Minneapolis PD. I had worked closely with their SWAT commanders through the years. So I knew them well. The FBI/MPD basic school became the standard for SWAT teams throughout Minnesota, North Dakota, and South Dakota. So it was a natural next step to add MPD SWAT officers to our team. The mix resulted in a 20-man SWAT team with K-9 capability, emergency medical capability, and explosive ordnance disposal capability.

Sheriff Chuck Zacharias, John Moore, Bob Waters, Mike Burke,
Rollie Martinez, Brad Urban

Mike Sitari, Eric Kleinberg, Steve Marston, Chris Omodt, Mike Snyder

Ramsey County SO and Edina PD SWAT graduation

The U.S. marshal helped us by swearing in all of the officers as special deputy U.S. marshals. This gave the officers the same jurisdiction as the FBI agents. The officers were proud of their status as deputy U.S. marshals. We were proud to have them with us as equal partners. This was law enforcement cooperation at a level I had never before seen.

The areas that the Minneapolis FBI/SWAT team normally covered included North Dakota, South Dakota, and Minnesota. We were also subject to being called anywhere in the United States. We needed a transportation capability. We had been training with Northwest Airlines (NWA) in an effort to prepare us to combat an airplane hijacking. Northwest was extremely cooperative, making aircraft and crews available. Their chief training officer, Vic Britt, was invaluable offering us expert knowledge about different type aircraft. The Minneapolis/St. Paul International Airport Police trained with our joint team. This cooperation paid dividends as you will learn later in this book.

Since many of the NWA pilots were also members of the Minnesota Air National Guard and the U.S. Air Force Reserve, they helped us to get an agreement between the guard and the FBI to fly us and our equipment in C-130 aircraft. The commander of the guard agreed to fly us to actual operations. This was a great advantage because instead of driving for many hours and arriving tired, we were able to fly with our vehicles and equipment. We arrived fresh and ready to go.

The spirit of cooperation was at an all time high. Now it was time to use it. In July of 1985, our team was ordered to go to northern Arkansas to participate with other SWAT teams in surrounding the compound of a radical white supremacist group known as the Covenant, Sword, and Arm of the Lord (CSA). Our team loaded on C-130 aircraft and departed for Arkansas. One of the K-9 teams that went with us was Dave Dobrotka and Spike. Spike was nasty. We offloaded on a very hot day. The tarmac had melted and when Spike started to walk his paws sunk into the asphalt. It was painful, so it was up to Dave to clean his paws. This was the only time I saw a police dog try to attack his handler. It took K-9 officers Ron Johnson, Luke Koerner, and Dave to hold Spike down so his paws could be cleaned. When it was over, Spike was meaner than ever. But to show how well trained we all were, including Spike, he was able to rejoin the effort. I guess dogs have short memories.

The first order of business was for us to attend a briefing. The FBI Hostage Rescue Team (HRT) Commander, Danny Colson held the briefing. Steve and I knew Danny well from our days together on the New York FBI bank robbery squad. The HRT was the primary team during this operation. The SWAT teams were there to augment the HRT. Each SWAT team leader was asked to tell Danny what resources they had. When it came to my turn, I told him we had a 20-man SWAT team, three K-9 teams, three medics, and two EOD personnel. Colson was surprised at the extent of our resources and a little jealous. For all of us, SWAT was an additional duty. We all had regular assignments. For Colson's men of the HRT, their full time duty was HRT missions.

After the briefing, Steve and I were visiting with Danny and he told us he really didn't want us there, but he needed our unique resources. He said he would have much preferred to handle the situation with his men alone. We took this as a compliment.

A siege of the CSA compound developed as negotiations with the occupants went on. The negotiators were trying to get those occupants who were wanted on federal charges to surrender. After the surrender search warrants were to be executed.

The weather was extremely hot and humid. Our medics, Mike Peach and Mike Murphy, made certain that all of the SWAT members, not just the Minneapolis team, drank a lot of liquids. The medics mixed up gallons of electrolyte drinks. They certainly prevented dehydration.

The siege dragged on. We worked around the clock. The terrain was heavily wooded and we could see the armed occupants of the compound. We had a sector of the perimeter which we were required to staff around the clock. To some members who had not seen combat in the military, this was a scary job. One of my young members was Mike Mines, an FBI agent from New Jersey. This was Mike's first mission of this nature. He said to me privately that he didn't know what to do and was concerned he would screw up. I told him to stick very close to one of our veterans, Lenny Matthys. Off they went into the woods. The next morning I asked Mike how it went. He said he felt much better. Training is surely necessary. But there is no substitute for actual combat. Even with all of our men we were stretched thin. One day medic Mike Murphy came to me and said he noticed how tired everyone was. He volunteered to work on the perimeter so someone else could rest. I knew that Mike was a Vietnam veteran in the U.S. army. So He got an M-16, gear, and went on the perimeter.

Eventually, the occupants surrendered peacefully. Morale among our group was high. I was extremely proud of our performance.

After we got to Minneapolis, everyone went back to their regular duties. I was the director of training. One of the subjects I enjoyed teaching was defensive tactics. That term means unarmed combat. The vast majority of resistance that police and agents face is physical, not with guns or knives. So it is just as important to know how to fight as it is to shoot. I received my initial defensive tactics training from an FBI agent Chin Ho Lee. Chin was a naturalized U.S. citizen. He was born in Korea and served in the Republic of Korea (ROK) army. He was a world-class teacher of several martial arts. His contribution to the law enforcement profession was that he adapted techniques from various martial arts to our needs and abilities. When I was teaching a class and a student would describe a situation that was new to me, I would call Chin at the FBI academy. In one case a student officer described a situation where he was trying to arrest a very muscular, strong suspect. The suspect would not allow the officer to handcuff him. He crossed his hands in front of his chest and leaned over the trunk of his car. The officer could not move the suspect. I had never encountered that type of resistance. So I called Chin and he said, "That is the old turtle." He described how to press in the middle of the suspect's back and his arms would pop out. I told the officers what Chin said. Then we practiced with the strongest member of the class. One officer, using the point of his elbow, pressed the suspect and his arms popped out like magic.

Chin left the FBI after 15 years. He told me that the officials at the FBI academy were angry with him because officers and agents were calling the

Al Garber and Chin Ho Lee

academy and asking for him only. I think he was just too skilled for the academy.

We had just wonderful cooperation from so many people when we needed training facilities. We needed a large gym-type facility to conduct a defensive tactics class. Lew Holtz, who was the head football coach at the University of Minnesota, let us use the indoor football practice facility. He wrote me a letter which said in part: "... Just want you to know that I have the utmost respect for your profession and the difficult job you do. If there is anything I can ever do for you, do not hesitate to call on me." It was signed, "Sincerely; Lew Holtz, Head Football Coach, University of Minnesota."

When I was in New York, I heard a lot of complaining about many topics. I remember telling one of my friends if he thought things were not being done right he should get promoted and do something about it. A supervisory position opened up in 1986 in the Minneapolis FBI. I applied for it hoping to get promoted so I could fix some things. Larry Lawler was the agent in charge. He was a former Oakland, California, police officer. We got along well. He asked me if I was sure I wanted to be a supervisor. He reminded me that as training coordinator and SWAT leader I was, in fact, if not officially, a supervisor. I told Larry I was sure.

My last operation as SWAT team leader was one of the most unique in terms of tactics and the person we arrested. William Charles Longbehn, also known as William Sisson and "Peg Leg," had one leg. He was dealing in methamphetamines which he brought from San Diego. He was also an outlaw biker type, who fancied himself as a modern day pirate. We found photos of him dressed as a pirate wearing his peg leg. His peg leg had a skull with two jewel eyes. He also used the alias DDDCP which stood for "dirty deeds done cheap."

He did his dealing from his home at 1959 North Lexington in St. Paul. He was indicted on 19 counts relating to meth. Our SWAT team was tasked with arresting him on September 10, 1986. The night before the arrest Steve Gilkerson and I did a recon to make a plan. We determined that he had a very large bull mastiff dog. We also suspected he had guns. There was a large window in the rear of his house. Just inside the window was the phone. The front entrance faced a long driveway.

The plan was to divide the team into two elements. Steve led one element which was to make their way to the front door before first light. The second element, which I led, was to scale the high wooden fence in the rear and then position us near the large window.

One of the investigators was to call into the house when we told him we were in position. When Longbehn came to the phone, agent Tom Trautman who was with me was to break the window with a baseball bat. Tom was to clear the window of glass and then I was to point my submachine gun at Longbehn. When the situation was controlled, we would deal with the dog.

Everything went according to plan and the call was made. Peg Leg came to the phone naked, hopping with out his peg leg. But, before Tom could break the window, Peg Leg said, "Fuck you," and hung up. The investigator called again and Peg Leg came back to the phone. This time he talked to the investigator. Tom broke the window. I got the drop on him. At the same time, Steve broke the front door and peeked in as he was instructed to do. He saw the huge dog and Longbehn's girlfriend. He told her to control the dog or he'd shoot it. She complied. She put the dog in a pickup that was in the driveway. We then arrested Longbehn.

Later we found that when he answered the phone he turned on a phone recorder. We listened to the recording that recorded the breaking glass and some yelling, "Don't fucking move or I'll shoot you." I can't figure out who would talk like that.

Assistant U.S. Attorney Paul Murphy prosecuted the case before U.S. District Court Judge Edward J. Devitt. Longbehn was convicted and Judge Devitt sentenced him to 60 years. The judge stipulated that he was not eligible for release until he served at least 20 years.

Longbehn was released from federal prison on March 7, 2008. During his time in prison he filed numerous unsuccessful appeals.

I have been asked many times by people who are interested in what we did if I was scared. Honestly, I was never scared. I was very concerned and always thinking of what I would do if things turned bad. I don't believe you can do this job if you are scared or if your fear dictates your actions.

On December 7, 1986, I was in the St. Paul, Minnesota, FBI office when Larry Lawler called and told me to come to Minneapolis. When I got there, I was told, "I am going to change your life." Then he told me I was being promoted.

In the FBI, supervisors are more managers than leaders. They are administrators. Normally they are expected to be in the office. They insure that necessary reports are prepared and deadlines are met. Only in unusual cases are supervisors expected to be at the scene. I always thought this did not make sense. If supervisors only got out of the office when big cases or emergencies occurred, how could they be expected to have the necessary experience to be successful. The result as I saw it was that inexperienced supervisors often were responsible in the most important cases. I thought

I was going to change that mentality by being on the street whenever I thought on-scene leadership was necessary. I thought that the agents would know how interested I was in their well being by my interest in what they were doing. I wanted to see them in action so I could evaluate them and offer constructive advice. I believed my experience would help the agents who worked for me.

Not long after being promoted we were told to go to Sioux Falls, South Dakota, to try to arrest two of the FBIs ten most-wanted fugitives. They were bank robbers named Conners and Dougherty. They were supposed to be hiding in a house. Since I was now the SWAT supervisor, Steve Gilkerson became the SWAT leader. So Larry Lawler, Steve Gilkerson, the rest of the SWAT team, and I went to Sioux Falls. After contacting the police, Steve and I set off to make a plan. After the plan was complete, we presented it to Larry. He said that the plan was good except for one part. That was the part where I went with the team to the house. He told me I was no longer team leader. Now I was the supervisor and I should be at the command post (CP) with him.

I listened on the radio as the team approached the house. As was our standard operating procedure (SOP), the team quietly surrounded the house. They waited for any signs of activity in the house. There were none, so they announced their presence. There was no response. I heard Steve on the radio. He gave the order for K-9 officer Ron Johnson and his security element to approach the door. They got the door open and I heard Steve say the dog is in. I felt uneasy hearing two of my best friends Steve and Ron risking their lives while I was in the safety of the CP. At this point, I had doubts about whether being an FBI supervisor was what I wanted.

In April 1987, police dog Bravo had to be put to sleep. It may seem strange but I felt very sad for Bravo and for Ron Johnson. I wrote an article entitled " A Tribute to Police Dog Bravo." Here is that article:

A TRIBUTE TO POLICE DOG BRAVO

Bravo was born in September 1978. He was trained as a police dog by Minneapolis police officer Ron Johnson in 1980. In 1983, Bravo assumed the unique duties of operating with the Minneapolis Division, FBI SWAT team. At the time, many canine handlers, including Ron Johnson, as well as many SWAT team members, doubted that a police dog could operate successfully with the SWAT team.

The primary doubt was that a police dog could be trained well enough and be skilled enough to differentiate between SWAT members and suspects. Bravo and Officer Johnson proved all of the doubters wrong. Bravo operated successfully with the SWAT team on numerous occasions until physical disabilities caused Officer Johnson to retire Bravo from everyday patrol duties in December 1986. Nevertheless, Bravo, because of his exceptional skills, and Officer Johnson because of his commitment to the SWAT team, continued to operate with the SWAT team until early 1987. Through hours of patient training and with a remarkable skill to know what his duties were, Bravo was an exceptionally talented and valuable animal. I can say with certainty that Bravo saved the life of at least one suspect and possibly the lives of SWAT team members in one instance when he distracted the suspect long enough for the SWAT team to disarm and arrest the suspect.

A special bond developed between the SWAT team members and Bravo. Officer Johnson as well as other canine handlers understand the sadness when Bravo had to be put to sleep in April 1987 because of increased physical disabilities.

Submitted by Allen Garber, Supervisory Special Agent, Minneapolis Division, FBI, 4/10/87.

Now back to my supervisory experiences. Larry Lawler was transferred and replaced by Jeff Jamar. Jeff had the misfortune to become the incident commander at the infamous Branch Davidian compound incident which occurred near Waco, Texas. When Jeff introduced himself to the staff, he insisted that he be addressed as Jeff. With my military, SWAT, and FBI experience, I found it hard to call him Jeff.

Jeff Jamar and I developed an unusual working relationship. I know he respected my investigative and SWAT experience. But he made it clear to me very early that he wanted me in the office unless I specifically asked for permission to leave. He told me that when he phoned my office he expected me to answer.

On July 28, 1988, I received permission from Jeff Jamar to accompany the SWAT team to the St. Paul/Minneapolis Airport. We had a great working relationship with the airport police. Duke Fathol Greene of Kenai, Alaska, was wanted by authorities on the Turtle Mountain Indian Reservation at Belcourt, North Dakota, for attempted murder. He was reported to be armed with a submachine gun.

Our agent in Minot, Jane Turner, got information that Greene intended to fly from Minot to Minneapolis disguised as a woman. The plan was for agent Turner to fly on the same plane with fugitive Greene. She was to get off the plane directly behind Greene. That way there was no possibility of a mistake in identifying him.

Some of the agents and uniformed airport police were in a stairway adjoining Gate 75 on the Green Concourse. Steve, two other agents in street clothes, and I were in the gate with other people to welcome the incoming passengers. Jane Turner came up the ramp behind what looked like an attractive young lady, who was actually Greene. He wore a brown wig, high-heeled shoes, a brown skirt, and a multi-colored shawl. He carried a small purse.

As he neared us, we went into action. Steve and I knocked him on his backside. Before he knew what was happening, he was handcuffed. The uniformed officers came out of the stairway. Other passengers were yelling, "Stop beating that lady." The police told everyone what was happening just as one of the agents pulled off Greene's wig. We checked his baggage and found a 9 mm submachine gun with ammunition. Later we also found out he was a military deserter.

The technique we used to knock Greene to the ground was one we practiced many times. Once again, this case proved that the biggest advantage SWAT teams have is the ability to plan and then to execute.

On a Saturday in March 1989, I got a call from Captain Bruce Erickson of the Apple Valley, Minnesota, Police Department. I knew Bruce well from training. He told me that Willie Johnson and Larry Hill, who was blind, had escaped from a state prison and were now holding Lois Platt and her two children hostage. They were in her townhouse in Apple Valley. Bruce asked me if our SWAT team could help. He explained that both escapees were violent and threatened to kill Platt and her kids if the police tried to rescue them.

I called Jeff Jamar and asked for his permission to assist. He said we could help but that we should not get "too involved." I had no idea what that meant, but I was glad he gave us permission to help. I called Bruce Erickson and told him we'd be on our way. I called Steve Gilkerson and told him to get his SWAT team going.

We met at the command post. Bruce was the incident commander (IC) which meant we worked for him. That was fine with me. Bruce, Steve, and I listened to the police negotiators trying to convince Johnson and Hill to surrender. It was very clear that they intended to kill the hostages if they didn't get what they wanted. Captain Erickson asked us to set up a sniper team across from the front entrance to the townhouse. He said that under the circumstances he believed that the fugitives would kill unless we killed them first. I agreed. Steve sent a sniper to set up. They had a direct view of the front door. I remember them telling me that the owner of the home they were set up in offered them cookies and milk, but they had to decline.

Jeff Jamar called me to ask what the situation was. I told him what our part was. He didn't say anything. I assumed he thought we were not too involved. He did not call back. I called him when the operation was over.

Among the SWAT teams there was the Burnsville, Minnesota, team led by Sgt. Bill Micklus. Bill was also a good friend. We had trained together. He was one of the instructors at the SWAT school that the FBI sponsored. We all trusted each other. The SWAT teams took turns being on standby in case an emergency assault became necessary. The negotiations continued. When the negotiators reached a consensus that, if the police did not act, Plat and her children would be killed, Captain Erickson asked for my advice. Steve and I talked with Bruce. I could feel the pressure he was under. He was about to make a life-and-death decision. When he made his decision, I encouraged him not to bring any more stress on himself. He had made a decision and that was that. His decision was that an emergency assault was necessary to save the lives of the hostages. Bill Micklus's team was on standby so they were given the mission. The outcome was that, when the Burnsville SWAT team entered the townhouse, blind Larry Hill tried to attack the officers and was shot and killed. Johnson was subdued. Bill and his team were truly heroes.

I then called Jeff Jamar and told him the outcome.

Although this case was a success, my relationship with agent in charge Jeff Jamar continued to be strained.

On Monday May 8, 1989, I was involved in the fourth event of my career involving a surveillance that ended with the arrest of a bank robber as he was in the act of robbing. This one occurred in Rochester, Minnesota. FBI agent Dave Price had gotten information from the Winona County, sheriff's office about a bank robbery that was about to occur. A little bit of background is that agent Dave Price had been stationed in Rapid City, South Dakota, in June of 1975. He was the first agent to arrive at the scene of the murders of agents Williams and Koler.

The information Dave received about the bank robbery was that an informant had been recruited by William Charles Hendricks to rob a bank. Hendricks would not tell which bank they were to rob. So we had to follow them using an assortment of cars, vans, trucks, and planes. They arrived at the Marquette Bank in Rochester.

My job was to coordinate the arrest. I was observing the arrival of the robbers from a vantage point about 100 yards away. Steve Gilkerson and Dave Price had gotten into the bank just before the robbers arrived. I told them on the radio that one robber was getting out of the parked car and approaching the bank. The robber pulled down a ski mask. Steve and Dave were able to get out of the bank by a back door. They approached the corner of the bank as I kept them advised of the robber's location. As Steve and Dave confronted the robber from behind a ballistic shield, other agents and police confronted the getaway driver.

The arrests were successful. They required careful coordination and precise execution.

 But then on October 22, 1989, an incident occurred that would put our problems on hold. At about 9:30 p.m. on Sunday, October 22, 1989, I got a call from Agent Al Catallo of the St. Cloud, Minnesota, FBI office.

Catallo told me that Jacob Wetterling, age 11, had been kidnapped at gunpoint as he was walking home in St. Joseph, Minnesota. He said a search was underway. I called Jeff Jamar. Jeff agreed with my plan to go to up to St. Joseph if Jacob was not found by daylight Monday.

So began a case that was to reach national proportions and was to affect me forever. I arrived in St. Joseph at about 9 a.m., Monday, October 23. St Joseph is a small town about five minutes west of St. Cloud. When I arrived, I went to a command post which had been set up in a community center. I spoke to Al Catallo, Sheriff Charlie Grafft, and the St. Joseph police chief. Jacob had not been found. Jacob, his brother Trevor, and their friend Aaron Larson had gone on their bikes to the nearby Tom Thumb convenience store.

Jacob's parents Patty and Jerry had gone to a party nearby. Jacob was left at home to babysit his younger brother Trevor, age 10, and his sister Carmen, 8. Arron Larsen, 11, joined them. With the parents' permission Jacob, Trevor, and Aaron took off on their bikes and scooter for the Tom Thumb store. On the way back, as they approached an intersection about a mile from the Wetterling residence, an armed man appeared. He wore a mask and carried a handgun. He asked Trevor his age. The he told Trevor to run. He did the same with Aaron. He said if they looked back, he'd shoot them. They ran. They looked back to see the man holding Jacob.

They ran home and the sheriff's office was called. Jacob was gone. The investigation that followed was like no other in my experience. It grew to monumental proportions. It drew nationwide media attention.

The case quickly outgrew the command post. It was moved to the Stearns County Sheriff's Department in St. Cloud. The effort to find Jacob is so extensive that I cannot begin to describe it. There are numerous aspects that are of particular note.

Jeff Jamar arrived on October 23. He asked me to accompany him to meet the parents. We sat in their living room and Jeff described the efforts so far. He told them to be patient. Patty just exploded. She screamed you can ask me to do anything but don't ask me to be patient. Throughout the investigation Patty was persistent and demanded to know when an important development occurred. Jerry, on the other hand, was calm and didn't ask many questions.

Because of Jerry's demeanor, some suspected he knew more about the kidnapping. But I don't believe it. His history shows his behavior has been consistent throughout his adult life. He is just not outwardly emotional. Later he was polygraphed with no indication of deception. I know that he loves his children as much as we love ours.

In 1989 law enforcement was not yet computerized. Captain Jack Kritzek, of the sheriff's department, saw early on that, if the information coming was not computerized immediately, we would lose control. So he set up a system to record all information. Jack deserves high praise.

I was the FBI supervisor on the scene. I reported daily or more often to Jeff Jamar in Minneapolis. I was in charge of the investigation. The sheriff, Charlie Grafft, was the overall person in charge. The outpouring from the community was overwhelming. At one point there were over 70 investigators working full time. People and businesses provided food and beverages for us. There were nearly 20 people answering phones.

As the information was developed, it was categorized into "A" or "B." A meant the information was acted on immediately. B meant action would take place soon but not immediately. There were evaluators who looked at each piece of information coming in and assigned it either A or B. Two of these evaluators were Steve Mund and Frank Whippler. Steve was an investigator for the Stearns County sheriff. Frank was the chief deputy sheriff for Benton County. Both were great investigators and hard workers. Both have become friends forever.

There was an immense amount of pressure on all of us. Some of the pressure came from the community, the parents, and the media. But most of the pressure was self-imposed. Everyone desperately wanted to find Jacob. We were not used to being unsuccessful and most of us had children. Steve Mund was very critical of my performance in directing the investigation. At one point, I had had enough from him. I asked him to talk with me privately. I told him that there was enough pressure and that the last thing I needed was for a key player like him to always be critical. That was the turning point in my relationship with him. He became one of my best supporters. He was there to help in any way from then on.

One of my duties was to brief the parents regularly. They were so understanding. They knew how hard we were all trying to find Jacob. Patty especially just wanted to be kept informed. She offered suggestions but she was never a hindrance to our efforts.

Our days were 12–16 hours. Every day began with a briefing. Each team of investigators would be given their assignments. There was discussion about what the investigators thought should be done. In the end it was my decision about which way to go. I had plenty of help, but the ultimate decision was mine. About 10 a.m. I would get a splitting headache. I called it my mid-morning headache. My principal assistant was FBI supervisor Terry Wyllie. Terry did not have a criminal investigation background but he was a source of relief and comfort to me.

When the kidnapping occurred, Steve Gilkerson and his SWAT team were training at Camp Ripley, Minnesota. I called Steve and asked him to come and help. He brought the entire SWAT team. Minneapolis Police Chief John Laux gave permission for the MPD officers who were members of the SWAT team to help. They arrived and immediately were assigned to investigative teams.

Suspects began to surface. Each one was investigated as if they were the kidnapper. In one case, an inmate at the Stillwater State Prison told us that another inmate said he kidnapped Jacob. We put a recording device in the suspect's cell. We heard him talk about kidnapping Jacob. We introduced an undercover agent, Carmen Piccarillo. We recorded Carmen's conversations with the suspect. All of this took place in the old shabby Stillwater prison. The warden Bob Erickson did everything we asked for. I remember walking in the dark corridors behind the suspect's cell. The warden knew every inch of that old prison.

The suspect told the undercover that he wanted to pay to have his car destroyed. We arranged to get the car. We brought it to our garage where a team from the FBI lab went over it from bumper to bumper. I never saw a car torn apart like that one. It was like in the movie *The French Connection*. The lab men were not able to get any evidence.

We obtained a search warrant for the man's rural farmhouse. I went there with others to search the house. We searched totally and completely without finding anything. The only thing left to do was talk to the suspect. Minnesota Bureau of Criminal Apprehension (BCA) agent Dennis Sigafoos and I went to the prison. We had the suspect brought to a room where we met him. I asked him if he kidnapped Jacob. He didn't respond. Dennis tried to convince him to tell us where Jacob was for the parents' peace of mind. He said nothing. We told him that we would leave a piece of paper and a pen in the room. We would leave and when we came back we hoped that someone would draw a map of Jacob's location. We left. After ten minutes we returned. The suspect had returned to his cell and the paper was blank. We never found out if this man did it.

In another instance, a similar crime had taken place in Cold Spring, Minnesota. A young boy was kidnapped and later released. Cold Spring is a town near St. Joseph. It was apparent to us that there was a strong possibility that the kidnapping of the boy in Cold Spring was related to Jacob's abduction. A suspect was developed. We were able to find the car the suspect owned at the time of the Cold Spring incident. Our lab found fibers in the car that were similar to fibers from the boy's coat.

We surveilled this man for weeks without success. Finally, we convinced the county attorney to charge the man with the Cold Spring kidnapping. This proved to be a bad mistake. First, we did not tell our BCA partners of the facts until the suspect was charged. Second, the county attorney really didn't want to charge him. But we insisted so he went ahead. Criminal profilers from the FBI Academy flew up to St. Cloud to offer us advice on how to interview the suspect after we arrested him.

The whole thing turned into a comedy of errors. Steve Gilkerson was selected to interview the suspect. The profilers set up furniture in certain places in the interview room. They placed a flag and special lights in the room. They scripted the interview for Steve. They told him he had to say exactly what they told him to. This all sounded ridiculous but we did what they said.

The man was arrested and brought to the interview room. Before Steve could say anything the guy said he wanted a lawyer. That was the end of the interview. The charges were dismissed. We never were able to get any evidence against him. The BCA agents and the county attorney were furious at us.

Another element we had to deal with was the psychics. Jerry Wetterling was contacted on several occasions by people who claimed to have powers that told them where Jacob was. I never believed any of them. However, I thought that giving us information which came from psychic power might have been a way for a person to pass us legitimate information without having to name a source. So we acted on most psychic information. None of it panned out.

We conducted massive ground searches. The searches got progressively wider. Lt. Kent Christianson, Hennepin County, Minnesota, Sheriff's Office, coordinated these searches. Volunteers on foot, on horseback, and on ATVs searched for days without success.

One of the teams developed a suspect who told some young kids that he kidnapped Jacob and threw his body in a lake. Divers searched the lake without success. We tracked the suspect to King County, Washington. I went out there and worked with local detectives. We found the man who insisted he was just trying to impress some young girls. He gave us an alibi which we were able to substantiate.

After weeks of 12–16 hour days, we were worn out. But I wanted to keep going. Jeff Jamar told me to give some of the troops the weekend off. I objected, but he said they needed the time off. Now I know he was right. I didn't take any time off. I just couldn't leave.

The number of investigators was gradually reduced. The support from the community began to become less noticeable. The hardest thing for me was to tell Patty and Jerry that we were leaving. They knew we were running out of leads and said they understood. I felt like we were deserting them.

The kidnapper was never found. Jacob was never found. I have been asked many times if I think Jacob is dead. While logic may say he is, I see no reason to believe he is dead. I see no harm in hoping he is alive. The case has been reviewed many times by various law enforcement agencies. They all find something they would have done different. That doesn't surprise me.

My belief is that the kidnapper is either a very unique criminal who has not told anyone he did it or he is dead. I say this because my experience is that almost all criminals tell someone what they have done. That's how we catch most of them. It is a very unusual case in which we don't hear about a crime and are then able to get some evidence. This is an unusual case.

Patty Wetterling has become a spokesperson for kidnapped children and their families. She has been very active with the National Center for Missing and Exploited Children. She and Jerry founded the Jacob Wetterling Foundation. The foundation started out to publicize Jacob's abduction. It has evolved and now offers training to law enforcement agencies and other non-profit organizations. It provides speakers who offer advice to parents and schools. Patty is still the driving force behind the foundation. However, she is more in the background. She made two unsuccessful bids for the U.S. congress. We still have infrequent contact.

As the years have passed, the FBI and the Minnesota Bureau of Criminal Apprehension have gone on to other cases. The Stearns County Sheriff's has become the only agency still investigating. Leads come in infrequently. The case investigator is now an experienced detective. In 1989 he was a new sheriff's deputy.

An interesting phenomenon has occurred. As I said earlier, law enforcement officers are not used to failure. We all failed, and not because we didn't work hard enough. So the only avenue left is to review the work already done to look for new avenues. When new avenues cannot be found, criticism of the work done occurred. Those of us who worked as hard and as long as was humanely possible are now criticized for "botching" the investigation. There is no point for me to divulge who is now saying this. I understand that criticizing is a substitute for not having any new avenues to explore.

Another more dangerous phenomenon that has occurred is that as new investigators take over they have personalized this case. The result is that unless a new lead has been the result of their work, they are reluctant to follow it. There is nothing I can do about it. But Patty understands this and does something about it. She maintains a cordial relationship with the Sheriff's Department. In her own unique way she presses them for answers without being offensive or insulting. On October 22 of each year she bakes chocolate chip cookies and delivers them to the Sheriff's Office to thank them for their work and to encourage them to keep looking.

I still occasionally receive information or leads. I always pass them on to the case investigator at the Sheriff's Office. But, since I am no longer working, I don't know the results. Occasionally, I also receive calls from other police officers or investigators asking me what they should do with information they just received. Recently, I got a call from an FBI Agent who had worked on the case more than 15 years ago. But, like so many others, he cannot forget or stop thinking about Jacob. The agent had been thinking of a new angle. I put him in contact with the case investigator. Since then I have received several calls from the agent. He is frustrated because he doesn't know and can't find out if his information was acted on. I have told him there is nothing he can do about it except keep trying to contact the current investigator. That's the way these things work out as time passes.

The sheriff's officers assigned the case are justifiably tired of the cases being reviewed again and again by various "cold case" units. So far the results of the reviews have not found Jacob.

Every October 22, I call Jerry and Patty. We just chat and reminisce. I call because I want them to continue to know that I still care and I remember. On October 22, 2008, when I called, Jerry reminded me that in 2009 it will be 20 years since Jacob was kidnapped. He remarked that it would be a fitting tribute to Jacob if my book was published on October 22, 2009. I don't know too much about those things work, but that is now my goal.

Assistant U.S. Attorney Jon Hopeman was assigned the case from the prosecutors prospective. He told me something that was so true. He said the more work that was done the more work remained. Investigation led to more investigation.

On my return to Minneapolis, I assumed my duties as supervisor of the violent crimes squad. In October and November of 1990, my squad was working with agents in Milwaukee on a gang of bank robbers. On November 7, 1990, the gang arrived at a home in Brooklyn Park, Minnesota. Brooklyn Park is a suburb north of Minneapolis.

We were working closely with Milwaukee agents and the Brooklyn Park Police. We were able to determine that on November 8, 1990, the gang was going to rob a bank. We didn't know which one so a surveillance was instituted. I joined the surveillance on the morning of November 9. We watched them buy rubber gloves and nylon stockings. Gloves are often worn by bank robbers to hide their fingerprints. Nylon stockings are favorite masks of bank robbers.

The problem was that we did not know which bank they were going to rob. Since we were very concerned with the safety of bank employees and customers, we planned to arrest at the last possible moment before they entered a bank.

The gang stole two vehicles and a set of license plates. Finally, we tailed them to an intersection where two banks were located. One was the Twin City Federal Savings and Loan (TCF) and the other was the First National Bank of Anoka (FNBA). They split up so we had two arrest scenes, each containing dangerous robbers who had guns.

Three members of the gang, in one of the stolen vehicles, were arrested just outside the FNBA. Two of them were wearing nylon stockings and had rubber gloves. One was armed with a loaded pistol in a holster. There was a loaded shotgun on the floor of their stolen car.

A traffic jam resulted during this arrest. The second group of gang members was in the parking lot of the TCF in a van and a stolen car. Before they could be arrested, they fled. Steve Gilkerson and I were in a bureau car. We pursued the van. Steve was driving as we pulled alongside the van. I leaned out of the front window and pointed a submachine gun at the driver. I ordered him to pull over and he did. He was arrested.

Then we heard on the radio that one of the stolen vehicles was spotted nearby. We drove to that area and saw the stolen vehicle. We saw an occupant jump from the car and run. We went after that robber, chasing him across lawns until we caught him hiding under the porch of a Minneapolis police officer. During the chase, we ran over a tree in the officer's yard, which we replaced later. That officer became a good friend over the years. He still tells that story.

What was very unusual about this case was that two banks were being robbed simultaneously by a group of very dangerous armed criminals. Even though we had a plan, the day was really saved by courage and good training.

The robbers were convicted of conspiring to commit bank robbery, aiding and abetting the use of a firearm during and in relation to a crime of violence, and aiding and abetting attempted bank robbery.

On another occasion, Agents Dag Sohlberg, Kevin Crawford, Bloomington Police Detective Bob Vaughn, and I went to the Dillon Inn in Bloomington to try to arrest a bank robber. There were two robbers who committed five or six bank robberies. We were especially concerned about these robbers because they physically assaulted bank employees and threatened customers and were armed.

We arrested one of the robbers earlier that day When arrested he had a piece of paper that said Dillon Inn and a room number.

We went to the Dillon Inn and got the key to the room. We found some crack cocaine hidden in a trash can. We expected the other robber to return to the motel. I gave the clerk a copy of the police artist's sketch of the robber. We got a room next to his, gave instructions to the clerk to call us if the robber returned, and waited.

At the same time another group of agents and police were staking out the nearby Fantasy Inn.

What followed was the most violent confrontation I had ever been involved in. Kevin was watching the hallway when he saw the clerk accompanying the robber. We didn't know how the robber arrived. As he put his key in the door, Kevin stepped into the hallway, drew his gun and said, "Stop. FBI." He ran a short distance into a small stairway. We caught him and the fight was on. He fought like no one I had ever seen.

He kept trying to get at my gun which was in my holster. Kevin who is a big strong guy, about 6´4˝, hit this guy square in the nose. There was blood everywhere. Bob Vaughn, who is also a tough guy, was punching him in the kidneys. I was twisting one of his arms behind his back and over his shoulder. He would not give up. Finally, we got him cuffed and brought him into our room. Kevin was wearing a white sweater that was covered with blood. The robber's nose was obviously broken. He cursed us and said take the cuffs off and we'll see who the tough guy is.

We later found out that he had arrived by cab. He had the cab wait. On the floor in the rear of the cab was a paper bag containing a gun, money, and crack cocaine. We later learned that both of these robbers had recently been released from a California prison after serving time for a robbery in which a police officer was shot. The next day we brought him before U.S. Magistrate J. Earl Cudd for his initial appearance. His face was a swollen mess. The judge asked him what happened and he said he couldn't remember.

Despite all of the good work by my squad I was still having basic differences with agent-in-charge Jamar. He told me many times that I was spending far too much time out of the office. In 1991, the Minneapolis FBI underwent an inspection. Periodically inspectors from FBI headquarters inspect field divisions.

As the inspection was proceeding it became apparent to me that the focus of the inspection of my work was on what I thought were minor administrative details. One of the inspectors told me he was a former Cleveland police officer and he would have loved to work on my squad. Nevertheless, he was very critical of my administrative performance. When the inspection was over, Jeff Jamar called me into his office. He told me he would like me to continue as a supervisor but I would have to change my ways. He told me specifically I would have to significantly curtail my activities on the street.

It really was decision time for me. I lived for the action of investigating violent crimes and arresting the criminals. This was a reality check for me. Had I become a supervisor to satisfy my ego or had I really thought I could change the way FBI supervisors perform. I decided that my ego was not worth the frustration I would have to endure if I continued to be a supervisor. I also knew now that I wasn't going to change anything about FBI supervisors' performance. So I made the difficult decision to give up the supervisor position and return to street agent.

Now the pressure was off me. I was back doing the things I liked to do.

I would again be close to the action. That was now my job. I didn't have to answer questions about why I was close to the action. The only difficult part was having to work with those agents who had worked for me. Fate was smiling on me. Jeff Jamar was transferred. The new agent in charge Nick O'Hara assumed his duties in December 1991.

Nick and I hit it off immediately. I was assigned to the violent crimes squad. He made me SWAT team leader again. Steve became the assistant team leader. In January of 1992, Nick asked me to be part of the new Minnesota Fugitive Task Force. This unit was being formed to chase and arrest the most violent and dangerous wanted persons in Minnesota. Personnel were chosen from the FBI, MPD, Alcohol, Tobacco and Firearms (ATF), Anoka County Sheriff's Office, Hennepin County Sheriff's Office, St. Paul PD, the Minnesota Bureau of Criminal Apprehension (BCA), and the USMS. The unit was to be led by the FBI. All non-federal members were to be sworn in as special deputy U.S. marshals.

Nick held a meeting of all the selected members to determine who would be the leader. I was honored that the members chose me to lead them. So Nick appointed me as leader. My best friend and fellow FBI agent, Steve Gilkerson, was also assigned to the task force. This effort was unique to Minnesota. The level of cooperation was never higher. My morale was never higher. This was the beginning of one of the best assignments I had in the FBI.

We were given all the resources we needed. We had an office in a renovated office building near the Metrodome in Minneapolis. The office provided quick access in and out of the building. Parking was behind the building and the entrance to the main highway, Interstate 35W was about a mile away. The sign on the office door read "AG/SG and Associates." I think you can guess that AG/SG stood for Al Garber/Steve Gilkerson. The original members besides Steve and I were Don Rogenbauer, ATF; Vern Lee, St. Paul PD; Mike Longbehn, Anoka County Sheriff's Office; Bruce Preece, BCA; Jim Scheu, MPD; John Dillon and Dan Nordine, USMS; Tony Thompson and Al Anderson, Hennepin County Sheriff's Office; and Dick Birrenbach, Ramsey County Sheriff's Office. Each of these guys brought a unique personality to the task force. The one thing they all had in common was that they loved the hunt. All they wanted to do was catch the bad guy and they did. In the first year we arrested over 300 violent fugitives. Some thought we would run out of work. What we found was that there were more fugitives hiding in Minnesota from other places than anyone imagined.

The personalities of the members were really interesting. Don Rogenbauer, the ATF agent, was a carpenter. He fixed some of our mistakes. In one case in south Minneapolis, we saw the wanted person inside walking around. We knocked on the door without a response. So we used a battering ram to break open this beautiful wooden door. After the arrest, we found out that the fugitive was a friend of the owner. The owner did not know the friend was wanted and was not home when we came knocking. So for the sake of good public relations Don fixed the door. It was as good as new.

Mike Longbehn was the most compassionate cop I ever knew. We were on surveillance in downtown Minneapolis on October 6, 1992. Mike saw a young mother berating her young daughter. The mother slapped the little girl, not very hard, but hard enough to make the girl cry. Mike walked over and asked if he could help. He got the mom to tell him she was frustrated over many things and took it out on her child. Mike must have talked to her for thirty minutes convincing her that the child didn't deserve that kind of treatment. In the end the mother apologized to her daughter and to Mike. She never even knew he was a cop.

Dan Nordine, a deputy U.S. marshal, really impressed us with his down-to-earth attitude. He was very serious about his firearms skills. Even though cops seldom have to use their guns, we know that when we have to shoot we have to hit the target.

Jim Scheu, MPD, was unorthodox to say the least. We were after a very dangerous fugitive in south Minneapolis. Jim and I were covering the back. One of the rules I had been taught for years is that you should not bring your gun so close to the suspect that he could grab it. We trained to retain our guns in the event a suspect got hold of it. So the bad guy came down the stairs in the back of this south Minneapolis house. He didn't see Jim or me.

We were standing very near the stairs. As the suspect reached the ground Jim stuck his gun in the suspect's mouth and told him to freeze. This violated the rule but it worked. In this situation, Jim and I were so close to him that we couldn't back off before he saw us. Rules are guidelines.

Vern Lee was a St. Paul police sergeant. I had met Vern under not so pleasant circumstances. There was not much respect for the FBI from the St. Paul police I knew. One night we were chasing a bank robber in St. Paul. We were working with the police. I had a St. Paul police radio in my car. Vern was not aware I had the radio. As the night went on everyone became impatient with our inability to find the robber. I heard Vern say on the police radio, I wonder where the FBI is, probably drinking coffee while we do the work. I answered on the police radio this is the FBI supervisor and we are not drinking coffee. The next day Vern called to apologize. I would not accept his apology. However, we worked together again and became very good friends. Vern was always there when he was needed on the task force. He carried a sawed-off shotgun and often told me he didn't need to run very far. Vern died of cancer. I was with him the day before he died. He was a fine man and a great cop.

Dick Birrenbach was a Ramsey County deputy sheriff. St. Paul is in Ramsey County. Dick was also unorthodox. We were looking for a killer in south Minneapolis. Dick and I were together in a bureau car. I was driving when we saw the fugitive walk up to an outdoor phone booth. As I drove toward him, Dick leaned out of the car, pointed his gun at him and screamed a series of obscenities ordering the fugitive to freeze. It worked. The guy was terrified that this crazy cop would shoot him. The rumor was that Dick had fallen from the good graces of the sheriff and that was why he was assigned to the fugitive task force. He was a great investigator and would work nonstop until the job was done.

Al Anderson, Hennepin County Deputy Sheriff, and I were at an apartment building on Elliott Avenue south in Minneapolis hunting for a fugitive. The fugitive was a former University of Minnesota football player. He was wanted on drug charges. As we were looking for the name of his girlfriend on the apartment directory, the fugitive walked into the lobby. Al turned to say something to him and the guy knocked Al aside and ran. We ran after him. Citizens were directing us to where the fugitive had run. We were not going to catch him. As I rounded a corner, I saw a green pickup truck heading right at the fugitive, who slipped as he tried to evade the truck. The driver turned out to be MPD officer Dan Ungarian. Dan had the guy at gunpoint for us. All we had to do was put the cuffs on him.

Sometime later, ATF agent George Gillette joined the task force. George was a real go-getter. He liked to use mace. We called him our hoser. He always carried mace during an arrest. One of the factors that made us successful was that we usually overwhelmed the criminal. Each member of the arrest team had a job. George's job was to hose down the fugitive with mace when needed. I often heard George hose him down. In one case George sprayed this guy with a form of mace that turned yellow and sticky. After the fight was over, the guy was complaining loudly about the guy who sprayed that ---- all over me. It was very effective and usually ended the fight.

Another rule we tried to follow was to notify the local police when we would be in their area. We wanted to avoid the disaster of the police not knowing who we were and mistaking us for criminals. Police have only seconds to react to a person with a gun. So it is extremely dangerous for plainclothes officers like us unless the police know we are in the area. However, there are some instances where we do not have the time to notify the police.

This happened to Steve Gilkerson. Other members of the task force were conducting surveillance in downtown Minneapolis. They were after James Garecki who was wanted by Hennepin County authorities for armed robbery. He was one of the county's ten most wanted fugitives. On two other occasions he had escaped from the task force. Steve was on another assignment and arrived after the surveillance had begun. The police had been advised that there was surveillance on a certain address. What they didn't know was that Steve arrived late and had decided to stay a block away.

As Steve was sitting in his car, he saw Garecki running from the area of the surveillance. Steve took off on foot after him. The chase went through Dayton's Department Store. Steve had his gun drawn and was yelling, "Police! Stop!" An MPD officer, Bob Thunder, was on foot patrol nearby. He heard a radio call of an Indian male with a gun running through Dayton's. Steve and I knew Bob Thunder well from our work together. Steve finally caught up to Garecki. Bob Thunder arrived moments later and saw Steve holding Garecki at gunpoint. Bob recognized Steve and said, "You're no fucking Indian." The other task force members never even knew Steve had caught Garecki. Sometimes you just have to act even if it is dangerous.

As the task force members gained experience and began to know each other, we really became a good team. Therefore, there was no need to use the SWAT team. The task force was in practice a SWAT team. The best example I can think of where the task force conducted a SWAT operation was in Granite Ledge Township, Benton County, Minnesota. Foley is the county seat for Benton County. It is about 60 miles northwest of Minneapolis.

In 1992, Frank Whippler was the sheriff. Frank had worked with the Jacob Wetterling task force. Steve Mund was Frank's chief deputy. Steve had also worked on the Wetterling case. So I knew them both well. We had gotten information that a man wanted for armed robbery was hiding in a trailer in Granite Ledge Township. I called Frank and told him we were coming there.

Task force members Al Anderson, Tony Thompson, Vern Lee, Steve Gilkerson, John Dillon, George Gillette, Mike Longbehn, Dick Birrenbach, and Jim Scheu along with SWAT paramedic Nancy Larson and I arrived at the Benton County sheriff's office. Steve Mund, Sheriff's Investigator Mike Tice, and Sheriff Whippler met us there.

Earlier in the day, Mike Tice had followed the suspect's girlfriend and determined that she was alone. Thus we figured the suspect was alone in his trailer house.

Nancy had enlisted the help of the local ambulance and crew. I wrote an operations order using SMEAC (situation, mission, execution, administration, command). I delivered the order and asked if there were any questions. The local paramedic asked me if this was for real or was this training. Everyone laughed as I said this is the real deal. The plan called for us to approach the trailer home through the woods, form a perimeter, and call on the suspect to surrender.

Minnesota Fugitive Task Force, 1990
Rural Benton County
Standing, left to right: Doug Brinkman, Jim Scheu, (small insert) Dick Birrenbach,
Mike Longbehn, George Gillette, Steve Mund, John Dillon, Steve Gilkerson, Vern Lee
Kneeling, left to right: Mike Theis, Al Anderson, Al Garber
Holding Defender shield: Tony Thompson

I was the leader. I got in trouble with the FBI boss because
I authorized the use of tear gas to flush out a criminal.

All went well as we left the sheriff's office. We were able to form a perimeter. We could see someone moving inside the trailer. We called on him to surrender. There was no response, except we could see someone moving rapidly from window to window. We were using trees for cover but it was becoming obvious that we could be shot from inside the trailer.

FBI policy was that tear gas could not be used except with the permission of the agent in charge. We were far out in the country but I attempted to call the Minneapolis office of the FBI using a cell phone. I could not get through. Frank Whippler and I agreed that we better either deliver tear gas or move out of sight. Moving out of sight was not an option because the suspect could escape. So after several warnings we delivered tear gas. After a few volleys, the suspect came out. His eyes were swollen and he was coughing and gagging. He was easily taken into custody. Once we got inside the trailer we found 12 loaded guns at various windows. It looked like he intended to shoot it out. The paramedics treated the suspect and he was off to jail.

But that is not where the story ends. He was not the person we were seeking for armed robbery. He had small amount of drugs in the trailer and, for some reason we will never know, he would not give up.

When I got back to Minneapolis, I was summoned to the assistant agent in charge's (ASAC) office. The ASAC was Rick Lind. He was mad. He chewed me out for using tear gas in violation of FBI policy. He told me that I knew that SAC O'Hara was out of town and that because Nick O'Hara and I got along so well, I thought I could get away with this violation. I tried to explain the dangerous circumstances we faced and that I tried to contact the office by cell phone. He wasn't buying any of my explanation. Later he sent me a letter reprimanding me.

I know I acted properly. The safety of the officers was more important than policy.

The fugitive task force was looking for a particularly vicious rapist. The investigation led to a house in south Minneapolis near Powderhorn Park. The task force assembled in the park. We asked for the assistance of MPD K-9 team of Officer Don Schwartz and Matrix. I knew Don Schwartz well. He had been shot about a year ago and I visited him in the Hennepin County Medical Center (HCMC). They met us and a plan was given. We all went to the house. Once there, we established a perimeter so he couldn't escape. Steve Gilkerson and I quietly approached the house. We were able to look in and saw the fugitive walking around.

With everyone in position, we knocked on the door. We saw the guy run downstairs. We told the woman who answered why we there. She denied the fugitive was there. We told her what we saw, but she still denied he was there. I told her we had a police dog but she continued to deny his presence.

Don Schwartz and Matrix came to the door and Don called. He said several times he had a police dog and the fugitive should surrender. So Matrix started to search with Steve and me providing protection for the K-9 team. Matrix went down into the basement and began rummaging through a pile of clothes. Soon there was screaming as Matrix pulled this guy out of a pile of clothes. Before Don could call Matrix off, the guys pants were shredded. All that remained of his pants were the waistband.

We got the guy handcuffed and transported him to the Hennepin County jail. We knew the jail would have us take him to the HCMC for treatment but we thought we'd try to get the jail to accept him. We brought him with pants shredded and his legs bleeding. The jail nurse took one look at him and said, "What's this?" She said we'd have to take him to HCMC. So we did. We arrived at the emergency room and were greeted by a female doctor. She asked what happened and we told her. We also told her this guy wanted for a very vicious rape. She said she would not treat him unless we removed the handcuffs. I told her we couldn't risk that. She insisted. So I told her I would remove the cuffs but I would wait in the reception area. With that she changed her mind and treated him. We then brought him back to the jail.

Two of the most interesting and challenging SWAT operations occurred in 1992. Super Bowl XXVI was held at the Minneapolis Metrodome on January 26, 1992. By this time our SWAT team was truly a joint MPD/FBI SWAT team. We had been training and operating regularly. We were given the mission of preparing for incidents that could occur inside the stadium, including hostage situations in the luxury boxes or elsewhere inside.

We shared this responsibility with the MPD Emergency Response Unit (ERU). The ERU leader was Sergeant Charlie Dodge. Charlie was a great SWAT officer and a good friend. Reluctantly he agreed that most of the officers who were members of both MPD ERU and our joint SWAT team could operate with us.

We were assigned an area in the depths of the Metrodome as our assembly area and command post. We began extensive preparations. At the first meeting Nick O'Hara was there with us. As each leader and key participant introduced themselves, Nick would write their names and organizations on three-by-five cards. When he didn't hear name or agency, he asked me. He told me that, if he was going to work with these officers, he wanted to know their names. That's one reason Nick was so respected by the police.

We began by installing a radio system that would operate anywhere inside the Metrodome. This was a difficult task that required installing radio repeaters in strategic locations. Our SWAT radio tech, Dennis Kelly, was excellent and accomplished this feat. We tested the radio system from many locations inside.

Next, we went to the manufacturer of the glass used in the luxury suites. We obtained samples so that we could see the effects of shooting through this glass. We did this by using bullet traps borrowed from Caswell Industries. We mounted the glass samples in these traps and placed them in the Metrodome. During the night, sometimes at 3 a.m., we shot through the glass. We found that due to the conditions in the Metrodome and due to the construction of the glass our bullets were not doing the job. We consulted with Federal Cartridge Company and the FBI Firearms Unit. As a result, a new bullet was designed, tested, and authorized for our use. This was accomplished in record time with great efficiency.

We practiced locating suspects who committed a crime and then fled inside. We used our K-9 teams. One of the team medics, Nancy Larson, agreed to play the part of a suspect. The K-9 team in this training was Officer Dave Dobrotka and Spike. Spike was the mean dog who had gotten tar in his feet during our trip to Arkansas. He was mean and had an exceptionally hard bite. Nancy was wearing a bite sleeve so she could take a bite on her arm. She had done this on other occasions. She was told when to run from the dog. The K-9 team located her hiding place and she was told to run. She ran with Spike going after her. She extended the sleeve to Spike and he took it. Dave called him off but he didn't let go immediately. After the training was over she told me she thought her arm was going to explode because of the pressure of Spike's bite. The dogs are a fearsome weapon.

As Super Bowl day neared we began having some trouble from a group of Los Angeles police officers who had been hired by the National Football League (NFL). These officers said they were in charge of security and our SWAT team could not go in certain areas of the Metrodome. It took some effort to get the powers to be to tell them that they should stay out of our way.

Super Bowl day came without further incident. We didn't get much chance to see the game. Our area was not in view of the game. We saw the game on TV just like everyone else. The exception was that two or three of our members were allowed to change to civilian clothes and walk into the runway to the field for about 15 minutes each.

In May 1992, Los Angeles erupted in riots and looting after the Rodney King police incident. Our SWAT team was told to prepare to go to LA. We had no idea what we would face there. So we took every piece of equipment we could load on military aircraft. I felt like we were preparing for war. We had enough ammunition to fight a war.

Upon our arrival in LA, we were assigned to the Long Beach fire department. I got a helicopter tour of the devastation in Long Beach. I had no idea that the looting and burning had spread outside LA. I was briefed by a Long Beach police commander. He assigned our team to a fire station. We were to lead and follow the fire engines. Firefighters had been subject to sniper fire. Their main concern was that they would be ambushed as they responded to a false alarm.

We slept at the fire station. When the firefighters responded, we were with them. They expressed their appreciation for our presence. On one occasion they were dispatched to an apartment house. Upon arrival there were no signs of fire. The firefighters were suspicious. So our SWAT team entered the building and found no signs of an ambush. The firefighters then entered to look around.

We actually had it pretty good compared to other teams. We slept on the floor of the firehouse. The firefighters fed us very well. Most of all we felt we were performing a meaningful job. I don't know if our presence prevented more bloodshed, but there was no violence when we were present.

Then the mission was over. We loaded onto military aircraft for the trip home.

In the early morning of Sunday September 19, 1993, Minnesota State Patrol officers attempted to arrest Peter John Butler and Wanda Claudette Butler as they were driving near Granite Falls. They were wanted for kidnapping Michelle R. Bright. Bright was kidnapped in Minneapolis, driven to Duluth, and eventually to Sioux City, Iowa, where she escaped. During the kidnapping Bright was brutally beaten.

During a high-speed pursuit with the Minnesota State Patrol, the Butlers lost control of their car and became mired in a field near Granite Falls. Both fled. Wanda Butler was captured hiding in a field near the abandoned vehicle.

Our SWAT team was summoned to search for Peter Butler. Butler was extremely dangerous. He had served a lengthy sentence for murder in New York State. He was believed to be armed. The weather was cold and rainy. The area to be searched was rural and contained mostly open fields. Open fields are dangerous to search because the chance is great that the fugitive would see us before we saw him.

The SWAT team included a K-9 team consisting of MPD officer Ron Johnson and Kodiac. We also had SWAT medics Gordy Vosberg and Mike Peach with us. We used the K-9 team out front with the rest of the team providing protection for Ron and Kodiac. We searched for two days. In the afternoon of September 21 as we were searching, we received word from a custodian of a local church. The custodian said he had gone to the Hawk Creek Lutheran Church on Renville County Road 60. As he was cleaning he entered a room and saw a man dressed in black sitting on a couch holding a gun.

The church was several miles from our location. We quickly drove to the church. We immediately established a perimeter around the church. We didn't know if the man had fled. We were certain it was Butler. It was because the team was well trained that we were able to quickly get into position.

Once we were in position we called into the church for anyone inside to come out. After numerous unsuccessful attempts to get a response we decided we would have to search the church. A plan was quickly put together. Even though we did not have the opportunity to put a detailed plan together we still used the military operations order format. I always carried a card with the outline. The plan was for us to get the front door open and call for the K-9 team.

Agent in Charge O'Hara approved the plan with one exception. He said he was going in with us. I knew Nick was an experienced agent and was well trained with firearms. However, he had not trained with us. But he was the boss and there was no time to argue.

We got the door open and called for the K-9 team. Ron and Kodiac came to the door. Ron announced that a police dog was about to search. There was no response. Kodiac began to search. In a minute or so we heard him alerting, indicating he found someone. We saw the room where Kodiac was alerting. Ron called Kodiac back. Steve and I entered carefully. I saw a man dressed in black sitting on the couch. He had a gun in his left hand and he was looking down. I ordered him to drop the gun. There was no response. We approached and knocked him to the floor. I began to handcuff him. I thought he was resisting so I twisted his arm back and as I applied the cuffs I heard a loud crack. His arm had broken. It was only then that I realized he was dead. He had shot himself behind the left ear with his .32 automatic. There was a small trickle of blood behind his ear.

We called the medics in. They told us we had handcuffed a dead guy. The crack was his arm breaking because it had stiffened in death. Steve and I took a lot of kidding over this. I guess you would call it dark humor.

It had long been my intention to retire from the FBI at the earliest possible date so that I could pursue my dream of becoming a police chief. FBI agents are eligible to retire after serving 20 years and reaching age 50. I reached both of those qualifications in 1992. I began to apply for chiefs jobs. While I had a good resume including a master's degree in public administration, I had never been a police officer. I applied but was unsuccessful for chief's jobs in Minnesota cities of Plymouth, Roseau, Rochester, Maplewood, Hibbing, and Duluth, and the University of Minnesota. I also applied unsuccessfully for the United States Marshal position. I was really getting discouraged until my friend and mentor, former Minneapolis police chief Tony Bouza, gave me advice. He said it didn't matter how many no's I got, all I needed was one yes.

The application process was an education. A search firm conducted the search for the chief in Roseau. Roseau is a very small town in northern Minnesota. Its population today is about 2700. The person from the search company told me I was not being considered because Roseau was too small and I would be bored.

Rochester is a city today of about 97,000. I was interviewed on numerous occasions. I took off from work on at least six occasions to travel the 90 miles to Rochester. I really thought I had a chance for that job. In the end I was a finalist with Rochester police lieutenant Roger Peterson. I had known Roger for many years. He was an outstanding candidate. After what I was told was the final interview, I heard nothing for about two weeks. Then I read in the newspaper that Roger got the job. I never heard from anyone in the Rochester city government. I am guessing that the city fathers wanted Roger all along but felt it would look good to have a nationwide search.

My experience in Hibbing was even stranger. I had met a city council member during some training I had conducted for the Hibbing police. Hibbing is on the "Iron Range" in northern Minnesota. Its population is about 17,000. When the chief's job opened up the council member told me to submit my resume to him and he would carry it forward. I did that. I was invited to go to Hibbing to participate in the annual police versus fire hockey game. I did that also. Then I heard nothing. When I found out that a chief had been selected, I asked a friend on the department to try to see what happened. He told me the council member never brought my resume to the attention of the search committee. Apparently he wanted someone else to get the job.

I also applied for the position of United States Marshal for the District of Minnesota. I had no understanding of the politics that were necessary for that position. The senior U.S. senator of the current president's party gets to nominate a candidate or candidates. If both senators are of the opposing party then the senior U.S. representative of the president's party gets to nominate. I didn't know any of this and I simply applied. I was interviewed by a board. The interview went well. After it was over, one of the board members who I knew told me the interview went well but I had no chance because one of the people interviewed had been active in President Clinton's campaign. I didn't get the job this time.

The final city I applied at was Champlin, population about 20,000. It is about 25 miles northwest of Minneapolis. That process was also interesting. There were several interviews that included the mayor, city council members, and a neighboring city chief. Again I made the final selection process. The finalists were Captain Dick Stumpf, a long-time Champlin officer; retired Minneapolis police deputy chief Roger Willow; and Mound chief Len Harrell. Roger was an old friend with whom I had played hockey and worked.

After the final interviews, but before the decision was made, I got what was the last assignment in my FBI career.

I had been told by Mayor Steve Boynton of Champlin that I was a finalist and the decision would be made in about two weeks. The FBI Academy called and asked if I would be interested in being a member of an evaluation team that would travel to Chile and Bolivia to evaluate how U.S. aid was being used. I was to be a member of a four-person team composed of two FBI agents and two employees of the U.S. State Department. The mission was to take about two weeks. I asked Mayor Boynton if my leaving the country for two weeks would influence his decision about the chief's job. He assured me it would not. I notified the FBI Academy that I would accept the assignment. I was fortunate to be given this opportunity. Normally field agents were not given this opportunity.

I travelled to Washington, D.C. for a briefing. I met the other members of the team. The FBI agent was a Spanish speaker. The two state department men were retired military officers under contract. My job was to evaluate how U.S. aid, which had been given to SWAT units of the Chilean and Bolivian police, was used.

The plane trip from Washington, D.C. to Santiago Chile took about 12 hours. It was not a pleasant trip. The plane was packed with many crying restless children. On top of this, I was suffering from a bulging disc in my neck. I was in constant pain. We arrived in Santiago and then were driven to a very nice hotel. Santiago was a modern clean city with a heavy police presence. At almost every corner there was a uniformed officer carrying a sub-machinegun.

The Chilean National Police are called Carabineros. Their SWAT teams are called Grupo de Operaciones Policiales Especieles (GOPE). GOPE gave us a demonstration of their skills such as sniper shooting, helicopter rappelling, and parachuting. They were well equipped and were in excellent physical condition. They told me that they appreciated U.S. aid but they did not need any more equipment. They needed training, particularly in hostage negotiations and dealing with airplane hijackings. The officers and their leaders were very open and anxious to share information.

Their training lasts for one year. It includes six months of theory and six months of practical training. They train in the mountains, jungles, and desert. Their training reminded me more of U.S. Army Rangers than police.

Up to that time four members of GOPE had lost their life; one in a helicopter crash, two in bomb blasts, and one had drowned.

They received a 35% raise in pay and retirement benefits. They earned these benefits. All of those we visited with showed high levels of firearms proficiency, martial arts, and tactical knowledge. They are very well equipped with different firearms, night vision equipment, and body armor. I was surprised when I asked them about their K-9 capabilities and about their use of some of the tactics we used. They said they had no K-9 capability and were not aware of the tactics I questioned them about. One of the contributions I made was to describe some of our tactics and our training methods. I often wondered if they ever adopted our tactics.

We met with their leaders who told us about their units. We visited a GOPE unit that was about to go on an operation. I was impressed. At the end of our week in Chile we met with the U.S. ambassador and members of his staff. I gave my findings, which were positive.

We left Santiago bound for LaPaz, Bolivia. The experiences I was about to have were vastly different. I suspected there might be a problem when medical personnel met our flight at the LaPaz airport. They told us that altitude sickness would likely affect us. They cautioned us that this illness could be serious or fatal. Almost immediately after we left the airport I got a headache and stomach ache. If you have never experienced this illness I can only describe it as always present.

As we drove through the countryside I saw people who looked like their spirit had left them. The houses were run down and the streets littered. We arrived at our hotel. We were cautioned to drink only bottled water. A representative of the U.S. Embassy told us that an employee had recently died of altitude sickness. We were given oxygen bottles and told that extra oxygen might help. We all looked pretty funny sitting around wearing oxygen masks. It didn't help.

The next day we walked to the National Police Office. The streets were littered and beggars were everywhere. When we arrived at the police station, we were led into the local commanding officers' office. The police station was in a particularly run-down area. But when we entered the colonel's office it was like we had passed into a luxury home. The colonel was well dressed and polite. We spoke briefly and I requested that I meet with their SWAT commander. Their SWAT team is The Grupo De Accion Immediata, known as GAI.

I met the commander and he introduced me to some of his team members. I was impressed by their openness and sincerity. I was also impressed by their lack of training and their limited capabilities. They had minimal equipment. They told me candidly that they knew they were lacking in many areas but they also knew they would be called on in the most dangerous situations. We spent many hours together discussing tactics and equipment. But I was not there to train; only to evaluate. I wish I had had more time to train these highly-motivated officers. I felt compassion for them. They really were dedicated and they got little support from their government.

I met with one of their subordinate commanders to discuss their lack of equipment. He told me that they had received a lot of equipment from the U.S. government. But eventually all of it disappeared. He either would not tell me where the equipment went or he did not know.

The team says it is a full-time unit. But in reality they have no regular training and they have additional duties. GAI members receive no extra pay or incentives. Some members of the team were trained by the French and some attended U.S. training. As a result of our talks with the commander, he said training would begin soon and be conducted regularly. We have no way of knowing if training did occur after we left.

I was very impressed by the interest they showed in our visit. They were just cops doing the best they could with limited resources. I felt a common bond with them.

Other officers and other government officials told me that the police were so underpaid that bribery was commonplace and expected. Bribes plus salary provided a livable income.

We wandered through the city looking in the many shops. I found National Hockey League (NHL) jackets from the Chicago Blackhawks and the Philadelphia Flyers. I came halfway around the world to find NHL jackets.

The altitude sickness continued but it was not to the point where I couldn't do my job. Finally, it was time to meet with senior Bolivian police commanders. The meeting also included members of the U.S. ambassador's staff. I was candid in my comments. I recommended that no more aid be given to the police until accountability was increased. I have no idea if my comments were acted upon.

We were all happy when the week ended. We drove to the airport and boarded our plane. It took only minutes and the altitude sickness was gone. Shortly after we were airborne, we were all offered an opportunity to change seats to first class. I learned later that our team leader had spoken to an airlines official. Although the flight lasted more than 12 hours it seemed like minutes. The good food, movies, and comfortable seats made the memories of Bolivia fade.

Chief Al Garber and Officers Brian Wentworth

Champlin
Police Service

After arriving home, I found out that Champlin had not made a deci-sion about their chief's position. A few days later I was sitting in my living room at 11:30 p.m. when the phone rang. It was Mayor Boynton. He said, "You're our man." I was so happy, as was my family. The FBI had been a great career, but now I was about to embark on a new adventure. I retired from the FBI on October 30, 1993, and became Champlin Police Chief on November 1, 1993.

The first day was something else. First, I arrived in the parking lot of the police department and locked myself out of my car. Captain Stumpf called the Champlin towing company. The tow truck driver unlocked my car with my cops watching. What a start. I really admired Dick Stumpf for the way he treated me. He really wanted to be chief. But when I got the job, he treated me kindly and did everything I asked of him. Unfortunately, shortly thereafter, Dick suffered a heart attack and never came back. He died about a year later.

I thought I knew police work. Was I in for an education. When citizens need any kind of immediate aid they call the police. The police really are the first line of defense. I rode a lot with the officers on patrol so that I could learn what they did. The first time I rode was with a veteran officer Greg Holst. We answered a theft call. When we arrived at the victim's home, we were told that a middle school student had about 100 CDs stolen from his locker at the middle school. The student told us he knew who stole them. He gave us the name and address of the thief. He said he had been told by a friend that the CDs were now in the suspect's bedroom. Greg took notes and told the parents and the student we would look into it.

We left the driveway and, instead of going to the suspect's house to see if the CDs were there, we drove the other way. I asked Greg what he was doing and he replied that he was going back on patrol. I said why don't we get the CDs back. He told me that he was a patrol officer and that detectives would follow-up sometime later. This made no sense to me but I kept my mouth shut thinking maybe I don't understand police patrol. As I became more experienced I realized that there was no reason why we didn't follow-up. Greg's mentality was that he answers emergencies and patrols, nothing else. I changed that.

In the winter, when the patrol officers were in the office, they left their squad cars running. We had a garage attached to the police department where cars could be parked. The garage was heated and it was within seconds of the patrol break room and the report writing area. I couldn't understand why the officers kept their cars running. We could save a significant amount of gas if the cars were parked in the heated garage and turned off. I got no argument from the officers.

The city of Champlin is about seven square miles. I couldn't understand how the officers could patrol for eight hours and not become bored if there were few calls for service. I learned that they filled up their shift with many different activities. Some ran radar; some did traffic enforcement; some talked to citizens; some checked almost every car they encountered using the in-car computers; while others stayed in the residential neighborhoods looking for anything they could investigate.

I was learning fast that I really didn't know much about what the police did. But I was willing to learn and I was a pretty good judge of people. Thus

I learned who to rely on for information. For me the best part of being the chief was that I could have the officers try new approaches and I could institute new programs. I also learned that I had no understanding of the relationship between elected officials and me.

The police are the first line of defense for the people. When people are afraid, confused, and don't know where to turn, they call the police. Emotions are often running high when the police arrive. Citizens expect their police to know what to do in all situations. The more experience an officer gets the more the officers know where to get answers to all sorts of problems. It doesn't matter whether it is a big city or a small city like Champlin; officers face a wide range of problems. The role of the police is very different from the role of the FBI. Normally the FBI is not the first law enforcement agency to arrive at the scene of an incident. The FBI is an investigative agency and as such usually arrives after the police have made the scene safe and secure. When the FBI does arrive first, it is because the agents know who they are after and have planned beforehand. The police seldom have the advantage of planning for what they will be confronted with when they answer a call for help or when they happen on a crime in progress.

Patrol officers enforce state laws most of the time. Seldom do they enforce federal laws.

So in many ways the job of a patrol officer is far more dangerous than that of an FBI agent. Patrol officers face the unknown more than any other officers including detectives and police SWAT teams.

Thus training for police differs from FBI training. Police must know state laws. FBI agents must know federal laws. Officers must be skilled in emergency medical procedures, responding to crimes in progress, handling domestic quarrels, using a whole host of lethal and non-lethal weapons, testing drunk drivers, and mediating all sorts of arguments. Police and FBI agents both train in the use of firearms. FBI agents must become skilled interviewers. They learn how to prepare all sorts of reports and affidavits. Simply put, police officers are trained to deal with the unknown; FBI agents are trained primarily to investigate known situations. Both jobs can be very dangerous.

Satisfaction is derived from different places for FBI agents and police. Police officers gain satisfaction from seeing firsthand from their constituents how police service has helped them. An example is seeing a heart attack victim whom the officer has saved by using an AED. FBI agents gain satisfaction by solving the crime, arresting the suspect, and convicting the suspect. Both groups gain a great deal of satisfaction by working with other hard-working, courageous, honest, like-minded individuals. My fondest memories are of those officers and agents with whom I worked and risked my life.

Most of the time the police are faced with situations that have little to do with serious crime. So the uniformed police have to be generalists. They must be emergency medical responders. They must deal with animal problems. They have to be mediators in neighbor disputes and domestic arguments. They must know the laws. And above all they must respond when the citizens call. This sounds like an overwhelming job.

Sometimes my common sense and experience were insufficient to allow me to understand why the police did certain things. The city mechanic told me that he replaced brakes on the police cars about every 12,000 miles. This sounded unreasonable to me until one night I was patrolling with veteran officer Kevin Wagman. We got a medical emergency call of a person in full arrest, which means the person has had a heart attack and is not breathing. Kevin slammed the accelerator down and we were off. At every stop sign he had to jam on the brakes and then speed off. Seconds mean the difference between life and death. By the time we reached the victim's house, the brakes were burning. We ran in the house and were directed to the victim who was on the floor, unconscious and not breathing. Kevin used the automatic external defibrillator or heart-start machine. I was of some help. Other officers arrived to administer oxygen. Even though paramedics had been summoned, the police arrived first and went into action. I never again questioned why brakes on police cars are replaced so often.

For the first two months of my tenure as police chief I lived about 45 miles from Champlin. The commute was too long and I couldn't become a member of the community when I left every evening after work. So my

Photo by Nadine Lemm

Life saving award

Champlin Police Chief Al Garber presents the Life Saving Award to officers Kevin Wagman (center) and Sean Gormley (right) Jan. 15 after the officers saved the life of Champlin resident Michael Katchman. He and his wife, Mary, thanked the officers at the presentation.

Police received a call Dec. 12 around 5 p.m. that "a man was down." Garber said the roads were slippery and snowy that evening, and Gormley arrived at Katchman's home five minutes later. He brought the heart start machine (automatic external defibrillator) to the bedroom where children said Katchman had collapsed. Gormley could not find a pulse or breath and Katchman's eyes were open and fixed dilated.

The machine was attached to Katchman, and Gormley shocked him and called on Wagman, who brought oxygen, to assist. Both officers began CPR and brought Katchman back to life.

Gormley rode along in the ambulance and continued CPR. Katchman has now recovered.

"These machines are wonderful," Garber said about the defibrillator.

Healthspan Paramedics assisted Champlin Police as well.

Garber said this award has only been presented once before.

© Champlin Dayton Press

family and I moved to Champlin in January 1994. Moving in January in Minnesota is never a good idea. I picked the coldest day of the year to move. It was about 20 degrees below zero. To make matters worse I tried to save money and had a moving company only move the heavy items. It took eight round trips to complete the move. I felt like for the first time in my professional life I was part of a community.

One evening I was sitting in my living room listening to my portable police radio. I listened to it all the time. I really was in a learning mode. I had completed first responder training a few days before this time. I heard a call broadcast saying police were needed for a full arrest. The address was my next door neighbor. I ran outside to my police car and retrieved the oxygen kit. My neighbor was standing in her driveway screaming that her father had a heart attack. I went into the house and found her father unconscious and not breathing. I was beginning CPR when I heard sirens. In a matter of seconds Officers Terry Cassem and Sean Gormley arrived. Terry brought the heart start. Together we applied the paddles and shocked the victim. He started to breathe, so Sean applied oxygen. By the time the paramedics arrived he was conscious and breathing. I was learning first hand how important competent police were to our community.

I think the cops laughed a little when they saw some of the things I did. I brought the same enthusiasm I had in the military and the FBI to the police. Only sometimes the results were not what I intended. In one instance, I was on patrol with Officer Kim Bonde. We answered an alarm call at a residence. When we arrived, I told her I'd cover the rear. With that I got out of the car, jumped over the fence and split my pants right down the back. I can only imagine how hard it was not to laugh at the chief. My response after the incident was over was to look for more rugged pants that could be worn on patrol and look similar to the normal uniform pants. I found a dark blue military-type pants and authorized them for wear. The cops liked them but one of the council members asked me why the police were looking more like military.

Again I was on patrol with Kim when we heard a call about a car stolen within the last few minutes. When the location of the theft was given, Kim said she had an idea where the car would go. We drove to Andrews Park and, as we arrived, here comes the stolen car. The thief lets the car roll as he jumps out and runs. I ran after him without my flashlight and portable radio. The foot chase lasted about 100 yards and I gave up. The thief who was later caught by other officers was a teenager who easily outran me. When I got back to the car, Kim politely told me that she had known other cars stolen from the area and they usually ended up at Andrews. As for why she didn't run as I did, she said she believed the kid would outrun me and she used her radio to tell other officers to head him off.

I had a great deal of experience in arresting armed and dangerous suspects. So when we got word of a dangerous wanted person being at a home in Champlin, I got some of the officers and went to the house. Among the officers were those assigned to patrol that day. I reasoned that we could use the patrol officers if they were not answering calls. We all parked a block or two away from the house. We surrounded it and called for the suspect to surrender. He came running out of the back door where I was. I tackled him and applied the handcuffs. I thought everything went well. But then we heard a radio call for a possible heart attack. Since we parked our police cars a block or two away, we had to run to the cars to respond. Officer Perry Guertin and I got to our cars first and responded. We found a woman in bed and obviously dead for a long time. But I learned that patrol officers cannot be used for any purpose that would slow down their response to an emergency.

The officers knew that I cared deeply and my enthusiasm was evident. Champlin did not have a lot of violent crime. We had our share of domestic assaults, fights, suicides, and drunk drivers, but shootings were extremely rare. One morning I was sitting in my office when Kim Bonde came in and calmly asked me if I would like to go the scene of a shooting in town. I jumped up and said "WHAT?" She quickly explained that a teenager had shot himself while showing off for his friend. We raced to the scene where we found an overweight teenage boy holding his stomach. He had shot himself in the side of the stomach with his father's gun. The bullet went across his stomach through layers of fat and exited. The paramedics came and determined there was no life-threatening injury.

The other side of my duties consisted of interacting with the mayor and council. Mayor Boynton who had appointed me did not run for reelection. The new mayor was Bruce Johnson. I attended council meetings and advocated for my police. I tried to get more money for equipment and more officers. The mayor appointed a citizen public safety commission and directed that I work with them on law enforcement issues. I got along well with these citizens and convinced them to advocate with me for more funding and positions.

In addition, off-duty officers went to council meetings to show their interest.

Things seemed to be going well. In mid-December of 1994, my immediate superior City Administrator Kurt Ulrich gave me an outstanding performance evaluation. Then the bottom fell out. On December 28, 1994, Mayor Johnson called me to his office. He presented me with a letter that shocked me.

The letter said in part:

> Chief Garber has been adequate in the area of constituent service. Concerns with the chief lay in the area of both policy and performance.
>
> The management report for the police department submitted by Chief Garber was unacceptable. Instead of outlaying options for the policy makers to review, only one scenario was presented and that one was outside the existing budget.
>
> The chief has presented proposals to the council that have been outside the parameters of the city budget policy.
>
> As staff liaison to the public safety commission, chief Garber has brought matters before the psc that were outside the parameters of the budget policy and outside the spirit in which the psc was created.
>
> Chief Garber has placed items on the council agenda without regard to the ramifications of city-wide decisions that are under the charge of the council and without respect to other departments that understand said ramifications and thus, refrain from such action.

At a September 1994, council meeting, Chief Garber, presented a proposal to restructure the police department staff to the city council and permitted uniformed Champlin officers to attend. This action demonstrated a complete lack of leadership and are grounds for a total lack of confidence in Allen Garber's ability to: comprehend the chain of command; respect the process of citizen rule of law (over military, or in this case paramilitary).

The chief is a personable individual. At the time of his hire his record of achievement and skilled interview gave the appearance of an individual who may excel at this new challenge despite his lack of experience in this position.

The question remains: Is this a case of untapped potential or a misinterpretation?

<u>Objectives:</u> Chief Garber must be demonstrative in establishing confidence from his elected superiors. Policy must be followed. It must be clear that the operation of the police department is driven from the top down not vice versa.

The mayor rated me unsatisfactory. I saw that I had choices. I could fight the mayor. This would be a certain loss of my job. I could make excuses. I could accept the mayor's critique and work hard to correct my shortcomings. I chose the latter. So I wrote a letter to the mayor and I met with him. I told the mayor that I would fully comply with his instructions. I told him I believed that my shortcomings were a result of my lack of experience in the political arena. I vowed to use his personnel review of me "as a critical tool to move forward and not to look back."

Conditions began to improve almost immediately. I told the mayor it was very important to me that he not give up on me. He said he had not. My superior, City Administrator Kurt Ulrich, helped me a lot. He told me in the presence of the mayor that I was an excellent leader and that I had the genuine respect of the police officers. He also said I was not afraid to make a decision. He told the mayor he counseled me to distance myself somewhat from the police employees so that I could be viewed more as a member of management. After this meeting, Mayor Johnson and I shook hands. He grasped both of my hands warmly and said he would expect better communications between us.

We then began to meet the first Wednesday of each month. The meetings were highly productive and allowed both of us to get to know each other better. Mutual respect was the result. Strangely my relationship with the officers remained strong. My second in command, Al Bruns, gave me a big boost when he told me that the majority of the officers were behind me. He told me I was doing a great job. I got to know Al well enough to know he meant every word. Al became chief after I left.

In fact, things became so positive that on November 12, 1996, the Champlin City Council passed a resolution nominating me for the Minnesota Chiefs of Police Officer of the Year Award.

The resolution read in part: "Whereas Champlin Police Chief Allen Garber has distinguished himself with meritorious service above and beyond the call of duty, and Whereas Chief Garber had responded expertly to Champlin's ever changing needs of public safety . . . , and Whereas Chief Garber has brought creativity in achieving results . . . , and Whereas Chief Garber has demonstrated a deep understanding for the concerns of the citizens; the needs of the victims; the rights of the accused; and that understanding has manifested itself in the operation of the Champlin Police Department, and Whereas the Champlin City Council recognizes and commends the distinguished and meritorious service of Chief Garber. . . ." After being awarded this resolution, I thought, "Boy, we have come a long way."

As I look back on this experience with the mayor and council, I realized that I learned a lot from my FBI experience. I gave up my supervisor's position because I chose not to be the kind of supervisor the FBI wanted. I tried to change the supervisor position but I realized that there was no chance for me to change the FBI. So I gave up the position. Now in Champlin I was told what kind of a chief the elected officials wanted me to be. I carefully thought about the changes I would have to make to survive. My conclusion was that they were not asking me to do anything unreasonable. They demanded I do my job in a way that had not occurred to me. I also considered that I was new to the chiefing job. Sure I was shocked and disappointed with the mayor's comments. But I guess the best way I can put it is I wanted to remain chief, so I changed. As I was changing my style, the elected officials got to know me better. They appreciated my enthusiasm, sincerity, and willingness to learn. So it all fell quickly in place.

Once I had the elected officials behind me, I could concentrate on making the efforts of the department better. I was concerned that the officers were going back to the same houses time and time again. Certain households had repeat problems and kept calling for police assistance. The officers answered the call, solved the immediate problem and were on their way. The best example of this was a couple who lived in town. The man was grossly overweight and often fell out of bed. His wife couldn't get him back in bed so she called the police. This happened more than 30 times in a month. Another example was a house where the children, who were teenagers, were constantly disturbing the neighborhood with their noisy and rude behavior. Neighbors called the police. The police came and told the kids to be quiet. The parents would promise it wouldn't happen again, but it did. Since we only had two, three, or four cops on duty at a time, these types of calls were eating up our manpower. The result was that we were calling our neighboring police departments for assistance on almost every shift.

I was talking to my old friend and former competitor for the Champlin chief's job, Roger Willow, about our problem. Roger was one of those people who I listened to and who freely gave advice. He told me he had had a similar problem when he was commander of the 5th precinct, Minneapolis Police. The way he solved this problem was he assigned an officer to the problem address. The officer was tasked with solving the problem. This approach was called problem oriented policing (POP).

I took this approach back to Champlin. I explained the idea to my officers. My second in command, Al Bruns, was given the task of keeping track of which officer was assigned which problem. The officers were skeptical that this was another theoretical solution that would not work. Some of them also took offense and told me they had been solving problems for years. I told them the difference was that now we would keep track of the problem addresses, whereas before, the officers who chose to solve problems only knew of problems they encountered.

POP cases worked great. The case involving the overweight guy who kept falling out of bed was assigned to Sgt. Rose Mary Mengelkoch. Rose Mary found out the couple had a son who lived in a nearby city. When she told him of his father's falling out of bed and that the police simply couldn't keep coming back, the son hired a nurse. The nurse was not there 24 hours a day, but the nurse did dramatically cut down on our calls. In fact, the son thanked us because his mother and father never told him.

There were numerous other cases involving nuisance complaints. These usually involved junk and trash on a property. These situations may not seem like very important police issues, but they are quality-of-life issues. Neighbors become concerned because of depreciating property values and public health hazards. In every case an officer was assigned and worked with the property owner. We were not always 100% successful. But we cut down our repeat calls dramatically. The citizens supported this approach and the elected officials encouraged us to continue.

Another issue that I knew was important was juvenile crime. The type of juvenile crime in Champlin did not rise to the level of serious felonies. Most of the crimes involved vandalism, fighting, and drug use. If we did not address these kids now we would be addressing them later as adult criminals. There was a curfew ordinance in Champlin but it was difficult to enforce because the police were often busy with emergencies. Taking these kids home and talking to their parents involved a significant amount of time. Juvenile-type offenses skyrocketed when school was not in session.

Sergeant Jim Kurtz suggested we establish a curfew center. I asked the neighboring chiefs if they were interested in sharing the costs. They enthusiastically accepted my offer. The curfew center was established at our indoor ice arena, which wasn't used when school was not in session. We hired a civilian and each department provided an officer. The way it worked was that if an officer encountered a juvenile out in violation of the curfew, the officer brought the juvenile to the curfew center. The officer gave some brief details to the center staff, then the officer was through and free to resume normal duties. The staff called the parents or responsible adult, who were required to come to the center to get their child. Juveniles who were arrested for serious offenses were not brought to the center. Violent juveniles were also not brought to the center. The curfew center was a resounding success. Juvenile crimes nearly stopped when the center was open. The word was out that if you were out after curfew you would be picked up. Parents made sure they wouldn't have to come to the center in the middle of the night to get their kid. The cops loved it because they didn't want to be burdened with these kids all night. As you can imagine the politicians loved this approach.

While answering calls for service and investigating crimes were the immediate priorities of the department, solving problems continued to be the next on the list of priorities. Statistics showed that while calls for police service were decreasing city wide, they were increasing dramatically in the multi-family areas of the city. In 1996, a survey was conducted on 144 apartment units compared to 166 single-family homes. The apartment units were responsible for 352 calls. The 166 single-family homes had 174 calls for service. Citywide, in 1996, the department experienced a drop in calls for service of 900. At the same time calls for service city wide to multi-family units rose 10%.

Inspections of our apartment buildings showed early signs of decay such as broken security doors, hallway carpets dirty and burned, and landscaping in poor condition. The overall quality of life for tenants was going down. The drop in quality of life resulted in more crimes with tenants as the victims. This was not the picture of Champlin that I wanted to see. I met with council members, members of the Economic Development Authority, and other city department heads. The conclusion was that the police department was the appropriate agency to take the lead in stopping these problems before they became any worse.

Fortunately, I found an officer who would take on these responsibilities with enthusiasm and professionalism. His name was Kevin Wagman. Kevin was an experienced officer who was one of our best. I use the word fortunate because to many police officers solving quality of life issues is not "real police work." If this effort was to produce the desired results, we needed someone who wanted the job. Funding was not a problem. We were able to get grants from the Federal government and from Champlin's Economic

Development Authority. The grants enabled us to add a patrol officer to replace Kevin Wagman.

We were off and running. We sent Kevin to Crime Free Multi- Housing course offered by the Mesa, Arizona, police department. We named the effort "Livable Housing Unit (LHU)." Finally, in August of 1997, the LHU began operation. I gave Kevin the flexibility he needed to do his job. He worked when he needed to accomplish his mission. I gave him a police vehicle which he could take home so that he could respond whenever he was needed. Kevin found additional training in crime prevention through environmental design. Environmental design dealt with landscaping that minimized hiding places in and around apartment buildings where potential muggers and vandals could hide. He met often with building managers and owners as well as tenant groups. He became their police officer. The patrol officers continued to respond to calls for service, while Kevin worked on overall problems.

LHU teamed with the building department, fire department, and planning department to form a civil enforcement team. When problems could not be solved by the LHU, the civil enforcement team would meet to see if any other department could help. Sometimes there were building codes or fire codes that could be used. The results were really amazing. As the apartment buildings would satisfy certain criteria, they were awarded Crime Free Multi-Housing Certification. The managers proudly posted their award signs on the property. The added result was that occupancy went up because people wanted to live in these buildings. The tenants were happy, the owners of the buildings were happy, the managers were happy, and the elected officials were happy.

Security doors were maintained, lighting in and around buildings was increased, and hedges and shrubs near doors and windows were kept trimmed. In one year the calls for service for the two busiest apartment complexes dropped 38%. Juvenile-related calls dropped 43%. Thefts dropped 44%. Even more impressive is that during the first year of LHU's operation, occupancy went from 75% to 100%.

Every building manager in town was interviewed and every one knew

Officer Wagman and what he was doing. Each one said they knew him well enough to call on him.

When the other officers on the department were interviewed, every one said they had referred cases to Kevin. The officers wanted him to let them know the outcome of problems they referred. They also wanted him to consult with them so they could have input. All in all the officers supported the LHU.

The high point of this effort was when the International Association of Chiefs of Police (IACP) recognized the LHU in its 1998 Webber Seavey Award for Quality in Law Enforcement. Kevin and I flew to Salt Lake City, Utah, to receive this recognition.

Then on November 23, 1998, the Champlin mayor and council passed a resolution which said in part:

> WHEREAS the Champlin Police Department recognized an increase in calls for service in the multi-family areas. And
>
> WHEREAS the Department formed the Livable Housing Unit to deal strictly with these areas, and
>
> WHEREAS Officer Kevin Wagman was assigned to address the problems in the multi-family area using a one-on-one approach, and
>
> WHEREAS Officer Wagman and Chief Garber recently . . . accepted the Webber Seavey Award for Excellence in Policing.
> NOW THERFORE BE IT RESOLVED by the Champlin City Council that the outstanding efforts of the Champlin Police Department, Chief Garber and officer Wagman in forming the Livable Housing Unit and receiving the Webber Seavey Award are hereby recognized by the City of Champlin.

With these successes and the positive feedback that followed, I began to appreciate how rewarding being a police chief could be. Being a chief allowed me to realize that chasing murders, robbers, and rapists, while very important, are not the only issues that are important to a community.

All new ideas and programs that police chiefs bring to their jobs have a "shelf life." That means that no matter how good a program or approach is there comes a time when it is discontinued. Frankly most new programs or approaches are of little lasting value. The exceptional programs produce results that significantly impact public safety. But ultimately a new chief comes in and changes even the exceptional programs. Usually the program is eliminated. However, sometimes it is renamed to give the new chief's stamp.

In my case I eliminated the two motorcycles my predecessor purchased for the PD. I thought that for a small department like Champlin motorcycles were a luxury we could not afford. I did not meet any resistance from the mayor and council when I eliminated them.

The POPS cases, the curfew center, and the LHU ran their courses and were eliminated after I left.

But the effort that disappointed me most by its elimination was the GAP for Runaway Youth. The background begins with the sad fact that police departments in our area did little to find runaway kids. Champlin was no exception and I later found out that few PDs in the U.S. did any more. When a parent or other responsible person reported their son or daughter had run away, an officer took a report and tried to assure the parent that the child would likely return on their own. When there was evidence of foul play, we did investigate. But usually there was no such evidence. Often the child's description was entered in the National Crime Information Center (NCIC) so that if a law enforcement agency inquired about a child they would learn that the child was a runaway.

The particular event that drove me to do more to find runaways involved a dad who reported his teenaged daughter had run away. He had no idea where she was. We took a report. Several weeks later the dad asked if we had learned anything and the officer said no. Weeks later I got a call from the police supervisor who asked that I come to the police station. It was about 2 a.m. The officer told me the dad was there with some very disturbing information about his daughter. When I arrived, the father told me he had been contacted by his daughter that night. She told him she had been taken to Detroit and forced to become a prostitute. She had escaped and was calling him from a pay phone. The father asked me if we were going to do anything now.

Of course, we did. We phoned the police department in the Detroit suburb where the girl was. They found her. Her father went there and brought his daughter back to Champlin. We interviewed her and she told us that she hung out regularly at the Northtown Mall, which is near Champlin. One night she was convinced by some guys who she had gotten to know to go with them. They gave her a story of excitement and adventure. Once they had her they took her to Michigan where she was told she had to prostitute herself or she would be killed.

At that point, I was ashamed of what we hadn't done. I knew that Patty Wetterling, whose son Jacob had been kidnapped in 1989, was active with the National Center for Missing and Exploited Children (NCMEC) so I called her. She told me that NCMEC conducted a course for law enforcement executives that dealt with runaways. I attended that course in 1997. It was excellent. There were chiefs, sheriffs, and other police executives from all over the U.S. None of them were doing any more than Champlin. We learned that NCMEC is a valuable source to locate missing kids, if the police will use them. Police cannot do the job alone. They must partner with social services, courts, and parents. There is a lot the police can do. Police taking a report and telling parents that the child will return on their own were not enough.

I returned to Champlin energized by what I had seen and learned. I spoke to my neighboring chiefs, Wade Setter of Brooklyn Park, Craig Gerdes of Plymouth, and Sherman Otto of Maple Grove. I encouraged them to attend this course. Each of them did. When they all got back we met and came to an agreement to form a runaway unit. We agreed to share the cost. Craig Gerdes would provide office space. I agreed to keep the books and apply for grants. The next task was to select and hire a coordinator. The person hired would be a licensed peace officer. The Champlin PD would be the hiring agency.

We formed an interview board of Chad Lanners of the YMCA, William Moore from Hennepin County Family and Children Services, and me. We advertised the position. We had two applicants. One was my old partner Steve Gilkerson. The other was retired Minneapolis Police Sgt. Bob Egeland. I knew Bob for years having played hockey with him. Bob's last position with the MPD was supervisor of School Liaison Officers. The interview board selected Steve. It was a hard decision for me because I knew them both to be fine men who would do an excellent job.

Officer Kim Bonde of the Champlin Police suggested the name of the unit be "GAP." The letters did not stand for anything. The GAP was to become a runaway unit that would bridge the gap between runaways, the police, the families, and the social services system. It is important to understand how unique this effort was. Police traditionally view their role as enforcement not social service. Police like to respond, investigate, and make arrests. This approach required that their role be expanded to include not only finding the runaways but also finding out why these kids ran away, connecting willing families with social services, and following through with probation officers and courts. Because this role was foreign to police we chose Steve Gilkerson to be the GAP officer because he did not have a police background. His view was not narrowed by police experience, yet he had a very extensive investigative background. The officers were pleased with this arrangement. They would not have to deal with runaways except for taking a report and forwarding the report to Steve and his partner social worker Paul Cunningham. The effort worked so well that, when new Champlin Police Chief Dave Schwarze eliminated the program in 2005, he told Steve that Champlin did not have enough runaway kids to justify the administrative time his department's staff had to devote to paying its bills.

The logic of this escapes me to this day. The GAP was so successful that the number of runways was significantly reduced. So do away with the GAP.

But now to get back to the workings of the GAP. The partners were the police departments of Champlin, Plymouth, Maple Grove, Brooklyn Park, Osseo, and Dayton, Hennepin County Family and Children Services, the YMCAs Point Northwest for Runaway Youth, Northwest Hennepin Mediation program, and Northwest Hennepin Family and Children Services.

The goals of the unit were: conduct active investigations to locate runaway youths; provide parent and guardians of the runaway with information and resources to deal with their child's behavior; provide earliest intervention available in identifying youth with drug and mental health problems and getting the help necessary to treat these problems (experience would prove that one or both of these problems exists in approximately 90% of the cases the GAP would become involved in); and keeping the youths out of an overburdened juvenile justice system.

I worked with Patty Wilder who was then the Executive Director of Northwest Hennepin Family and Children on getting grant funding. Patty was a master at writing grants. She knew where the money was. At one point she said that GAP ought to be an acronym for something. I told her the reason why we suggested the name. As a result of her efforts along with Steve and me, we got significant grants from the Minnesota Department of Economic Security and the U.S. Department of Justice. The GAP was totally funded by grants. It did not cost the police departments one cent.

In January of 1999, I had the honor of swearing in Steve Gilkerson as a Champlin police officer. The support was overwhelming from the elected officials and even the police unions.

In its seven years of operation Steve Gilkerson located 260 runaway children. He handled 2,645 runaway cases. Think of this effort of one dedicated police officer. Here are some wonderful statistics: 90% of the parents felt supported by the GAP; 94% of the parents would recommend the GAP to families in similar situations; 88% of the parents said the GAP helped them either resolve the issues or better deal with them; and 88% of the parents credited the GAP with increasing their knowledge of resources and services.

Here are some of the heartwarming stories of the GAP's efforts:

> To Chief Al Bruns Champlin Police:
> Your officer Steve Gilkerson at GAP for runaway youth found my 16-year-old daughter. She ran away December 17, 2003. I notified the police and did everything they suggested. By the end of January I felt the police were not answering my questions or sharing information they had. Once I talked to Steve Gilkerson I knew my contact with him would be much different. Steve listened to the whole story and gave me some ideas to work on right away. Then Steve was able to use his resources

and knowledge to do some searches and put the pieces together. He called me on Friday, February 13, and told me where he thought she was staying. Steve arranged for me to meet with the Minneapolis Police because he suspected she was staying there. I did exactly that and we were successful. My daughter is now getting the help she needs and I thank Steve Gilkerson for finding her. Sincerely, . . .

Here are comments of another parent:

Steve was the one who finally brought our son in the last time after he'd been gone for five days. He encouraged us to have a plan when we got him off the streets. He helped us set up the plan. . . . If we hadn't, I don't know that we would ever have gotten him off the streets. . . . The plan worked perfectly.

Another parent commented:

Steve would come out to the house every time she ran away. When she was on the run, I would call him, talk to him, and give him any information I had. She would usually end up in juvenile hall, or the police station or something. She was a registered runaway. She was now in the system. After about the third time she got caught, Paul (Cunningham, Hennepin County family and Children Services) stepped in and said, "Ok, we're going to get a court date, you're going to go to court." . . . Before, it was like she was nothing to nobody.

Another father said:

My wife will tell you Steve Gilkerson saved her (my daughter's) life." The daughter who had runaway said, "Yeah, I agree. I very much agree. I think if I was still doing what I was doing, I don't think I 'd even be alive to be doing it."

Of all of my efforts as chief I am most proud of the GAP and of the singlehanded efforts of my best friend Steve Gilkerson.

On June 7, 1997, Cpl. Tim Bowe of the Minnesota State Patrol was shot and killed. He was a member of the State Patrol Special Response Team (SRT) team. Shortly after midnight on June 7, 1997, the Chisago County Sheriff's Office received a call of a man shot at a residence in Fish Lake

Township, which is approximately 10 miles west of Cambridge. The area is rural. The report was that three men were doing drugs at the residence when one of them pulled a gun and shot one of the other men in the chest. The wounded man, Jason Leibel, 24, his mother, Jacqueline Steele, and another man ran into the house and called 911. Four Chisago County deputies and three Isanti County sheriff's deputies responded. Trooper Bowe heard the call and also responded.

The officers parked their cars and walked toward the residence. They saw the suspect's vehicle parked in the driveway. The suspect was lying on the front seat of the car with his legs sticking out. Around 1 a.m. the officers started to approach the suspect's car. The suspect fired one or two shots from his .40 caliber handgun, hitting trooper Tim Bowe in the chin.

They returned fire. It was later determined that the suspect, Joseph S. Lindstrom, of Arizona, died of a self-inflicted gunshot to the head. Trooper Bowe was med evaced to the St. Paul Ramsey Medical Center where he died at 2 a.m. on June 7, 1997. He was 36 years old and had been with the State patrol for 15 years.

I had been a member and leader of SWAT teams for over 25 years. The president of the Special Operations and Training Association (SOTA), Deputy Sheriff Pat Erickson, approached me and asked if I would work with him to put together a ceremony dedicated to Cpl. Bowe. I had been the president of SOTA, which an association of SWAT members in our area. I accepted Pat's offer and embarked on one of the most emotional experiences of my career.

Tim Bowe left a widow, Denise, and two young children. I met with Denise and asked her if she would permit SOTA to honor Tim. She emotionally agreed. Seeing her alone with her grief and her two children was almost too much for me to bear. Someone suggested that SOTA present her with Tim's duty weapon and an American flag in a shadow box. She thought this would be a fitting tribute.

I asked the State Patrol's chief firearms instructor if they would allow us to do this. He said they would and gave me Tim's gun. In April 1998, SOTA held its annual banquet, an awards ceremony. Colonel Ann Beers, the Chief of the State Patrol was there along with our special guest Los Angeles Police Chief Darryl Gates. It was a touching evening for everyone including Denise Bowe. When I made the presentation to Denise, I think everyone was crying.

The State Patrol gave everyone who attended the funeral, which had been held earlier, a card. It read, "Dear Friend—In my memory do an act of kindness each day. It is lighting a candle in a world of darkness. With Love, Cpl. Timothy J. Bowe—June 11, 1997."

Another interesting note is the action of Chief Gates toward me. He was known as no friend of the FBI. He knew I was a retired FBI agent. He gave me a copy of his latest book which he signed "Best wishes to Al Garber, an FBI agent that I respect, from Darryl Gates."

I have occasionally run into Denise Bowe after that day. She always has a nice hello.

In April 1998, Colonel Ann Beers wrote me a letter in which she said:

> Please accept my sincere thanks for the time and effort you put into honoring Corporal Tim Bowe at the Special Operations banquet. . . . I am well aware of the personal input you had in making the event special for Denise Bowe and the State Patrol Special Response team. I am sure the impact of Corporal Bowe's death had on the team members did not go unnoticed. Through your efforts, they were able to proudly demonstrate their admiration for Tim, as well as their grief in his tragic death, to their peers. Thank you for providing all us that opportunity.
>
> If I or the State Patrol can ever be of service to you or your agency, please do not hesitate to ask.

But, as we all know, life goes on, so it was back to being police chief for me. I learned that the officers of my department would either make me successful or not. So I always looked for opportunities to heighten their morale. Police officers thrive on the diverse nature of their job. Sometimes it is a good idea to create opportunities for the officers. With my background in SWAT, I decided to create a SWAT team. However, a department as small as ours did not have the funding or the personnel to staff a top notch SWAT team. So I asked my neighboring chiefs and the county sheriff if they would be interested in a joint team. The responses were interesting. Chief Setter of Brooklyn Park was not interested because he thought his city was large enough to need its own team. The sheriff Pat McGowan was a long time friend of mine. I met him when he was a detective sergeant with the Minneapolis police robbery squad. He was also a hostage negotiator. I played hockey with him.

Pat told me he did not want to be part of a joint team. He said he would allow his team to perform SWAT duties in Champlin, but only if I understood that he or his designated official would be in charge. I told him that would not be acceptable. He said that after the incident was over he would tell me the results. I asked him to put himself in my shoes. I answer to the mayor and council. I am responsible for public safety in Champlin. What do you think their response would be if I told them that a critical incident was occurring in Champlin but I didn't know what was going on because the sheriff was handling it? The sheriff listened to me and then said either he would in charge or his SWAT team would not be available.

The other chiefs, Sherman Otto of Maple Grove and Craig Gerdes of Plymouth, liked the idea, and our joint SWAT team soon became a reality. We all signed a mutual aid agreement. The agreement said that the police chief of the city where the incident was occurring would be the incident commander. The other chiefs would assist the incident commander. Each city accepted responsibility for the actions of its officers on the team. Each city was responsible for equipping its officers. This agreement worked well. The most common occurrence was a domestic assault that developed into a barricaded hostage situation. In every case, the joint SWAT team which included hostage negotiators successfully resolved the situation.

Then an incident occurred which almost caused me to dissolve the team. The incident occurred in Champlin late one night. A man had beaten his wife and when police responded he refused to come out. Friends told us he had numerous guns in the house. The SWAT team responded and after several hours he surrendered. His wife said he had hidden a gun in his attic. The SWAT team, which was dressed in military camouflage clothing, left the scene after the suspect was taken into custody. That left uniformed officers who were dressed in their patrol uniforms to search the insulation-filled attic. I didn't know what had occurred until we held a debriefing at the police department later that night. I noticed that the SWAT team was clean and rested while patrol sergeant Rosemary Mengelkoch's uniform was covered with fiberglass insulation. I asked her how she got so dirty. She told me that the SWAT team left the residence and that she and her other patrol officers had to do the searching and they found the gun. I asked the SWAT team leader for an explanation. He told me that SWAT does not search for evidence. They only deal with the suspect. I told him that was not the way it was going to be in the future. SWAT are not elitists and they would get their hands dirty in the future. That mistake never occurred again.

However, another incident occurred that would result in the joint team being dissolved. The team had been training at Camp Ripley, a military post near Little Falls, Minnesota. After the training, my supervisor, who was at the training, told me the training went well. About one week after the training, I got a call from Chief Sherman Otto of Maple Grove. He asked me if I knew of an incident that occurred at Camp Ripley where a SWAT officer pointed a loaded gun at another officer. When I replied no, Sherman told me one of his officers was the victim and a Champlin officer had pointed the gun. My lieutenant, Al Bruns, interviewed the Maple Grove officer who told us the whole story. It was pretty bad. The Champlin officer pointed a gun at the other officer's chest and said, apparently in jest, that he could shoot him anytime. The Maple Grove officer thought the gun was empty and this was a bad joke until the Champlin officer ejected a round from his pistol. Other officers took the gun from the suspect officer and dismantled it. It got even worse. Another Champlin officer who fancied himself as a knife fighter held another officer and put a knife to his neck saying he could cut him. This occurred after training was completed and the officers were in their barracks. There was some drinking but it did not sound like anyone was drunk. The worst part of it for me was that my supervisor who was there tried to cover it up and never told me anything. When I asked him to explain himself, he said he was going to "handle" it himself.

The Champlin Police Department is a pretty small close-knit group. The officers performed their duties with efficiency, professionalism, and pride. So this incident was a big deal. When I found out, it was late afternoon. I called the suspect officer and supervisor into my office. I immediately suspended each of them. I then called a meeting of all of the employees. I wanted them to hear what happened from me and not from the rumor mill. I told them as much of the details as I could. Most of them expressed shock and dismay.

I informed the mayor and council who were supportive. The mayor told me to do what I thought best and tell him after I did it. I consulted with the city attorney because I wanted whatever punishment I gave out to stick when it was appealed. He advised me that the most that would stand up would be a two-week suspension without pay for the suspect officer and four days for the supervisor. I really though this was light punishment, but I took the city attorney's advice. I also gave the officer in the knife incident four days off.

The suspensions of the officer who pointed the gun and the supervisor were appealed to an arbitrator. In the case of the suspect officer, he testified that he admitted to exercising poor judgment but this was his first offense. The arbitrator said he disagreed and that this was not a case of poor judgment; it was a case of no judgment. The arbitrator upheld the suspension.

The supervisor's arbitration did not go so well. His suspension was overruled. He was reinstated and got back pay for the four days I suspended him.

The officer in the knife incident took his punishment and apologized for his action.

The real impact was that the other chiefs told me that their officers would not work with the Champlin officers in SWAT capacity. The team was dissolved. In fairness to the other officers, they did not participate in this outrageous conduct. But they were lumped into the group that neighboring officers would not work with. This incident was the worst one I faced in almost six years as chief. The whole incident did not affect the attitude of the supervisor and the gun pointer. They said they had done nothing wrong. The other officer took this very seriously.

Sergeant Jim Kurtz was one of the shining stars of the police department. In a small department promotions don't happen often. I got the opportunity to promote Jim. I was never sorry I did it. Jim was an idea man. One of the ideas he proposed to me was allowing patrol officers to take their squad cars home. Our program was modeled after another small southern department. They gave their officers take-home cars and placed responsibility for the care of the car with each officer. Our program, as I proposed it to the mayor and council, worked like this: patrol officers who lived within 50 miles of the department would have a take-home car assigned to them. They would be responsible for routine maintenance, which they would pay for. They were allowed to drive to and from work, but they could stop at convenience stores or day care enroute providing these stops did not add more than five miles to their trip. Each squad was inspected at the start of each shift. Any abuse would result in the car being taken away.

Squads were assigned by seniority since there were not enough cars for each officer. Several cars were held back for duty use by officers who were not assigned individual cars.

As the department got new cars, we would trade them after one year's use. Since the cars were taken care of so well, they would bring top dollar. Eventually, we would have a fleet of all new cars. All of this made sense to me both for morale and for fixing responsibility. In addition, with regard to those officers who lived in town, the result would be citizens seeing a lot more police cars. The police union enthusiastically supported this program. The tough sell would be to the mayor and council. When other city departments found out about my proposal, they lobbied against it. They asked why the police are so special that they get take-home cars. I thought their argument was pretty funny. Can you imagine a public works employee driving a front-end loader or a dump truck home?

The city council approved. The effort was a real success. The officers took great pride in "their" squads. I remember seeing Officer Chris Larabee in the city garage one weekend. He was cleaning the tire rims on his squad with a tooth brush. The cars looked good and were all regularly maintained. We began to sell the one-year-old cars to other departments.

Looking back on this program, I think the mayor and council approved it because they had a lot of confidence in what I told them. Soon after I left as chief, the program ended.

There was almost an unlimited amount of funding available for local police departments through the Federal Community Oriented Policing (COPS) program. The money was awarded by the U.S. Department of Justice. I learned how to write grants with key words or phrases. I cannot remember ever being turned down. Grant money was also available from the Minnesota Department of Public Safety and a host of businesses and non-profits. The only funding that came with conditions was COPS funding. The conditions were generally that a city had to agree to fund the added officers for three additional years after the COPS funding ended. I was able to convince the mayor and council that the COPS conditions were not unreasonable because the city was growing and additional officers would be needed anyway.

Between grants and the city's budget process the police department was well funded. You must remember that the police officers' performance of their duties was the key factor in great confidence that the elected officials had in the department. Were it not for the normally outstanding performance of the officers, none of this funding would have been authorized. I was proud and pleased that I was performing my job in making resources available to the police and they responded with outstanding service.

On November 7, 1996, Minneapolis police officers conducted a raid at 2216 26th Avenue North. The raid went bad quickly. One officer, Mark Lanasa, was shot and hundreds of rounds were fired by officers in the front and in the rear of the house. The police department conducted an internal investigation while the county attorney's office looked into the affair from a prosecution standpoint. Chief of Police Bob Olson and Deputy Chief Bill Jones asked me if I would look into the incident from a different prospective. They asked if I could determine what steps they could take to insure this type of situation never occurred again. I knew both of them from both my time in the FBI and as Champlin chief. They promised that the results of my investigation would not be used to discipline any officers. I took them at their word and agreed to help them. This was a very difficult assignment because I knew I would have to promise the officer I had to talk to that whatever they told me would not be used to discipline any of them. My experience told me that without this guarantee most of the officers would not talk to me. I knew many of the involved officers from my SWAT days. If Chief Olson or Chief Jones double-crossed me, my reputation in the police community would be shit.

This is a summary of what I determined: The purpose of the raid was to execute a drug search warrant. A police informant purchased marijuana from the residence. When he purchased the dope, he said there was a man with a shotgun who was near the side door apparently providing security. The PD's Emergency Response Unit (ERU) was given the mission of executing the warrant. Sergeant Bob Kroll was in charge. He planned to use ERU personnel to enter the building. Police from the Public Housing Unit (PHU) were to be used to form a rear perimeter to prevent escape. The first sign of a problem was that PHU officers were not SWAT-trained and had not worked with ERU before.

Since the informant said that there was a man with a shotgun near the side door, Sgt. Kroll decided to deploy two flash bang diversion devices near the side door. These devices produce a very loud bang and a brilliant flash. They were to distract the occupants so that ERU officers could get into the residence quickly with the element of surprise.

Sgt. Kroll conducted a briefing in which he outlined the plan. However PHU officers were not given specific assignments; were not told the rules of engagement (when they could shoot); and were not given guidelines for seeking cover when they went into position. Cover means hiding behind something that will stop bullets, like trees, other buildings, and such. Finally PHU officers were not given the opportunity to recon their positions before the raid. So the first they saw of the area was when going into position just before the raid. While ERU was a well-trained unit with standard operating procedures, PHU did not have this advantage.

ERU had conducted many raids and in some respects became casual in their approach and execution. I remembered that as an FBI SWAT member and leader I always complained that the FBI didn't use the SWAT team often enough. It really had to be a big deal for the FBI SWAT to be used. In retrospect, I realized that one of the reasons our team never had anyone injured was that we really planned our operations well—we knew we were not used frequently and we didn't want to screw anything up. Anyway, ERU did so many warrants that they relied on one method and that was to enter the objective rapidly and dynamically. While this approach often provided the officers with the element of surprise, it also took away their ability to be deliberate and careful. Accidents happen when you move too fast.

So the raid began with the PHU officers going to the back only to find that they were in the open and vulnerable to being shot from the house. The flash bangs were deployed; ERU broke in the front door and entered. PHU apparently thought the flash bangs were shots. They saw a silhouette of a person in the window with a long gun. They assumed they were being shot at, and with no cover they had to shoot back in self-defense.

The ERU officers saw the man with the shotgun and received fire probably from the PHU officers in the back who were shooting into the house. ERU officers returned the fire. Someone shot Officer Mark Lanasa in the neck. His body armor collar stopped most of the round. According to Officer Jim Scheu, who was one of the ERU officers, and who was a trusted friend from the days of the joint FBI/MPD SWAT team, he heard rounds whistling past his head. So he returned fire clearly in an effort to save his life and the lives of the other officers. Jim rescued the injured Mark Lanasa, dragging him outside while returning fire.

Many, many rounds were fired by the police before the man with the shotgun; Andre Madison, was taken into custody. He was wounded twice.

My overall conclusion was that the officers acted in good faith shooting in what they believed was self-defense. In fact some, like Jim Scheu, acted courageously. My recommendations included that if non-ERU personnel were to be used with ERU they should both train together. ERU should be more selective in the raids they conduct so the numbers go down. This should allow more time for planning. The rules of engagement must be clearly explained. ERU should consider that in some cases dynamic entry is not to their advantage. If they had a smaller number of warrants to execute, or if the unit size was increased, they could use other tactics like waiting for suspects to come out of the house and arresting or detaining them outside, or sneaking into the house slowly and deliberately.

Recently, I asked Jim Scheu why all of the officers talked to me back then. He told me the others knew he had worked with me and asked him why they should believe me. He said he told them that he didn't know anyone who cared more about their welfare than me and that he trusted me "to the ends of the earth." Now I know why they talked to me.

Chiefs Olson and Jones kept their word. They visited me at the Champlin police department to go over my report. They thanked me for the many hours I spent. Of course, I told them I didn't want anything for my efforts. They brought coffee and bagels. We spent several hours going over the report. As a result of this effort the number of ERU warrants went down dramatically, and they did include non-ERU units in their training. At least for the time being my efforts were worth it.

One Sunday morning I was having coffee at my old friend Jack Reshitar's house. Jack has since passed away. His home was on the Mississippi River in Champlin. He was quite a character, a big bear of a man with a heart of gold. He had owned the Minneapolis landmark restaurant, Little Jack's, for many years. I met him years ago when he asked me to speak at Minnesota 100 Club meeting. The 100 Club is an organization of business people who support police. It had been a routine for us to have coffee together each Sunday morning. We talked about every subject we could think of. We watched the birds and ducks that he fed. Jack saw that I was becoming ready for a professional change. The Champlin Police Department was running well and I was running out of challenges. Jack told me that Governor Ventura was looking for a Commissioner for the Department of Public Safety (DPS). My initial reaction was that's not for me, too much politics. But the more Jack and I talked, the more I thought it would be an interesting challenge to work for Governor Ventura.

So I submitted my resume. I was surprised when I got an interview with one of the governor's citizen interview boards. The members were average citizens who asked common sense questions. There was not a hint of politics during the interview. I related very well with these average citizens. Then I got a second interview with another citizen's board. That went well also.

Still, since I didn't know Governor Ventura or his method of governing, I didn't think I was well known enough to get the job. I was shocked when I was asked to attend an interview with the governor. The governor, the lieutenant governor, Mae Schunk, and the governor's chief of staff, Steven Bosacker, interviewed me. The governor did most of the questioning. Almost immediately I felt a common thread between him and me. We talked about military experiences, including my time as a U.S. Army Airborne Ranger and his time as a Navy Seal. The lieutenant governor asked a few questions. She was a down-to-earth sincere person. Steven Bosacker asked only one or two questions. But it was apparent he was paying close attention to my answers. All in all the entire entire interview was a pleasant experience. I was relaxed as were they. Finally, the governor said he had great respect for my experience and felt we would work well together. However, he said, he had decided to give the PSC Commissioner's job to Charlie Weaver, a lawyer and former prosecutor. Then the governor asked if he could call on me in the future for help. I answered, of course.

I went back to Champlin never expecting to hear from him again. I read in the newspaper that his nominee for Commissioner of the Department of Natural Resources (DNR) was in trouble after DNR Conservation Officers disclosed that the nominee had received several citations for natural resources violations. I didn't know much about the DNR except that the agency and the commissioner were widely criticized in the press.

About two weeks after my interview with the governor I got a call from his personal secretary. She said the governor wanted to see me at noon today. I responded that I was conducting police training all day and I was dressed in military fatigues. She paused and then asked if I took a lunch break. I said, yes, but what about my dress. There was another pause and she said it didn't matter how I was dressed. So I showed up at the governor's office at noon dressed in fatigues. The receptionist did a double take when

I told her who I was and why I was there. I was ushered into the governor's office. He stood up and said, "I need your help; I want you to be DNR Commissioner." I replied, "Governor, I don't know much about the DNR." He said that didn't matter. I answered, "I accept." How could I refuse to help this governor who I had grown to respect in such a short time?

My respect for Governor Ventura began after my first interview with his citizen interview panel. I was impressed by these ordinary citizens and by the fact that their questions had nothing to do with politics. When I got my interview with the governor, lieutenant governor, and the chief of staff, I was impressed that an apolitical person (me) was being interviewed by the top leadership. When I actually talked to the governor, I found him to be easy to communicate with. I judged him to be a man who says it the way it is, not one who says the popular thing. I also greatly respected his military service. Military service is a very important responsibility of all citizens of this great country. It has been said that first impressions are often the most important. In the case of Governor Ventura, I was to learn that my first impression was right on the money. There will be more about that later.

I had no clue what I was in for. The chief of staff asked me not to tell anyone except my family for now. I promised. There were periodic calls from Steven Bosacker over the next two weeks. It was very difficult to face the new mayor and council and the police officers knowing I would be leaving soon. Finally, Steven told me when the governor would make the announcement of my appointment and I could now tell the elected officials. I wrote a letter to the mayor and to each council member. Then I personally delivered each one. It was not an easy thing to do. The elected officials had shown such great support for my efforts and those of the officers, I was sad to deliver these letters.

Then the next day I had a meeting of all police department employees. I wanted them to hear the news from me. The response from them was overwhelming to me. In six years a bond had developed between us that was difficult to break. However, the decision was made and I moved on.

*With Governor Jesse Ventura on Al's appointment as
the Department of Natural Resources Commissioner*

CHAPTER 5

Minnesota Department
of Natural Resources

W hat followed was like the best spy or thriller movie I ever saw. The media in Minneapolis and the surrounding areas were spreading all kinds of information about who would be the next DNR Commissioner. It seemed like everyone was mentioned except me. The chief of staff asked me to refrain from telling anyone else about my impending appointment. It always amazed me that although I told my mayor and council, and the governor and his staff knew, the word never leaked to the press.

The night before my appointment, the chief of staff Steven Bosacker asked me to meet with Acting Commissioner Ray Hitchcock. I was to meet Ray at his house which was in rural area about 60 miles north of Minneapolis. The meeting would take place at 11 p.m. and was scheduled so that Ray could give me an overview of the DNR. My instructions were to call Ray at home and tell him I was coming. Neither of us had heard of each other before that night. We did meet. Ray was gracious and had obviously prepared for this briefing. Ray had been a DNR employee for more than 35 years and had risen through the ranks. It really was a strange meeting between two people who never before met, one of whose identity was a closely-guarded secret.

So the next day my son Micah and I went to the governor's office. By this time I had told the Champlin police employees that I was leaving. My deputy chief Al Bruns and Officer Kevin Wagman were waiting in the large conference room that adjoins the governor's office, as were many representatives of the media. When the governor, Micah, and I entered the conference room, I heard someone in the crowd of reporters say, "Who the hell is that?" The governor introduced me and then the questions started coming. Why was I chosen? What was my background in hunting and fishing issues? What was first order of business?

The one answer I remember best was that my first order of business was to meet with the senior leadership of the DNR. I had asked Ray Hitchcock to arrange the meeting as soon as I could leave the governor. Some of the reporters forcefully asked me to meet with them right now. I told them I would meet with any of them after I introduced myself to the senior staff of DNR. This decision on my part to put my staff ahead of the media set the tone for my administration. It was very unusual for any commissioner to put anyone before the media.

I met with the staff. They each introduced themselves and told me a little about their backgrounds. It was a pleasant meeting. I was met with enthusiasm and politeness. I outlined my plan for the immediate future. DNR was an organization that employed over 3500 full-time and 500 part-time employees. The size did not overwhelm me. My idea was that every leader had a span of control. That means that I would directly supervise a small number of senior employees. So I would be supervising no more employees as DNR Commissioner than I had in previous positions. The key was to appoint or retain the right people as senior managers. My earnest belief is that it is the employees who make the agency a success or a failure. With that in mind I was going to spend the great majority of my time meeting my employees face to face statewide.

Then I met with members of the media. The reporter who made my antenna go up the highest was Dennis Anderson of the *Minneapolis Star Tribune*. He was obviously disappointed that a man like me, with little background in hunting and fishing, was chosen as commissioner. He asked to have his photographer take a picture of me in the outdoors soon after our first meeting. I agreed. I came to work in a suit and tie and the photographer asked if I would pose for an outdoor shot. I did, and the result was not very flattering. Here I was the DNR Commissioner responsible for all aspects of Minnesota outdoors dressed in a suit and tie. The article that accompanied the photo was no less flattering. That was the first and last time I let the reporter dictate the place and circumstances.

I spoke to my friend Howard Safir about my new job. Howard was then commissioner of the New York City Police Department. I met him in 1983 when I participated in the hunt for Gordon Kahl who had killed two U.S. marshals. Howard was then a senior official with the U.S. Marshals Service. He gave a key piece of advice about choosing people to work for me in the DNR. He said I had to have a person who I could confide in, not a career DNR official; someone who would give me unbiased opinions and someone not reluctant to tell me the way it is. He told this person would be key for me keeping the correct prospective and someone who would let me vent to. To accomplish this I brought former Champlin police officer Kim Bonde on board. I created the position of Special Assistant to the Commissioner. It was not easy convincing her to leave her chosen career as a police officer. She would prove to be the right person for the job in every respect.

Then I began my search for a deputy commissioner. Ray Hitchcock soon realized that he and I had completely different styles of leadership and different ideas about how to lead the DNR. To his credit he helped me greatly in the beginning and then made the choice to retire. I went to his retirement party and to this day have admiration for the way he treated me. The chief of staff suggested that I might want to talk to State Senator Steve Morse about the position. The chief made it clear that the choice would be mine, but Steve might bring needed expertise.

So Steve and I met for dinner at a Minneapolis restaurant. Steve had been a Minnesota state senator since 1986. He chaired the Senate Environment and Agriculture Budget Division. He was intimately familiar with the details of the DNR budget which at that time was some $280 million. He knew all the players in the senate and the house. Steve was an upbeat, friendly fellow who was cautious about accepting the post. He was quite an interesting person. His family farmed in southern Minnesota. He hunted and fished but was not avid about either. Although he had not attended college, he was obviously intelligent and had a wide understanding of the DNR's responsibilities. We had a long talk and ended with an agreement that he would get back to me. Shortly thereafter, he accepted the position of deputy commissioner. He proved to be a wonderful partner who was invaluable to me.

The DNR has wide-ranging responsibilities. It has the following divisions: Fish and Wildlife; Trails and Waterways; Waters; Forestry; Lands and Minerals; Enforcement; Ecological Services; and Parks. Each division had a director who was a member of the senior staff. They were key players so I interviewed each of them privately to insure they were the right person for the job with me as commissioner. The division directors are directly supervised by an assistant commissioner for operations. The assistant commissioner was Brad Moore, a career DNR employee. I liked Brad from the first time I met him. He is an avid hunter and fisherman, who realized that all elements of the environment depend on each other. I liked his prospective that the environment was more than hunting and fishing. I asked Brad to stay on and he did.

The support functions of DNR were: budget; engineering; licensing and education; and human resources. Each of these administrative bureaus had an administrator. I interviewed each of the current bureau administrators. The bureau administrators were directly supervised by an assistant commissioner for administration. I asked my former boss at Champlin, Kurt Ulrich, to take that position. He accepted. My management team was complete. Now it was full speed ahead.

The commissioner's position is very demanding. In the first year I travelled about 85,000 miles. I was constantly on the road. I was driven by my schedule. It seemed like everyone wanted my ear. I relied on my staff to tell me who I should meet with. I had an administrative assistant who kept my schedule, screened my calls, and generally kept me pointed in the right direction. I travelled by car or on DNR aircraft. I never ceased to be amazed by the reception I got in the outlying DNR offices. I had employees tell me that in over 30 years as a DNR employee I was the first commissioner they had met. In one employee meeting I was asked what I hoped my legacy would be. I told them I hoped I would be remembered as a commissioner who truly cared about the employees, both as employees and as people. DNR employees in general proved to be hardworking, committed, and nice people. They were not used to having a commissioner who would stand up for them when they were right regardless of who was beating them up. Decisions came hard for them because they saw long implications for their decisions. I repeatedly told them what I learned in the army, "DO Something." I had difficulty in understanding their reluctance to make decisions. My career had been in the military and in law enforcement where life-threatening decisions often had to be made. I couldn't understand how decisions that were not life-threatening could be so hard.

The budget process was something that required intense scrutiny. Steve Morse and Budget Director Peggy Adelmann handled most of the details. They were excellent and answered my questions which were many. There were times when I know they wanted to tell me to stop, but they didn't. It was my responsibility to represent the DNR at the governor's cabinet level. The governor would approve a budget and I believed that, after the decision was made, it was my duty to support the governor and his budget. That was not the way it had been done. I learned that the way it had been done was that the senior staff of the DNR would whisper in the ears of key legislators about what funding they really needed. The commissioner would do the same. To me that made the governor's budget meaningless. So I gave orders to my staff that, when they were called before the legislature, they answer all questions, but they must not lobby behind closed doors for more funding than the governor's budget called for. This order was hard for them to swallow. The worst director in this respect was Bill Morrissey, the parks director. Bill was an outstanding director. He was passionate about Minnesota state parks. The results he and his staff produced stood for themselves. The parks were clean, beautiful, heavily used, with almost no complaints. But Bill had a long career in DNR and kept lobbying in private for more funds. I would

Deputy Commissioner Steve Morse, Kim, and Al

get word from a legislator or someone on the governor's staff about Bill doing this. I would then tell Brad Moore, Bill's boss, to tell him to knock it off. It got so bad that I had to meet with Bill and tell him despite the great job he was doing he wouldn't have his job much longer if he continued to disobey my order. We reached an understanding and he stayed on.

A key to my success was for me to realize which issues were of sufficient importance for me to get personally involved. One of them again involved Bill Morrissey. He came in one day and asked me to sign a contract he had drawn up to widen the road in one of our most beautiful state parks, Itasca State Park in northern Minnesota. I had been there several times. The park was famous for its 250–300-year-old red pine trees. The park contains the headwaters of the Mississippi River. That great river begins at Lake Itaska.

So I asked Bill to explain why the road needed to be widened and what would be the impact on the red pines. He explained that, because recreational vehicles were being made larger and larger, the existing road was too narrow to allow these large vehicles to park off to the side to observe the natural beauty. He also told me that about 246 old red pines would have to be cut down. Finally, he told me that Clearwater County, Minnesota, officials wanted the road widened so it could have an alternate road for traversing the county. I refused to sign the contract. I told him that no construction would occur and I asked if he was clear on that. Then he told me he had made some sort of commitment to the county and asked if I would talk to them. I agreed to do that. Shortly thereafter, I met with the county engineer and other officials. I told them I would not approve widening the road. They told me it was important to them to get the road widened and if I didn't agree they would stop plowing snow in the park as they had for years. I said we would plow our own snow. That was the end of the issue and those trees were never cut down.

My way of doing business had always included confronting issues head on. I also tried to believe what people told me unless they had an obvious reason to lie or omit facts. Loyalty is very important to me. So when an employee of mine gains my confidence and trust I will defend that employee at all costs. I used all of these principals in addressing an issue involving the *Minneapolis Star Tribune*. The *Star Tribune* is the largest newspaper in the Minneapolis area.

In June of 2000, Ron Payer, who was my director of the fisheries department, came to see me. Ron was a 25-year veteran of the DNR. Literally millions of Minnesotans fish making Ron's position naturally high pressure. He was often criticized by all kinds of people who have an interest in fishing. These included all the various people who fish for specific species. Each group wanted the DNR to do more to produce conditions that were conducive to them getting more fish. Then there were those who were interested only in conservation. These people wanted more restrictions. There were also resort owners who wanted more fishing opportunities so they could have a better business return. Then, finally, there was the media who always delighted in pointing out where Ron and his staff were lacking. So criticism came with the territory for Ron.

It was immediately apparent, when Ron walked into my office, that he was very upset. He told me that over the years he had been called many names and accused of many things he had done wrong, but never in his 25 years had he been called a liar. I looked at this good man and loyal public servant and knew this was serious. He told me that a reporter for the *Star Tribune*, Dennis Anderson, had written an article saying Ron had promised no changes would be made in fishing limits but that after the legislature had appropriated more funds for the fisheries division and then adjourned for the year Ron now said there would be changes.

I read the article was written by Anderson that was published in the *Star Tribune* on June 2, 2000. Here is the article which Anderson entitled:

DNR LAID LOW, GOT THE DOUGH; ANGLING SUFFERS.

Oblivious, seemingly, to the notion of winning friends and influencing people, the Department of Natural Resources this week celebrated its $32 million windfall by announcing it will review Minnesota's game fish limits. The DNR's goal, implicit or explicit, is to reduce the number of walleyes, northern pike, bass and panfish that anglers can catch and keep.

The DNR's notice follows closely the end of the legislative session, during which many people argued on the agency's behalf that it should receive additional funding.

It worked. When the legislature headed home not many days ago, about $5 million in new money had been awarded the DNR from higher hunting and fishing license fees, $2 million was set aside for the DNR from the general fund and $25 million was shifted to the agency from a tax on lottery ticket sales.

It might come as news to the DNR, but that money was allocated with the expectation that the state's fish and wildlife population would be enhanced, not so conferences could be held to see how significantly fish limits could be cut.

It seems not by coincidence that the DNR stayed mum about its fish limit proposal during the legislative session. After all, how would it have looked for the agency to argue, on one hand, if given more money it could improve fish and wildlife management—while simultaneously arguing that fish limits should be reviewed and perhaps cut?

The DNR instead waited until it had its new money in hand and legislators were scattered to the hinterlands before announcing , as it did Wednesday in the voice of fisheries section chief Ron Payer, that fishing technology and angler pressure have increased , putting more and more pressure on the state's fisheries. It's reasonable to ask, whether, in light of these increases, some of the existing bag limits may be out of date. . . ."

Ron Payer told me that what Anderson left out was that bag limits had been a subject of discussion at the fishing roundtables for the last three years. Fishing roundtables are held every year and organized by the DNR. Any interested citizens can attend and participate. Ron told me that in his circles he was being called a liar. I asked my management team which consisted of the deputy commissioner, assistant commissioner for Operations and my special assistant to read the article and give their opinion about what we should do. We all knew what an honorable man Ron was. I asked for their advice about meeting with editor, Tim McGuire. They all advised me to go ahead. So a meeting was set up.

We went to office of the *Star Tribune* and met with McGuire and some of his staff. The meeting did not go well at all. McGuire told me he believed Anderson and that was that. He was obviously angered after I made my case. An argument developed and we left.

After returning to my office, I issued a directive to all employees instructing them that when they spoke to Anderson they should request that their conversation be recorded so that they could have an accurate record of the interview. I further instructed all employees that if Anderson refused to record the conversation they should decline to be interviewed.

The policy was adhered to almost entirely within the DNR. The result was that Anderson's articles became meek, mild, and not very informative. I knew that it was the DNR that had the critical information that reporters like Anderson need to be successful. In most cases, he refused to have interviews recorded and therefore received no information.

I received a call from editor Tim McGuire who told me my policy was unreasonable, unjust, and illegal and that he would sue me. I told him I did not respond to threats.

I must say now that looking back I had no idea how much I had angered and frustrated the *Star Tribune* and particularly its editor. I would later find out the consequences of challenging the media.

All of my actions were intended to vindicate Ron Payer and prevent a repeat for any other employee of mine. My motive had nothing to do with frustrating either Anderson or McGuire.

About six months later I rescinded the policy because Anderson's articles did not contain further lies, exaggerations, or untruths. I thought this was over. It was not. In February 2002, I was told by Dennis Stauffer, my media relations director that a reporter for the *Star Tribune*, Paul McEnroe had called an auto mechanic for the DNR and asked him about allegations that he had repaired my personal car. I couldn't understand why this in query was made because I had never had a DNR mechanic work on my car. I was told that the reporter found out that the DNR mechanic had worked on my state car which got a flat tire while it was parked in my driveway. So that inquiry ended.

Then at night in April 2002 my doorbell at home rang and it was a Champlin police officer. The officer told me that a man that I had served with in Vietnam had contacted the police dispatch and asked that I call him. The officer told me his name was Jim Barrett.

Although I didn't remember Jim, I called him. His story just knocked me off my feet. He said he was in my platoon in Vietnam when we both served with the 1st Cavalry Division. He was now disabled, suffering the effects of Agent Orange. He said he was overjoyed to find me. His life's work had been to create a website and to locate as many members of our former unit as he could. He told me he had been looking for me for 30 years and had been unable to find me until he received a call from a man who said he was a reporter, Paul McEnroe, from the *Star Tribune*. McEnroe asked him if I really served in Vietnam. He asked what kind of a leader I was. I knew from talking to Jim on the phone that he had to have been in my unit in Vietnam because he knew so many details. But I still couldn't remember him.

188

I was so angered and insulted by the questions McEnroe asked that I decided to visit him face to face. This may have been a mistake as I look back. But it was something I had to do. When I called him on the phone, he could not believe the DNR commissioner was actually calling. He immediately agreed to meet me and I went to his office. He tape-recorded our conversation. I asked McEnroe why he had asked the soldier I hadn't seen in 30 or more years if I had actually served in Vietnam. He told me he never asked Jim Barrett that question and he was only doing some background about me and had found Jim through his website.

He asked me a series of questions that showed me the depth of his investigation and how it was about me personally, not about me as commissioner. I asked him if this investigation was a result of my confronting his editor about Dennis Anderson's article about Ron Payer. He said absolutely not. He said he was investigating information he received about me and my administration.

I arranged to continue the interview at my office the next day. He questioned me about decisions I made as the FBI supervisor of the Jacob Wetterling kidnapping case. The case occurred on October 22, 1989, in St. Joseph, Minnesota. He told me there were allegations I had allowed Jacob's father, Jerry, to hear and participate in things he should not have been allowed to. He never cited any specific instances. He asked me about the DNR auto mechanic allegation.

He also accused me of stealing documents from the Champlin police personnel file of Sgt. Jim Kurtz, who was now heading the DNR's Office of Professional Standards. He said I was alleged to have stolen the documents so that Kurtz could pass the DNR's background check.

He asked a lot of personal questions about my life. He also told me he was puzzled how he could receive such glowing reports of my abilities and conduct from some people, and yet DNR Conservation Officer Union President Tony Cornish had such a low opinion of me and had made so many terrible allegations against me. I answered his questions despite the fact that he was looking for dirt not facts.

Subsequently, another Champlin police officer called me about a call he received from McEnroe. He said he had to talk to the officer about me and that this was a serious matter. McEnroe said he had been directed by his editor and the highest levels of the *Star Tribune* to take a serious look at Garber. The officer told McEnroe I was a good chief, treated people fairly, and was efficient. McEnroe asked if the officer had anything that was newsworthy.

Then the requests for information pursuant to the Freedom of Information Act came in droves to the DNR. He asked for all sorts of records. I knew it was time for legal representation. I went to Minnesota Attorney General Mike Hatch for advice and counsel. In Minnesota the attorney general is elected. I understood the AG and his staff to be the State's attorneys. So instead of hiring DNR attorneys as had been the practice, I had approached Mike early in my administration and asked for his legal representation. I told him I thought it was a waste of money and a duplication of efforts for the DNR to hire attorneys. He was very receptive and assigned two top notch attorneys to the DNR. So he and I had a mutual respect for each other.

So now when I explained what had occurred with the *Star Tribune* and the recent deluge of FOIA requests, he said he would gladly help. He assigned two other attorneys who had some expertise in FOIA matters. We worked countless hours sorting through records to make sure McEnroe got all he was legally entitled to.

I informed the governor of all of this. I assured him I had done nothing wrong. The governor was a source of strength to me by committing to support me because I had done nothing wrong.

These were difficult times for me. I was asked by numerous DNR employees how I could carry out my duties with all of the media pressure, I don't really know the answer. What I do know is that the battle was worth it. I am proud to have stood up for the integrity of Ron Payer and other DNR employees. I guess that is why there is an old saying: "That's why you get paid the big bucks." No story was ever written and McEnroe went away. Tim McGuire is no longer editor of the *Star Tribune*.

I cannot say with any certainty that our efforts to reform our conservation officers were directly related to the investigation by the *Star Tribune*. So I will leave it up to you to draw your own conclusions.

The Enforcement Division of the DNR is the law enforcement arm of the agency. The officers are called conservation officers (COs). Within a few days of the announcement of my appointment by Governor Ventura, I was visited by CO Union President Tony Cornish. The visit took place in my office at the Champlin Police. Officer Cornish told me that COs had been terribly mistreated by the current administration. He told me the COs had made every effort to improve their lot but had been unsuccessful. He said the best way to bring about reform that would result in fair treatment of the officers would be to appoint him as director of the enforcement division. I thought his initiative to speak to me was unusual, but I kept an open mind.

After assuming my duties, Cornish asked me to meet with a group of COs to hear their grievances. I was accompanied by Assistant Commissioner for Operations Brad Moore. We heard emotional and impassioned statements by them about how they had been mistreated over the years and especially by the current director, Leo Haseman. They were convincing with their picture of injustices perpetrated against them.

Leo had been with the DNR for 31 years. He had risen through the ranks of the COs. Brad and I had numerous talks with him about the concerns the COs raised. He denied almost all of them but was not very convincing in his denials. Meanwhile, during this time, Officer Cornish visited me several times. I finally told Cornish that he would have to go through the chain of command before bringing operational issues to me. Then Brad and I made a decision to ask Leo to resign. He was shocked but acted like a real gentleman. He retired with full benefits.

I hired Bill Bernhjelm to replace him. I had known Bill for years. He had been chief of police in Edina, Minnesota. I had great expectations that Bill would bring a new spirit and fresh leadership to the division. I thought that the COs would respond positively to Bill's leadership. I was to learn soon after Bill's arrival that leadership was not the problem. Rather, the problem was an ingrained culture of no one tells us (the COs) what to do.

As I travelled around the state, I began to hear stories from COs, from citizens, and from interest groups that got me very concerned about the way our COs did business. One lieutenant told me that he loved his job as a conservation officer because he was so free, but that he was injured and then promoted to lieutenant. Now he said he did not have to do anything. Bear in mind that this lieutenant said this to the commissioner of the DNR.

Another lieutenant told me he had no idea where the conservation officers he supervised were. In fact, he said to me that he had not seen one of them for six months. But he knew the CO was still alive because the lieutenant had signed his timesheets.

I asked a newly promoted lieutenant if he intended to spend time in the field supervising and interacting with the officers. He said he would not do this because, if he did, he would be viewed as a spy.

In part because of my belief that allegations against COs were not being thoroughly investigated by the enforcement division, and because there was no process for investigating complaints against any DNR employees, I established the Office of Professional Standards (OPS). It was shocking to me that the DNR which had as many as 4000 employees had no process to investigate complaints. Employees were in limbo for years as complaints were publicized but not investigated.

OPS investigated serious complaints against DNR employees. Its supervisor reported directly to the assistant commissioner for administration. The investigators chosen for the unit were experienced law enforcement officers who were not afraid to find out the facts.

OPS made a real difference. The investigators we chose were experienced investigators. Jim Kurtz, who had worked for me at Champlin, was the supervisor. The other investigators were Dennis Smith, a retired Golden Valley PD detective, and Dean Mooney who had been a chief and officer for two departments. Kim Bonde, our assistant commissioner for administration conducted the interviews and selected these men.

They conducted investigations that were consistent. Consistency is absolutely necessary if punishment is to stand the scrutiny of legal challenges and union challenges. The size and diversity of DNR made it critical to hold all employees to the same standards. This approach resulted in generally high morale throughout the agency.

Some of the noteworthy cases were:

A parks employee was responsible for collecting fees from the collection box in one of our state parks. The park manager noticed cash shortages on numerous occasions. The manager had no investigative experience. Now he had a means to refer the case to real investigators. Jim, Dennis, and Dean posed as campers. They put marked money in the collection box. Marked money means that they recorded the serial numbers of the bills. They photographed the employee removing the cash from the box. The found out that four of the envelopes that the investigators had placed in the collection box were missing from the park receipts. After three weeks of surveillance, they stopped the employee as he was driving his personal car. They found the marked money and thirteen collection envelopes containing cash in his possession. The worker was subsequently fired and criminally charged. Had it not been for OPS there probably would have been no investigation.

In another case, a fatal accident occurred in a state park. Two teenagers were killed and one was critically injured. About one month later a parent of one of the deceased teenagers called Assistant Commissioner Kim Bonde. He said a parks department intern had a party in a cabin located in the park. There was a lot of drinking. His child was at the party. The parent said he thought the DNR was covering up these facts. Kim assigned the case to OPS. Jim Kurtz was able to locate witnesses who said that the intern held the party as the parent described. There was underage drinking. After the party, the kids got in their cars and began to race. One of the cars sped through a stop sign and crashed into a tree. Two kids died and one was injured critically. The park intern was charged criminally and fired. There is no doubt that if there were no OPS there would have been no investigation.

A third case started when a citizen called Major Bill Everett of the DNRs enforcement division. The citizen claimed he was being harassed by a conservation officer (CO). Bill referred the case to OPS. Jim Kurtz and

Dennis Smith determined that the man had been arrested by the CO for illegally trapping fox. The arrest was based on a search warrant that the CO obtained from a state judge. The man claimed that the facts listed in the search warrant affidavit were lies.

Jim obtained a copy of the affidavit. It said that the CO was invited into the man's home and saw a fox pelt in plain sight. Jim found witnesses who said the CO snuck into the house when the man was not home and conducted a search.

The address that the CO listed as the man's address where the CO saw the fox pelt was not the address where the man lived.

The affidavit listed the man's occupation as a tanner of hides. In fact the man never was a tanner.

Jim presented these facts to the county attorney, who dismissed the charges. Then the county attorney called me and angrily told me he would never accept a case from a CO again

Ironically this same CO who was assigned to the southern portion of the state was found hunting in his state truck in the very northern part of the state. When he was asked why he was so far out of his territory, he responded that he was a Minnesota CO and could work anywhere he chose. It was partly as a result of his misuse of his unmarked state vehicle that we decided that all CO vehicles would be appropriately marked.

Time and again OPS proved to be a valuable tool both to charge employees with misconduct and to exonerate them.

As I learned more about the COs performance of their duties through OPS and through my sources, I had frequent talks with Director Bernhjelm. I told Bill I was disappointed that he had not been able to turn around the direction of his division. So in November 2001, I gave him directives that had a deadline of May 1, 2002. COs wore uniforms when on duty. However, their vehicles were unmarked. Many of them told me they need unmarked vehicles so they could work undercover. This made no sense to me because they were in full uniform. Furthermore, the division had an undercover unit. I suspected the real reason for unmarked vehicles was so they could be used for unofficial business and not be recognized.

I directed Bill to move the officers' offices from their homes to a nearby DNR office. There were numerous DNR offices throughout the state. I wanted the COs to be visible and accessible to the public. I also told him I wanted his supervisors to make personal contact with their officers. Other directives included establishing duty rosters so we would know when an officer was working and establishing a central communications system or directing officers to sign in by radio with their local sheriffs' dispatchers when going on duty. COs did not sign in by radio and therefore no one knew who was working. This was a safety and an accountability matter. Finally, I asked Director Bernhjelm to establish a standard report system and records retrieval system

What I did not understand was the political power of the conservation officers union. We were in for the fight of our lives. Conservation officers were stationed throughout the state. They operated largely without supervision or guidance. Over the years they had cultivated their local state representatives and senators. Often state senators and representatives spoke of "their conservation officer."

In order to free the COs from less important duties that did not require armed officers, we established a non-sworn position. This new position would handle such things as noise complaints in parks, littering on state lands, and parking complaints in state parks and campgrounds. One morning I was notified by a good friend that State Representative Rich Stanek was going to introduce legislation that would eliminate our non-sworn position. This intended action by Stanek took me by surprise because he was a Minneapolis police officer on leave to the legislature. Most law enforcement agencies in Minnesota use non-sworn personnel. These positions were absolutely essential to do the less important but very necessary tasks that sworn officers would not do and are not needed to do. I raced over to the state capital to talk to key legislators about this unwise legislation.

I learned that Stanek was carrying this legislation forward at the request of the conservation officers union and the Minnesota Police and Peace Officers Association. It was no coincidence that the president of the Minnesota Peace and Police Officers Association was DNR Conservation Officer

Captain Mike Hamm. I also received a call from the executive director of this organization who questioned DNRs legal authority to establish this non-sworn position.

The issue went away after the Minnesota attorney general issued an opinion that DNR could establish this position. I convinced key legislators that it was foolish to take away these positions from law enforcement agencies, including the DNR. A study group was formed and nothing more was done.

During this time, I went to the office of State Senator Doug Johnson. He was a long-time senator from northern Minnesota who I got along with very well. I went there to explain why it was so essential that all law enforcement agencies retain the ability to use non-sworn personnel to enforce misdemeanors. He told me that a local CO, Tom Fink, was the only DNR employee he knew well. He said that the COs, including Officer Fink, spend a lot of time with him. They had become friends and it was very hard for the senator to take a position in opposition to them.

Next, I was summoned to the office of State Representative Dennis Ozment who was the chair of the house environment and natural resources policy committee. When I got there State Representative Mark Holsten, chair of the house environment and natural resources finance committee was also there. Representative Ozment told me I had been unreasonable in not discussing the issue of non-sworn personnel enforcing misdemeanors with union president Cornish. When I told him I had had such conversations with Cornish and that, along with Director Bernhjelm, we had discussed the issue with many COs, Rep Ozment told me he wanted me to meet Cornish in Rep. Ozment's office. I objected and he told me not to forget that it was the legislature who gave and could take away the authority of the commissioner of the DNR. I left.

I knew that there were many COs who were conscientious and wanted to do their jobs. So I attended as many meetings with them and Director Bernhjelm as I could. I attended an awards ceremony with Bill. The ceremony disintegrated into an arguing match during which Bill Bernhjelm was booed, hissed and cursed. I was embarrassed for my friend Bill

Bernhjelm and I was pissed off at their conduct. After I spoke to one of Bill's majors who told me they had gotten rid of one director, Leo Haseman, and that if the director or the commissioner got in their way they would get rid of them too.

A friend of mine called me. He was a member of the board of directors of the Minnesota Peace and Police Officers Association. He told me their president, DNR Captain Mike Hamm, said that he would get rid of this administration and particularly me.

May 1, 2002, came and went. The only directive I gave Bill Bernhjelm in November 2001 that was completed was that the CO vehicles were marked with insignias. None of the others were done. I felt I had no choice but to ask for Bill's resignation. I still feel badly about doing that. I am not sure that anyone can reform them. They have too much political clout. Bill left as the gentleman he is.

The next director lasted until we left office in January 2003. The last director didn't accomplish much more.

Perspective is important to my story. The enforcement division had about 219 personnel. The entire DNR employed approximately 4000 people. Except for the enforcement division, the DNR functioned very well. None of the other divisions or bureaus presented any major problems. My issues with the *Star Tribune* occupied too much of my time, but hardly occupied any of the other employees' time. My relations with most of the other media were good and cordial. Sam Cook of *Duluth News Tribune*, Doug Smith of the *Star Tribune*, and Joe Felege of the *Outdoor News* were some of the journalists who were very helpful. The majority of the smaller media outlets were also positive.

Forestry interested me the most of any of the disciplines in DNR. Healthy forests are related to so many other aspects of Minnesota's great outdoors. Healthy forests mean healthy wildlife populations. Clean water means healthy forests. State forest land in Minnesota is about 46 million acres. Then there are many more millions of acres of privately-owned forest lands. Timber sales from state-owned lands provides about $15–$20 million annually in revenue. There are many competing interests in our forests. Hunters and their interest groups want certain types of forests. Nature lovers and bird watchers want other conditions. Loggers and the wood products industry want still other conditions. All-terrain vehicle lovers, snowmobile operators, dirt bike lovers, four-wheelers, and a host of other motorized vehicle enthusiasts have their interests. The daunting task of balancing all of the needs of these groups falls to the DNR.

We were constantly meeting with these groups to hear their concerns. On one occasion, we met with a group of folks who came to ask us to open more areas for them to use their 4-wheel-drive trucks. I knew something about this type of recreation, but I had no idea how intense this group was. One fellow and his wife came with their small child. The man made an impassioned plea to me. The more he talked, the more he became emotional, until he burst into tears telling me that his family stayed together by four-wheeling. If he and his family did not have this recreation, their family would be lost. It sounds bizarre, but he was serious.

An aspect of forest management that I became very involved in was fighting wildfires. Forest fires are a naturally occurring phenomenon. Forests regenerate through fires. The old forest burns and new growth starts. So the natural way is to let the fires burn. However, since man is in the equation, we cannot let the fires burn. People have built homes in the forest. Resorts have been built in and near forests. Timber provides a livelihood for many Minnesotans as well as a significant source of revenue for the state. So we have to have a strong wildfire-fighting effort.

One of the most effective pieces of equipment is the water scooping airplane. The state is particularly well suited for the use of these aircraft because we have thousands of lakes. There are always bodies of water near wildfires in Minnesota. We had been renting an aircraft called a CL-215. It is a powerful aircraft made by the Bombardier Company of Canada. It is capable of scooping 1400 gallons of water in about 10 seconds. The plane flies a few feet above the water surface at about 90 m.p.h. The water is scooped into the aircraft's tank and the plane continues to the fire location. It can stay aloft for almost four hours. The largest wild fire since 1985 occurred in October 2000, in area not far from Minneapolis. It was called the Carlos Avery Edge Fire because it occurred on the edge of the large Carlos Avery Wildlife Refuge. Unfortunately, at the same time, there was another large wildfire in the northern part of the state. Since the state didn't own these planes, we could only rent them and we were in competition with other states and provinces. The Carlos Avery Edge Fire took a number of homes before the CL-215s could arrive. I flew and drove the fire site and I saw lines of burned areas where the CL-215s had saved homes by just feet. On another occasion, I flew over a major fire near the city of Brainerd, Minnesota. The city has about 12,000 inhabitants. The CL-215s were available and saved the day. I saw the ring of burned area just outside the city limits.

We mounted an effort to buy two CL-215s. These are expensive aircraft costing then $1.5 million each. Then there were maintenance costs. Also, until we could train our pilots, we had to hire experienced CL-215 pilots. Working with State Finance Commissioner Pam Wheelock and Deputy Commissioner Peggy Ingeson, we came up with a plan to finance the purchase from the state's fire emergency fund. This fund was authorized by state law and was replenished as needed. Thus, we did not need legislative authorization. However, I knew that we had to get legislative buy-in or we would make some lasting enemies. So we testified before house and senate committees. The legislators supported us. The governor was very supportive. So on January 29, 2001, we took delivery of our fist CL-215. The only other state that had CL-215s was the North Carolina Division of Forest Resources. Everyone agreed that these planes were the single most important piece of wildfire fighting equipment we had. During the winter when our fire season is over, we rent the planes and crews to other states. It was a win-win situation.

Colonel Denny Lord, who was the operations officer for the Minnesota National Guard, asked me if the DNR could use the assistance of his helicopter crews who had been training in wildfire fighting. He asked if I would be interested in watching their training at Camp Ripley. I accepted. We went to Camp Ripley and watched his crews fill large canisters of water and attach then to helicopters. They would drop the water and repeat the process. The capacity of the helicopters to haul water was much less than our CL-215s. But it was clear to me that the helicopters could be valuable to drop water on hotspots or to simply add to the amount of water dropped on a fire. So I told Col. Lord I would set the wheels in motion to bring his crews into our operation.

When I spoke to Ike Anderson who was our fire operations person, he told me it was a good idea. But I could sense he had some reservations. Ike was a good man and I could speak freely to him. I asked him what his hang-up would be. He told me that DNR crews and the Federal crews we often worked with would not welcome the military. He said the military helicopter crews were not permitted by their regulations to look out of the helicopter windows to spot the area to drop water. He also told me the military helicopters were green in color and that presented a safety problem for the other helicopters. This made no sense to me so I relayed this information to Col. Lord who was a very experienced helicopter pilot with thousands of hours flight time. He told me it was nonsense about their pilots not being able to look out of the windows. He also told me that green helicopters are no less a danger for other helicopter crews than blue or purple helicopters. He told me the real reason for the objections were that the other crews didn't want to share their action with anyone else. He knew this because he had offered this help in years past and been turned down.

I went back to Ike and his supervisor Carson Bergland and told them we would integrate the National Guard crews. Both Ike and Carson were good men and conscientious. They admitted that the objections were not their objections and made no sense. They told me they would make it work. The partnership did work many times. The guard was valuable when our resources were stretched thin. During the fire season, that was a common occurrence.

I had the opportunity to meet a number of loggers as well as people in the wood products industry. I immediately took a liking to the loggers. They were hard-working people who depended on the forests for their livelihood. Many of them were 2nd, 3rd, and even 4th generation loggers. Often they were also avid hunters and anglers. When I heard certain conservationists criticize the loggers, saying they didn't care about the forests, I really became angry. It was plain stupid to think these hard-working people, whose whole lives were spent in the forest, didn't care. Of course they did. So I often spoke on their behalf.

As I travelled throughout the state, I didn't like what I saw in our forests. About 86% of the land that had been logged in Minnesota in the last 20 years was logged using the clear-cut method. This meant cutting everything down, and then 50 years later doing it again. This method left landscapes that reminded me of Vietnam after a bombing. The landscape would have a tangle of small regenerating trees. The primary tree type that was harvested and re-grown was aspen. The wood products companies had tooled to process aspen. Some hunting interest groups, like the Ruffed Grouse Society, told me they had to have young aspen forests so that the grouse could prosper. When I asked why so much of the forest had to be aspen, I immediately made enemies.

The more I learned about forestry the more I was convinced there was a better to manage our forests. I began reading about the Finnish model that advocated selecting trees in the forest of different ages and then logging them. The result was that were always some trees in the forest. The Finns claimed that their forests regenerated quicker than those that were clear-cut. In simple terms, they said that there were just so many nutrients and sunlight and, if the forest was a tangle of young trees all vying for the same amount, the growth would be slower than in a forest of different aged trees with different requirements.

The Blandin Paper Company, which had a large plant in Grand Rapids, liked what we were saying. Their headquarters is in Helsinki, Finland. They offered to host a trip for some of my management team and me to Finland. We would pay our own way and they would provide guides and hosts. The parent company of Blandin is UPM Kymmene. I spoke to the governor who gave the go-ahead.

Our host was Olav Henrickson, who was an official of UPM Kymmene and spoke English and Finnish. We were accompanied by J. Kevin Lyden, the president and CEO of Blandon. Both of these men were extremely knowledgeable and were eager to show us the Finnish model of forest management. What we saw was astonishing. First of all, the Fins grow primarily coniferous trees, meaning pine trees. They select trees in the forest for harvesting. The equipment they use has on-board computers that show the operator the boundaries of the area to be cut. Each tree to be harvested is marked. The equipment is very light on the land. It has wide tires that produce a less noticeable imprint. After the tree is cut, the slash—the limbs and leaves—are stripped off and left on the forest floor. The harvester backs over the slash material on its way out of the forest. I watched timber harvesting done in this manner and I couldn't tell the machine was ever there. The forests look beautiful, their wildlife is plentiful and their cords of wood per harvest is high.

We left Finland excited. to bring back what we learned. Upon our return, we started discussing this selective harvesting with all the interested parties. We were met with overwhelming enthusiasm by each group except the Ruffed Grouse Society which insisted that only young aspen forests would do. I decided to have a forest summit to bring everyone together to tell what we learned and how we could apply this knowledge in Minnesota.

In preparation for the summit, and to know who to invite, we embarked on a statewide effort to talk to as many people as possible. The results were very gratifying. I met and talked with many loggers. I thought they would be hesitant to listen to such major changes. I was wrong. These people understood the forest like no one else. They had one hesitation, and that was that the wood products industry in Minnesota was tooled primarily to process aspen. If the wood products industry was willing to invest in retooling, the loggers were all for the shift. One of the most interesting loggers I met was Lowell Pittack. He'd been logging for many years. His company was small but had the reputation for being efficient. He asked me to come with him to watch his loggers work. Much to my surprise he was doing the type of logging that I was proposing. He had state-of-the-art machinery. I watched him log an area and, when he was done, you could hardly notice he'd been in there. So Lowell was with me.

Another influential person was Jack Rajala. Jack is a third-generation wood products company owner. I had read about Jack and his huge efforts to bring back the white pine, which was once so prevalent in Minnesota. Jack and his family, workers, and volunteers have planted millions of white pines. I told him of my ideas for applying the Finnish model in Minnesota. He was just great in his support. Jack and I became friends. His book, *Bring Back the White Pine,* is a wonderful explanation of the value of that species and how to plant more of it.

Lowell Pittack and Jack Rajala are the true conservationists. They have spent their many years working, living, and enjoying the forests. Having them supporting our efforts was critical. It was also fun working with them.

We invited everyone we could think of to the summit. Governor Ventura agreed to open the summit. It started on June 13, 2001. It lasted three days and was attended by over 100 participants. All media were invited but they were asked to refrain from asking questions during the various presentations. The give-and-take was between the participants.

Our friend Olav Henrickson flew in from Helsinki and spoke. David Zentner represented the Minneosta chapter of the Izaak Walton League, a national environmental group, and spoke of the need for forest management policy to not be anti-industry but also not be driven solely by industry.

Representatives of Boise Cascade, Potlach, UPM-Kymmene, and Rajala companies spoke in support of cooperation, diversity, and forest management.

We invited our U.S. senators and representatives. The only one who showed was Senator Mark Dayton. Senator Dayton listened and then told me we had his support.

Many of the participants were long-time adversaries. It was great to see them in the same room talking and finding they had more in common than they would previously have admitted. I knew that change of this magnitude would be a lengthy process lasting far beyond my term as commissioner. But we wanted something concrete as an accomplishment of the summit. I had heard too many pie-in-the-sky ideas followed by nothing but studies costing the taxpayers millions. So, before the summit, we were able to get the cooperation of public and private forest landowners to agree to join their lands into a demonstration forest. They pledged that the selective harvesting, diversity model would be the way their lands would be managed. The area totaled 240,000 acres, not a large area by Minnesota standards, but not an insignificant piece. As part of the summit, participants toured the demo forest. Schedules for future meeting of the owners of the demo forest lands were set up. The demo forest continues today. It is the Bear River Demonstration Forest.

Another interesting person I met during my tenure was Lynn Rogers. Lynn is a renowned bear researcher. He's a very colorful guy. He's retired from the U.S. Fish and Wildlife Service. He lives in a beautiful rustic home near Ely, Minnesota. He has been a bear researcher for over 40 years. His manner in learning about bears is unique. I first learned about Lynn after the DNR Wildlife head, Tim Bremicker, came to me and asked me to deny Lynn's request to capture and radio-collar some bears. Tim also asked me to revoke those permits that DNR had previously given Lynn. Tim's request perked my interest. He went on to tell me that Lynn's practices were unorthodox and dangerous. Apparently, Lynn had close personal contact with the bears in order to collar them and study their behavior. Furthermore, Tim told me that Lynn encouraged others to engage with wild bears. Our DNR bear biologist, Dave Garshelis, backed up what Tim said. I wanted to learn more about bear research so I asked Dave Garshelis to show me the proper way to collar bears in the wild.

So Dave, some of his assistants, my special assistant Kim Bonde, and I went into the woods north of Grand Rapids. Using a tracking device which looks like a small TV antenna, we traced the movement of a female adult bear that Dave had previously collared. We were able to find the bear den that contained mama and two cubs. As we approached, momma ran out of the back of the den. We were then able to weigh the cubs, take blood samples, and place radio collars on them. All the while, mama was somewhere in the woods. We kept track of mama using the tracking antenna. Dave explained that by collaring the bears he could study their movements, their life span, and other habits. After we finished with the cubs, we placed them in the den. We left, but stopped a short distance away. We could hear and tell mama returned to the den. I asked why DNR was trying to deny Lynn Rogers permits to do the same thing. Dave told me that Lynn approached adult bears and interacted with them in a dangerous manner.

Some months later I still had not met Lynn. Kim Bonde and I were at a resort known as Vets on the Lake near Ely,. We were invited by American Legion people to interact with disabled vets. We went out on boats with them and helped them fish. At the end of the day, I noticed a flyer saying that Lynn Rogers would be speaking that night. He would also be showing a video. So Kim and I attended. Lynn didn't know who we were. I was impressed with this down-to-earth guy. He talked about how he gets very close to bears, but cautioned that less experienced people should not do what he does. Then he showed a video of him playing with bears, talking to them, and feeding them out of his hand.

After Lynn finished we introduced ourselves. He was cordial and offered to take us into the forest to see how he works. We accepted, and a few days later we were in the woods with him. He had his antenna and we were tracking one of his collared bears. I told him we didn't want to get too close to the bear. He said we wouldn't. As we rounded a corner, he was looking at his antenna when right in front of us less than ten feet away stood a full-grown, female black bear and two cubs. All I could think of was that both Kim and I didn't need to outrun the bear. We only had to outrun Lynn (that's a joke). What followed was amazing. Lynn talked to the bear saying "It's only me, bear." The bear was calm. The cubs climbed a nearby white pine. Lynn then told the bear we were leaving and that's exactly what we did. He apologized to us saying he didn't know the bear was so near. He also said this bear was one he collared and studied for several years and had even been in its den with the cubs. Unbelievable, but true. We became friends after that incident.

I approved his requests for permits to collar some more bears. My wildlife chief and Dave Garshelis were not happy with me. But I knew I was allowing a valuable researcher to do his work. Years later, Lynn opened the North American Bear Center in Ely. He invited me there. He gave me a grand tour and told me that if I had not given him his permits, his financial backers would not have funded the center. He told me the center was his lifelong dream and I had played a significant part in making his dream come true. He is still my friend.

All waters in Minnesota are publicly owned. That means that all lakes, streams, and rivers belong to everyone. The land that adjoins these bodies of water is often privately owned. In our state the DNR builds and maintains public access points for people to launch boats and engage in other water activities. My waters division director, Kent Lokkesmoe, advised me of a situation on the St. Croix River. A very wealthy and influential businessman owned land that adjoins a marina on the St. Croix River. He had erected a fence across the water so that no one could enter the marina by boat. Since he owned the land around the marina he had complete control of the marina. Kent told me this action was in violation of state law. Kent's personnel had asked the man to remove the gates and he refused. The man made an appointment to see me. We met in my office and he told me he would not remove the gate because he wanted to protect his house and dock that he had built on his land that adjoins the marina. I told him his action was illegal and that all Minnesotans had a right to use the marina. His response was he would not comply. I told him that if he did not remove the gate within 30 days we would remove it and have the cost added to his tax bill.

His response was what might have succeeded in any other administration except Governor Ventura's. He said he knew some very influential politicians and, if necessary, he would take this matter up with the governor. I politely told him to do whatever he wanted to, but the gate would be removed within 30 days. I never heard another word from him or any elected official. He removed the gate about 30 days later.

I tried always to treat everyone respectfully. Likewise, I expected the same behavior in return for and from my employees. Sometimes DNR employees made decisions that were not in compliance with the law or rules, but were made based on the employee's beliefs. One such case happened in St. Paul. I was asked by then-Mayor Norm Coleman to meet with him and some members of his staff.

I was told the issue was St. Paul's efforts to develop the land along the Mississippi River and its frustrations with the DNR. I got background information from Kent Lokkesmoe. Development along the river is governed by the Mississippi River Critical Area Plan. Communities wishing to develop land covered by the plan must comply with the elements of the plan. The DNR is tasked with insuring that the city complies with the plan. Kent told me that a member of his staff reviewed the city's plan and determined it was not in compliance.

So we met with the mayor and his staff. The DNR person responsible was present with us. The mayor told us about the proposed development. His staff members told me what our DNR person told then they would have to modify in order to gain DNR approval. We went over the modifications the city was told to complete. They did complete them. At the conclusion of the meeting I met with our people. It seemed to me that the city had done everything we asked.

I put this question to our responsible DNR employee. Has the city complied with the elements of the Mississippi River Critical Area Plan? He replied, yes. Then why have you not granted them approval to continue? He said the city may be in compliance but as a conservationist he would not permit development on the river land. I told him it was not in his or DNRs power to make judgments outside the law no matter what our personal feelings were. He still objected, so I told Kent to review the city's plans and, if he agreed they were in compliance, to prepare the approvals for my signature. A few weeks later Kent brought me the approvals which I signed. The multi-million dollar project went forward. I wondered how many other decisions were made contrary to law by well-meaning employees who thought they were above the law.

There were many people inside and outside the DNR who said the way I conducted business was different than any former commissioner. I don't mean that my way was better or worse, but it was my way. I think there was one other commissioner, Joe Alexander, who served from 1978 until 1991, who was a sworn peace officer. Joe had been a conservation officer before being named commissioner. I retained my status as a licensed sworn peace officer during my term. Most of the time I was armed. The same was true of assistant commissioner Kim Bonde. She also retained her license. There were many times when heads turned when I would take off my coat in an internal meeting and reveal that I was armed. But the employees came to understand that this was a result of our long backgrounds in law enforcement. One afternoon we left the DNR building to go to lunch. As were driving out of the parking lot, Kim called my attention to a car that was driving on the sidewalk across the street from us. I looked up to see the car trying to run over a guy who was running down the street. I drove at the car and as we stopped both of us got out, drew our guns and I yelled, "Police. Stop." Before I knew it, the car hit the guy who flew onto the windshield. We started to approach the car as the driver got out when Kim said, "Watch out, he's got something in his hand." He was holding something in his right hand behind his back.

The injured guy rolled off the hood and ran into the street. The driver chased him as I yelled, "Drop it." We saw that he was holding a hammer as he was chasing the injured person. We had taken positions behind our car and called for the injured person to run to us. He did. The driver then got back into his car and fled. We got the license number of the car. We got the injured guy behind our car. I used the police radio I had installed in my DNR car to call St. Paul police dispatch. I gave them the license number of the getaway car. Soon an ambulance and police were at our scene.

We learned that the guy who was being chased was on his way to court to testify against the other guy in a drug case. Later the police did find the car and the assailant. After it was over, I looked up to see many DNR employees looking out of the windows. I'm sure the six-story DNR building was tilting toward us. I heard someone say, "Look, the commissioner has a gun."

Sometime later, Deputy Commissioner Steve Morse presented Kim and me with a valor award. He designed the award and did all of the work. We thanked Steve.

Wildlife management is another of the most important responsibilities of the DNR. For those species that are hunted, the challenge is to set hunting seasons and limits so that the number of species is plentiful enough to continue to hunt them indefinitely. In some cases, the number of licenses is limited, while in others the number of animals each hunter can take is limited. This is a complicated task that considers science, politics, and public opinion.

In the case of the wolf the challenge was different. As a result of wolves being hunted almost to extinction, and due to decreases in their natural prey, they were placed on the Federal endangered species list. This action gave wolves protection under the Endangered Species Act of 1974. The task was to investigate unlawful killing of wolves and to keep track of their numbers. The DNR worked with the U.S. Fish and Wildlife Service. Wolves made a remarkable recovery in Minnesota. Thus, in 2000, the DNR had to create a wolf management plan for when the wolf was removed from the threatened and endangered list. The plan had to pass the legislature and be approved by the U.S. Fish and Wildlife Service. Wolves evoke more emotion in more people than any other animal we dealt with.

The International Wolf Center is located in Ely. The advocates for wolf preservation come from all over the world to Minnesota to champion their cause. Cattle and other livestock owners are vocal and influential. Their concern is wolves that attack their animals. Hunters, particularly deer hunters, see wolves as a threat to their hunting. There are those whose fear of wolves come from folklore and movies. They believe wolves are a threat to humans and pets. The media used the wolves as a platform to stir the pot. All in all creating a plan that would pass muster was a daunting task.

Our first attempt did not pass. The reason was that we did not have enough consensuses before we brought the plan forward. We devised a plan that divided the state into regions. One region was the area where wolves naturally occurred. The second area was where wolves migrated to but did not naturally occur. It was in this region that the majority of livestock were raised. The plan was sound in that it protected the wolf in its natural habitat and allowed for killing wolves that threatened livestock. The problem was that the first time we made our plan public was just before the legislature was to consider it. The press criticized our plan widely and succeeded in insuring it did not pass.

So we went back to the drawing board. But this time we invited all interested parties from the beginning. In fact, we had a wolf forum in Duluth. Anyone who wanted to attend could. It was a fiasco. I heard from kooks to scientists to hunters to wolf lovers. But it was worth the effort. We were sincere in letting everyone have their say.

Then we convened a series of meetings among the interested groups' representatives. The plan we all agreed to was almost identical to the plan that had failed. When the plan was finalized, we made it public so that anyone could take their shot at it. When we had broad-based consensus, we presented it to the legislature. It passed with flying colors. It was then approved by the U.S. Fish and Wildlife Service. Minnesota was ready to manage the wolf population so that it would never be endangered. This was a major accomplishment for me because I had come to be fascinated by wolves, and for the DNR because of the emotion and controversy the wolf had with so many people.

I met some very interesting people through the wolf issue. Dr. David Mech was a renowned wolf researcher. He had travelled worldwide and enjoyed a reputation as one the world's most knowledgeable persons in his field. Dave was a down-to-earth guy. He was very interesting to talk to. His support for our wolf plan was critical. Since he participated in the plan's development from the beginning, he supported it entirely. Another person who was interesting to talk to and work with was Nancy Gibson. Nancy was a naturalist and author who gave countless hours to the Wolf Center in Ely. She raised the Center's two arctic wolves Malik and Shadow in her home for the first six weeks of their lives. She was very helpful guiding me in the creation of the partnership that was so critical. Finally, the executive director of the Wolf Center was Walter Medwid. I marveled at Walter's talent for advocating for the wolf and not joining in the political controversy. He always said that his job was to educate people about wolves. He used education as his tool for gaining support.

Wolves are beautiful animals. They are very shy. In fact, in four years as DNR Commissioner, I saw a wolf in the wild once. There is an area of Minnesota called the Northwest Angle. To get to it by land you must travel out of Minnesota into Ontario and back into the Northwest Angle. The area is sparsely populated. It is a popular fishing area as it allows access to Lake of the Woods, which is a large lake with excellent fishing. I was travelling by car in the Northwest Angle with Paul Swenson, DNR's regional director, when we rounded a corner and, standing at the side of the road, was a grown wolf. I don't know who was more surprised, me or the wolf. We stopped and were face-to-face with each other for what seemed like an eternity before he slowly walked off.

So the wolf management plan that we put together was a satisfying achievement. We have guaranteed the survival of the wolf in Minnesota for many years.

Another wildlife species that is very important to Minnesotans is the white tail deer. The DNR sold between 500,000 and 600,000 deer hunting licenses during my administration. Over 200,000 deer were harvested during that time. Deer hunting season is extremely important to many Minnesotans. DNRs responsibility is to insure that the deer population stays at a level to accommodate these numbers of hunters forever. Deer hunters are a powerful political force. Chronic Wasting Disease (CWD) became a major concern. The disease is always fatal and affects North American Deer and Rocky Mountain Elk. The disease was discovered in a single captive elk in Aitkin County.

The discovery of the disease triggered a near panic among many people. We decided to initiate an aggressive campaign to stop the disease before it affected the deer population. But before we initiated our actions, we knew we needed public support. So we held a public meeting in Aitkin County. We publicized the event widely. Anyone who had an interest was encouraged to attend. The local high school auditorium was packed. Media coverage of the discovery, as well as the actions of the DNR, was widely publicized. The entire state was watching. The plan we proposed included harvesting large numbers of deer in the area and rapid testing of the carcasses by the U.S. Department of Agriculture lab. The issue was as important economically as it was to sportsmen. Major companies, including Gander Mountain and Cabellas, make huge sales each year to deer hunters.

Agreement with our plan was almost universal. Our conservation officers had the task of shooting a specific number of deer in each of the zones the county was divided into. Then other DNR people took samples of the carcasses and transported them to the USDA lab. The outcome was that no cases of CWD were discovered.

Then, as deer season approached, we told all hunters to be alert for deer who exhibited the signs of CWD. All in all we did it right. It was one of the few situations where the DNR got high marks from everyone.

One of the more interesting challenges we faced was called the consolidated conservation lands. The issue dated back to the late 1800s and early 1900s. Back then, a number of counties in Minnesota issued bonds to pay the cost of ditching millions of wet acres for the purpose of draining the land for agricultural use. Land was sold to individual property owners and ditches were dug. Not all these efforts resulted in suitable farmland; however, continued drainage problems combined with economic depression of the 1930s caused many landowners to default on their property taxes, which, in turn, put the counties at risk of defaulting on their ditch bonds. The state interceded, paying off the county ditch bonds in exchange for full ownership and management of the lands.

There were originally 1.9 million acres of consolidated conservation lands in seven counties. About 400,000 acres were sold to private parties. In 2000, the legislature passed legislation concerning management of 260,000 acres.

In 1991, then DNR Commissioner Joe Alexander issued a commissioner's order designating over 102,000 acres as state wildlife management areas. The 102,000 acres were the final consolidated conservation lands that were not designated for management by any governmental body. However the Minnesota attorney general ruled that the commissioner did not have this power.

Thus, the counties could have their say about the land. The counties all wanted the land back. The DNR solicited the counties' opinions and logic. There was a great amount of emotion involved. On one occasion I travelled to Aitkin County to meet with their county board to get their input. The first thing their chairperson said to me was he really didn't think the DNR would listen to him and his board. I responded that I had travelled over three hours to see them. If I wasn't going to listen, I would have stayed in my office in St. Paul. After that we had a nice conversation.

My deputy commissioner Steve Morse took the lead role for the DNR. Steve had dealt with many of the county boards when he was a state senator. Steve did a magnificent job of striking an agreement with the counties. At the same time, he convinced key legislators to also agree. Basically, the lands would be managed by DNR forever. The counties were to be paid sums of money in return. In 2002, the legislature passed legislation designating the last 102,000 acres into DNR management, thus bringing a 75-year controversy to a close. Steve Morse received the praise he was due.

Things were going well for DNR and for me. Everyone expected Governor Ventura to get re-elected. I expected to get four more years to continue our good work. Then the governor dropped a bombshell on us in a cabinet meeting. He announced he would not seek re-election. He simply said he did not want to subject his family to the scrutiny they had been subjected to in the last four years. That was that. There was no changing his mind. I was very disappointed. I knew that when a new governor was sworn in I was history. That was the way things worked. But it was not only me that was affected. All of the appointed positions in the DNR would likely be replaced.

Then fate intervened. When the United States marshals position became available after President Bush was elected, I did not apply because I anticipated staying with DNR for another four years. However, the nominee for U.S. marshal withdrew. So there was a chance I could still apply. I called Congressman Jim Ramstad and asked if the position was available. He asked why I had not applied before and I told him. He said he would be honored to put forth my name to the White House as a candidate. The way things worked for that position was the senior U.S. senator from the president's party got to nominate a candidate or candidates. Since both of our senators were democrats, Jim Ramstad, who was a republican U.S. representative got to nominate. I was thrilled to get the chance.

Eventually, I was summoned to Washington, D.C. for an interview. There were three candidates for the position. One was my good friend Roger Willow. If you remember, Roger was retired from the Minneapolis police and was a finalist with me for the Champlin police job. The other candidate was Len Harrell, retired Mound chief and also a candidate with me for the Champlin job. It is a small world.

The interview panel consisted of a White House person, an assistant attorney general, and U.S. Marshals Service Deputy Director Don Gambatesa. I don't remember most of the questions. However, I remember one that Mr. Gambatesa asked. He said, if you were asked by the chief judge in your district to pick his daughter up at the airport and take her home what would you do?

I knew that the U.S. marshal worked closely with the U.S. District Court judges. In fact, one of the primary responsibilities of the marshals is to provide security for the judges. However, I also knew the chief judge in the District of Minnesota. He was Jim Rosenbaum, a man I knew well for about 20 years.

So my response to the question was straight forward. I said I would respectfully decline to do this. I would tell the judge that his request was outside my duties. But I added that I knew Chief Judge Rosenbaum and he would never make such a request. I believe all of the interviewers liked my answer.

A few months later, I got a call from the White House telling me I was the president's candidate for United States Marshal for the District of Minnesota. I was very happy. But as time passed I had no idea how the process worked and how long it took. Every U.S. Judicial District, and there are 94 of them, has a U.S. Marshal. Marshals are nominated by the president and require an FBI background check and confirmation by the

U.S. Senate. Some states have more than one judicial district. Minnesota has one. I could not figure out why some states much smaller in area and population had more than one judicial district. I believe it has to do with politics. That is to say, the more judicial districts there are in a state, the more appointments the majority party has.

I had told the governor when I first applied for the position. I then told him when I was nominated. Now I decided to tell my senior staff at the DNR. They were disappointed, but they were also looking for their next jobs since Governor Ventura announced publicly he would not run again.

Before I get to my service as U.S. marshal, there are some things that need to be said about my tenure as DNR commissioner. I was part of history. Never before and probably never again will there be a governor like Jesse Ventura. He was not influenced by politics, politicians, or big money. I would never have had the opportunity under any of the other politics-as-usual governors. I was able to speak my mind and do what I thought was right. I was able to practice the type of leadership ability I had. The governor made enemies of the press, senior elected officials, and other financially influential people. That came with the territory for him. To a much lesser degree, the same was true of my experience. I didn't stand for any bullshit. I listened carefully to all sides and made my decisions.

The learning curve as DNR was steep for me. All of the disciplines were new. It was a challenge I attempted to meet by reading, travelling, listening, and using my ability to judge people. Constantly travelling throughout the state was my style of leadership. I was around the "troops." I learned from watching them work. Work and private life seemed to melt into one another. But it was a great ride.

To Allen Garber
With best wishes,

With the Compliments
of
The President

My Service as U.S. Marshal

The position of United States Marshal is unique in government service. Each U.S. marshal is appointed by the president and confirmed by the U.S. Senate. However, the Director of the USMS is also appointed by the president and confirmed by the senate. Thus, although the marshals answer to the director, his direct authority over the marshals is not clear.

The result is that marshals can be anywhere from ceremonial heads to hard working and involved. The USMS has very well defined areas of responsibility. They are responsible for the security of federal judges and prosecutors. They are also responsible for the security of federal courthouses. Deputy marshals transport federal prisoners from detention facilities to court, medical facilities, and other places. They investigate threats against judges and prosecutors. Service of all sorts of court papers is also one of the duties. A special division of the service administers the witness security program. This program provides security for certain witnesses. Finally, the service hunts for wanted persons or fugitives.

The USMS has the widest authority of any federal law enforcement agency. Thus, its personnel can work closely with local and state law enforcement on almost any issue, federal or state.

The process to confirm my nomination took almost eleven months. I don't know if it took so long because, in the big picture, confirmation of U.S. marshal nominees is not very important, or if our nominations were used as bargaining chips by the competing parties in the senate. I do know that I began to believe that I was not going to be confirmed. During the eleven months after Governor Ventura left office, I applied for several jobs, including police chief in Duluth, and Transportation Security Deputy Director for Minnesota. But finally on April 8, 2003, I was confirmed by the senate. On April 10, 2003, President Bush appointed me to the position of U.S. Marshal for the District of Minnesota. I found out in a phone call from Director of the Marshals Service Benigno Reyna.

I immediately called my friend Chief U.S. District Court Judge Jim Rosenbaum and asked if he could swear me in on April 11, 2003. He agreed and I was sworn in officially on April 11. On May 5, 2003, a ceremonial swearing-in ceremony was held in Judge Rosenbaum's courtroom.

I was off and running. As an FBI agent I had some dealings with the marshals. It was mostly when I turned a prisoner over to them. But I was to learn that I really didn't know what they did. I had known Chief Deputy Marshal Mike Ball for a long time. He was the face of the marshals service in Minnesota.

I met with him often in the weeks after I was sworn in. When I first reported in, I was surprised to see many deputy U.S. marshals at their desks. In fact, I was surprised to see how many of them there were. I asked Mike what they were doing, and he told me they were waiting for assignments to bring prisoners to court or to provide security in court.

I began to understand that Mike ran the show in every respect. He was a strong person who had been running the show for about 17 years. There was going to be a problem between him and me. It was my intention to run the show and become involved in the operation. He tried to accommodate me but it was difficult for both of us. He was used to ceremonial marshals and wanted me to continue the tradition. I wouldn't, and Mike chose to retire.

The deputy marshals were reluctant to talk to me. Their practice was not to speak to the marshal except to greet him. But little by little they began to talk to me. The more I learned, the more I was convinced that they were not being used in the most efficient manner. They were mostly young and just dying to become involved in the action.

The marshal also has operational control over a group of former law enforcement officers who are hired by a private firm under contract to the USMS. They provide building and courtroom security. These people are called court security officers and are known as "Blue Coats." While they are not employees of the USMS, the marshal must swear them in as special deputy U.S. marshals so that they can perform their security duties. So, if I chose not to swear one of them in, they couldn't perform their duties. The arrangement worked well because I respected them and had a lot in common with them. In fact, I had worked with many of them when they were law enforcement officers.

They were treated as a separate entity by Mike Ball. I was going to make them members of our team. I wanted to have the deputy U.S. marshals (DUSMs) and the court security officers (CSOs) work closely and communicate. I felt it was my responsibility to look out for everyone in both groups. The first sign that I was going in a direction that the marshals service headquarters didn't want me to go was when I requested winter clothing for the CSOs. As a part of their duties they patrolled on foot outside the federal courthouses. Minnesota winters can be brutal. I noticed that some of them were not dressed for the weather. When I asked why, I was told that there were not enough parkas and hats for everyone. I directed the person on my staff whose duties were to oversee the CSOs to see that they got the clothing they needed. After some arguments from headquarters, they got their clothing. I was told it was not the responsibility of the USMS because the CSOs officially worked for a private security firm. That sounded like bureaucratic double talk. Anyway they got their clothing.

As time went on, I began to have regular meetings with the CSOs. They responded by offering many sound ideas for improving security. They were perfect for the jobs they did. They were all retired cops of some sort. They knew how to speak to all kinds of people. They had to enforce security standards for everyone who entered the courthouses. They dealt with high-priced attorneys, judges, defendants of all types and federal employees. They knew how to watch without letting people know they were being watched. They had a smile and greeting for everyone and, at the same time, made sure that everyone complied with the security requirements. For such a large contingent of people, I received almost no complaints about them. On top of it all, they were a fun group for me to be around. The CSO program was one of the smartest things the USMS did for their judicial security mission. If young enthusiastic deputy U.S. marshals had been used for this mission, it would have been far less effective. Imagine how a young deputy would react if challenged by an influential judge or an important elected official. The sparks would have flown. But with the experience and age of the CSOs the reaction was measured and mature.

The strength of the USMS is at the same time its weakness. The deputies operate below the radar screen. In other words, they operate with little publicity or fanfare. If you ask most citizens, or even police officers, what the marshals do they don't know. But because they get little publicity they are also at the bottom of the food chain when it comes to funding. This situation has improved since I was marshal. But the service has to be careful not to become publicity hounds like the FBI. There is a balance that has to be maintained. It is this balance that has earned great respect from local and state law enforcement officers.

The marshals, more than any other federal law enforcement agency, are known for their willingness to get their hands dirty. Since they have the widest of jurisdiction, they are able to work with the local and state police far more than the FBI agents can. The marshals service does its job and doesn't try to do other agencies' jobs. The marshals are usually the first ones to answer the call for help.

From my prospective, the key to effective law enforcement is for each agency to do its job and not try to do things outside their missions. When agencies try to do other's jobs, the effort becomes confused and results in duplication of efforts. The USMS has as one of its missions to transport federal prisoners. We got into a problem with the FBI because in one case a high-profile prisoner had to be transported. By high profile I mean a prisoner who was extremely dangerous and had been widely publicized. The FBI SWAT team showed up at our office. When I asked the team leader what he was there for, he responded that his team would transport the prisoner. I told him it wasn't his job, but if he wanted to help us we would give him instructions. I knew him well and he told me that he was under orders from his boss to take over the mission from us. I showed him the door. To me this was far more than a turf battle. It was an opportunity to show the FBI boss that they should do their job and let us do ours. My response was not taken well.

I took our job of providing security for the federal judges and prosecutors very seriously. I believe that the judges, the courtrooms, and the prosecutors have to feel secure to perform their extremely important duties. If they can't do their jobs, our entire justice system crumbles. The federal judges in the district of Minnesota were all very intelligent people. They were all political appointees, but there were clearly reasons other than politics that got them where they were. I disagreed with them on many issues, but I stood firm when it came to security matters. I refused to operate with the "it can't happen here" attitude. In some cases, this brought me into conflict with a few of the judges. But, with the strong support of Chief Judge Rosenbaum, security was of utmost importance.

Sometimes it took a specific incident to win over a judge. One of the judges was not very enthusiastic about security. That judge went along with the program but used every opportunity to comply only with the minimum. The judge received a number of threatening letters from a particular person. There were implied but specific threats in the letters. So I went out one Saturday with my judicial security specialist. We found someone who knew the writer, and we asked a lot of questions about him. He appeared to be a person who might carry out a threat. We told the judge and immediately provided enhanced security. Then we went right to the man and confronted him. The judge completely turned the corner in terms of his respect for our concern and how we handled this matter. That judge became one of our biggest supporters.

I made it a point to know all of our judges well. I found them interesting people. When asked, I gave them advice on security matters for them and their families. They knew that they could call me anytime day or night. Our relationship was always business but, when I had a concern that involved a judge, I went right to them.

One of the important issues for me was how to use our personnel to the best advantage. We had enough people to do more in each area of our responsibility. Partnerships based on a willingness to be honest with each other are a cornerstone of law enforcement. So I started to look for partnerships. One of the first was to form a fugitive apprehension partnership. I had a lot of experience in this area from my time with the FBI.

I approached the FBI agent in charge. The fugitive task force that my old partner Steve Gilkerson and I started was still in operation. However, because of certain current considerations, the task force was reduced in size and resources. I offered to partner with the FBI. We had office space and other equipment available. I offered these resources but the offer was refused. The reason given to me was that the bureau never partners unless they are in charge. Furthermore, they never gave up any responsibility.

So with other partners we moved ahead. There turned out to be no duplication of efforts because there was so much work to be done. The members of each task force communicated and cooperated. The USMS and our partners pretty much stayed out of the headlines. The police were expected partners but some of the agencies that came forward were a surprise. One was the investigator for the U.S. Office of Housing and Urban Development. I didn't even know they had investigators. Another highly-motivated and talented group was the Minnesota Department of Corrections (DOC) fugitive unit. Other partners included the Alcohol Tobacco and Firearms Unit, the Ramsey County Sheriffs' Apprehension Unit.

I saw an opportunity for the USMS in Minnesota to make a real contribution to safety of the citizens. We had adequate resources and wide jurisdiction. So I looked for partnerships so I could assign our deputies to efforts that made a difference. Unfortunately, many law enforcement partnerships start out with good intentions but don't really make a difference. Murders were at an all-time high in Minneapolis. For many years, the Minneapolis police had a unit of the department that located persons wanted for murders and other violent crimes. The unit also located witnesses and conducted search warrants. This unit was known as the Violent Crimes Apprehension Unit (VCAT). The members of the unit performed their duties so that the homicide investigators could concentrate on putting the case together. VCAT was headed by an old friend, Sgt Al Kramer. Al was an old-school cop. He did not tolerate any nonsense. So Al and I had a talk about whether assigning some deputy U.S. marshals to his unit would be beneficial. Al was very enthusiastic about such a partnership. Not only would the deputies be added investigators, but they would also bring the USMS's technical and nationwide resources to the table.

I discussed the idea with Minneapolis Police Chief Bill McManus and another old friend Deputy Chief Tim Dolan. I told them that, since I knew Al Kramer, and his unit had performed at a high level for many years, I had no hesitation assigning deputy U.S. marshals to VCAT full time.

After discussing the idea with my staff, we assigned two DUSMs to VCAT. They would work for Sgt. Kramer on a day-to-day basis. Their USMS Supervisor, Chris Connelly, would keep track of their efforts and would be able to commit more resources of ours as needed. This was one of the best things the USMS did in Minnesota during my time as marshal. We picked two enthusiastic, hard-working deputies for the assignment. I went out with the unit on several cases. Once again, I learned that in police work there is more than one way to get the job done, and also that appearance of the officers is not the most important quality. Not all of the VCAT officers were in good physical condition. They weren't always as cautious as I had learned to be. But they all had great police sense, that is to say, they recognized danger before bad things happened. They were all just great in their ability to speak to people in a way that they didn't speak down to anyone. It didn't take long to figure out that our deputies assigned to VCAT were getting practical experience they would not otherwise get.

During the time when homicides were at an all time high in Minneapolis, the police department brought a guy named Chuck Wexler, the executive director of the Police Executive Research Forum (PERF). PERF is non-profit kind of think tank and head hunter recruiting agency for law enforcement agencies. Wexler was a very interesting man. His talent was facilitating the efforts of many different agencies and officers to address a common problem. So, with the blessing of Chief McManus and Deputy Chief Tim Dolan, Chuck invited all of the federal and state agencies that served Minneapolis to a meeting. The dynamics of the meeting were very interesting to me. The problem was mainly a Minneapolis police problem. I was willing to help in any way. The key word was "help." Not all of the agencies were willing to "help." Some of them wanted headlines and some would not make specific commitments. They made vague statements about cooperating, being careful not to make specific commitments.

For my part, I committed the services of many deputy U.S. marshals to concentrated efforts, after business hours, to finding wanted persons and other law breakers in the areas of the city where the homicides were occurring. One of the things that made me angry was when Tim Dolan or Chief Bill McManus would be absent from a meeting, and their own criminal investigations division commander would make undercutting remarks about the effort. I was quick to let Tim know he had a fox in the chicken coup. That summer proved to be an important time for the people of Minneapolis. Violent crime did decrease through the efforts of this partnership.

In April of 2006, Bill McManus resigned as Minneapolis police chief to take the job in San Antonio. Tim Dolan was appointed as acting chief until the mayor and council appointed a permanent chief. Tim invited me to go with him and the mayor, R.T. Rybak, to a Police Executive Research Forum seminar in Washington, D.C. on August 6, 2006. The conference was to be run by our friend Chuck Wexler. Its purpose was to give chiefs and mayors from the country's largest cities a chance to share ideas about combating violent crime in America.

This invitation grew out of yet another partnership between the Minneapolis police and the USMS. The USMS had conducted a nationwide concentrated fugitive hunt each year beginning April 4 to April 10, 2005. The operation was called FALCON. During this time, each USMS district mounted an intensive hunt for wanted violent criminals. We invited all of our law enforcement partners from around the state. Naturally, we concentrated our efforts in the most populated areas. It was a great effort and involved almost all of the city, county, state, and federal agencies. Unfortunately, there was no participation from the FBI. But that really didn't detract from the effort. It was a massive effort. In Minnesota it is the sheriff who holds warrants. So we asked the Hennepin County sheriff to bring warrants charging persons with violent crimes so we could intensify efforts to locate them. We learned that a number of wanted murderers were juveniles. For some reason, they slipped through the cracks. Only the ones who had been arrested and released had probation officers. The probation officers attempted to look for these violent juvenile offenders, but had limited success. No one else was actively looking for these kids. We took ten cases of juvenile murderers and formed a team headed by St. Paul Police Sgt. Dave Korus. Ten investigators or officers were assigned to him. He was told he had from April 4 to April 10 to find as many as possible.

Dave and his team arrested six of the ten in one week. This effort turned a lot of heads. Maybe these violent juveniles could be brought to justice.

After FALCON concluded, I asked Acting Chief Dolan to meet with me and the head of juvenile probation. We met, and what came out of the meeting was a new unit of the police department that was called the Juvenile Crimes Apprehension Team (JCAT). The unit was modeled after the very successful Violent Crimes Apprehension Team (VCAT). I committed two deputy U.S. marshals to the team. It was headed by Minneapolis Police Sergeant Ron Stenerson, another no-nonsense police professional. It began operation in August 2006. Tim, probation people, and I met with the juvenile judges to let them know they would be seeing a lot more violent juvenile offenders. The judges agreed to look more carefully at these offenders before they released them.

JCAT was a resounding success. The teams went out at 5 a.m. and found many of these violent people in bed. Cooperation from the community was exceptional. Sergeant Stenerson did a great job of selling JCAT to the community. Tips started coming in constantly. Many of these type offenders were arrested.

Earlier I wrote about how only a few of the many ideas that police leaders come up with really make an impact. JCAT was one of them. In fact, it continues today.

Many concerned citizens think that the problem of violent crime is not only a police problem. They are correct. Many factors combine to produce violent criminals. However, I have always believed that arresting and convicting these people is the police contribution to the effort. That is why I was so committed to committing maximum resources.

Now to get back to the PERF Conference in Washington. Being with the mayor gave me a great opportunity to tell him just how outstanding Tim Dolan was. The conference was attended by 170 chiefs, mayors, and other public officials from all over the U.S. Tim and the mayor spoke about partnerships that existed in Minneapolis. I had a chance to speak about what the USMS was able to contribute.

On January 9, 2007, Tim was sworn in as Minneapolis's new chief.

I had learned the value of a joint SWAT team from my experience as leader a joint MPD/FBI/Hennepin County Sheriff SWAT team. One of the first partnerships on my agenda was forming a joint USMS/MPD SWAT team. The leader of the Minneapolis PD SWAT team, Sgt. Mike Young was enthusiastic.

I visited with Chief Tim Dolan and, after we reminisced about the good old days of the FBI/MPD SWAT team, he gave his whole-hearted blessing. The selection process was really interesting. The process gave us the opportunity to see some of the best police officers Minneapolis had. The interview board consisting of USMS Supervisor Chris Connelly, my SWAT team leader Deputy U.S. Marshal Eric Arguello, Sgt. Mike Young and his Lieutenant, Otto Wagonfiel, and I.

It was quite an experience to see these experienced officers looking their best, proudly wearing their awards, and expressing their interest in becoming members of this new joint SWAT team. It is very unusual, in my experience, to have police officers try so hard to be partners with federal law enforcement. We picked nine top-notch people.

Shortly after the team was formed, we were off and running. In order for these officers to have federal law enforcement authority, it was necessary for me to swear them in as special deputy U.S. marshals. This is a special authority granted only to U.S. marshals. There is a process that includes concurrence from USMS Headquarters. However, before the formal process could be completed, our SWAT team was activated to attempt to arrest a guy who was wanted for the brutal rape and beating of a woman. The man was believed to be hiding on an Indian reservation in northern Minnesota. A case like this is exactly what a well-trained SWAT team is for. The area was sparsely populated and densely wooded. The people who lived there were not very helpful to law enforcement.

The situation was urgent so I used my authority to swear in the MPD SWAT members as special deputy U.S. marshals even though we had not received formal approval from our headquarters. Sometimes you just do what you have to.

Anyway we drove to the area. It took about five hours to get there. I met with the sheriff whom I had never met. I explained the situation to him. He offered any help. In fact, throughout the entire operation, which lasted about 18 hours, he was right with me. He even had food and beverages brought out to us. I will always remember Sheriff Keith Winger for his assistance and friendship. In fact, some years later I was able to return the favor by spending a day with him going over security in his new courthouse and making recommendations based on my experience.

Now to get back to the operation. The weather was cold with constant drizzle. Our SWAT leader Eric Arguello made a plan which I approved. It called for a discreet surveillance of the remote house where we thought the fugitive was hiding. It was even more dangerous because everyone in that part of the state had at least one hunting rifle and, even though it wasn't hunting season, some people hunted anyway. So the team made it to the area of the house undetected. After a few hours, we heard shooting. Eric told me over the radio that some of the people from the house were shooting into the woods apparently just because they could. The rounds were going over our team members' heads as they hugged the ground.

After watching for hours, we were able to contact the person who gave

U.S. Marshal Al presenting award to Butch Visger

us the tip about the fugitive's location. The source was able to go into the house and determine that the subject had left for Duluth shortly before we got there. So the SWAT team pulled out again undetected. We notified the Duluth police. Sometime later they arrested the man as he was raping another woman.

The SWAT team performed extremely well. Despite the fact that they were a new team, they really operated like a seasoned group. They took orders, executed them, and never complained despite the difficult and dangerous conditions.

The deputy U.S. marshal who had developed the informant and gave us the information was Butch Visger. Butch was a 20-year veteran of the USMS. He has since passed away after battling cancer. Butch was not a SWAT type. But he was typical of the fine hardworking people the service has. He never sought the limelight but I came to know him and respect him greatly. I visited him and his wife many times as he fought cancer. I will always fondly remember Butch Visger.

All in all, that operation was a great way to start. On August 22, 2006, I received a letter from one of the team members, MPD Sgt. Bill Palmer. Bill got promoted and had to leave the joint SWAT team. I would like to quote some of his letter. It will give a sense of the level of respect we had for each other.

He wrote:

> By now I am sure that word has reached you that I have been detailed to sergeant and I have been informed that my time in SWAT has come to an end . . . my new commitments as a shift supervisor bring new challenges. . . .
>
> The United States Marshals Service District of Minnesota Special Response Team clearly has been one of the highlights of my career. I will always fondly remember being cold, wet, and covered with mud and loving every minute of it on an Indian reservation in northern Minnesota. Of course, the bullets flying over my head did put a slight damper on the day but it was still one of the best days of my career. . . . The team gave me a sense that the mission we were called to accomplish meant something in the real scheme of things, not just another day of 911 calls and drug warrants. I will miss those assignments more than I can describe. I only wish I had discovered the federal service a bit earlier in my career.
>
> Thank you for the opportunity to participate in the team and I hope that in the future I will have the chance to work with you again.
>
> Sincerely,
> William J. Palmer

Bill Palmer made me think how lucky I was to work with officers, deputies, and agents like him in my career.

On April 7, 2005, during the USMS nationwide fugitive operation, FALCON, our teams of law enforcement were looking for Eric Byron Baker. Baker was charged with narcotics violations in Ramsey County.

About a week before this, a team of state agents raided the house where Baker was living. They did not locate him, but they did find narcotics and a number of guns.

We knew the car he was driving. A team headed by MPD Sgt. Ron Stenerson located the car at 25111 Kettle River Boulevard in Wyoming, Minneosta. The area was rural with a few other homes nearby. When Sgt. Stenerson went to the door and announced his identity, there was no response. Other members of his team heard movement inside the house. One of the members saw a person in the house that looked like Baker. Repeated attempts to get a response from anyone inside were unsuccessful. They also heard a dog.

Since this was the residence of a known associate of Baker, his car was there, and a person resembling Baker was seen in the house, Sgt. Stenerson had his team make a perimeter around the home. This was a potentially dangerous situation given Baker's previous possession of guns, and given the fact that the occupants knew the police were there to arrest him.

Sgt. Stenerson notified our command post of his situation. I told him to hold his position and be sure his people had good cover. Cover means a position that gives protection from gunfire. I activated our joint SWAT team. We would later use our entire team including hostage negotiators. The negotiators are an important element of most SWAT operations where someone is holed up in a building. The plan is usually that the initial responding officers make a perimeter to insure that the person does not escape. When the SWAT gets there and gets organized and briefed, they take over the positions that the initial responders established. The negotiators attempt to make contact with the person(s). The object is a peaceful and safe surrender.

The MPD hostage negotiations team had been training with our team. Included in the training was Kim Bonde, who was an experienced negotiator and a special deputy U.S. marshal. I had witnessed her successfully negotiating the surrender of armed barricaded persons on two occasions when she was a Champlin cop.

We established a command post near the Wyoming residence. The SWAT team led by Deputy U.S. Marshal Eric Arguello arrived and was briefed. He placed his team in position.

The negotiators set up their operation. Kim tried repeatedly to contact someone in the house by phone. Finally, she made contact with a woman. She identified herself and asked if Baker was inside. The woman said we were at the wrong house. She never answered if Baker was there. Then she hung up.

During this time, we were able to get the phone number of the owner of the house. I spoke to him and he told me his son lived in the house with some friends. He said Baker had been there but didn't know if he was there now.

After some time, Kim was able to contact a man in the residence. This guy would not say if Baker was there. Finally, she was able to convince the people to come out. A plan was devised where one of the men who came out would safely tie up the dog. The plan worked well and a girl and two men came out and were detained by the SWAT team. Each was questioned but would not tell us if Baker was there. One of the men said we would find out when we went in.

I called the owner of the house back and told him, if his son and the others refused to tell us if Baker was there, we would have no choice but to deliver gas to the house. I explained how dangerous we thought Baker was. The owner agreed to talk to his son on the phone. His son refused. I got the owner back on the phone and he told me to do what we had to.

The decision to gas the house really was not that difficult to make. Given the facts as I knew them, I wasn't about to endanger our team by asking them to enter the house. The local police officer and the sheriff were told of our intentions.

So we delivered gas, a lot of it. Our procedure was that if the decision was made to deliver gas, we used enough to insure the person(s) inside could not endure the atmosphere. No one came out. So we delivered more gas. No one came out. We eventually searched the house and found no one. I have no idea why the people wouldn't tell us if Baker was there. Just about every window in the house was broken by the gas rounds.

The Wyoming Fire Department boarded up the windows so no one could go in.

The operation was a classic barricaded suspect SWAT operation. All the right decisions were made starting with Sgt. Stenerson's decision to pull back and form a perimeter. Years later Baker was arrested in Mexico on gun possession charges. He was sentenced to a lengthy prison term. The owner of the house tried to get the USMS to pay for damages to his house. So far he has been unsuccessful.

One of the duties I have described is when I swear in law enforcement officers as special deputy U.S. marshals. The swearing in was thought to be ceremonial and not significant. I did not have this opinion. I thought it was an honor for me and for the officers. I knew many of the officers and had a great deal of respect for them. I made sure each of them understood their responsibilities and authority. I had someone photograph every swearing in that I did. I offered a copy to each officer and I kept an album. Once again, law enforcement is a team effort. Each element does its part. My part was to grant federal law enforcement authority to officers who needed it.

One of the most unusual partnerships we formed was with the Inspector Generals Office of the Department of Housing and Urban Development (HUD). There was an investigator assigned to their office in Minneapolis. My supervisor Chris Connolly established a dialogue with him. The agent, George Adams, was a real go-getter. HUD was trying to insure that people who got free or subsidized housing deserved them. We learned that many persons wanted for serious crimes were living in subsidized housing.

An effort which became known as Operation Clean House took shape. The goal was honorable. It was to arrest wanted persons in these housing units so that law-abiding, needy people could get housing. Since most of the housing was in low income areas, we had to be careful to make our intentions clear to community leaders and housing officials. We also had to consider the fact that, if we publicized out efforts, arresting these people would become very hard. So we told a limited number of people of our operation. All of these people bought into the idea.

So we formed a large contingent of officers from many departments and agencies. On April 15, 2005, we swooped down on the housing units where we believed fugitives were hiding. We made many arrests. In addition, HUD started the process to kick out people who harbored these fugitives. It was a noble effort to free subsidized housing units for those who deserved them.

I found that, except for required firearms training, no other training was required by the USMS. One of greatest concerns was that we would face an active shooter situation. The phrase *active shooter* evolved from the shootings at Columbine High School. Minnesota suffered its active shooter tragedy at Red lake Minnesota where ten people were killed. Active shooter situations have been over in minutes. The killer just keeps shooting until he is killed.

There is no time to summon a SWAT team. Officers on the scene have to act with what they have and what they know. So we began intensive training at the court buildings. The deputy U.S. marshals and court security officers would be the officers to respond. One of the keys to success was to become intimately familiar with the building. We had to train at night because the court houses were in use during the day. We needed the cooperation of the judges and other occupants of the court buildings. With one exception, all of the judges allowed us unlimited access to their courtrooms, offices, and other areas. One judge had his clerk call and tell me the judge would prefer we didn't train in any of his space. I really couldn't understand why he didn't want us prepared to deal with an emergency in his area. But I didn't want to argue. I did tell the chief judge of the situation. He offered to intercede but I told him not to.

Several of the judges asked to participate in the training by playing themselves in a scenario. After considering their offer, I told them that it would be better if they didn't know our tactics. I feared in a real situation they might inadvertently reveal our actions. They understood. I assured them that we would be as prepared as possible. Since none of the active shooter situations had been resolved successfully to date, there was little information for us to draw on. I went to the most experienced SWAT officers I could think of in our area. Sgt. Charlie Dodge of Minneapolis Police SWAT, retired MPD SWAT Sgt. Mike Quinn, retired FBI SWAT Team Leader Steve Gilkerson, USMS Supervisor Chris Connolly, USMS SWAT Leader Eric Arguello, St. Paul Police SWAT Sgt. Dave Korus, and I devised tactics that we believed would work.

Then we practiced as often as possible. The deputy U.S. marshals were really great. After a full day's work, we would train in the courthouses where they were assigned. I watched their efforts develop. These deputies were mostly not SWAT-trained, but they had experience in the courthouses and they had courage and determination. We used simunitions for realistic training. Simunitions are training ammunition fired from real guns. The ammunition stings when it hits you, but it does not cause serious damage. By using this ammunition there was no question about who was shot. The training was as realistic as any I had been involved in. We achieved a level of proficiency that made me very proud of the deputies.

The incident that occurred on March 21, 2005, on the Red Lake Indian Reservation left ten people dead and numerous students wounded. The Red Lake Tribal Police Officers who responded courageously cornered the shooter who then shot himself. These officers saved untold lives by exhibiting courage and aggressiveness. The action was recorded by cameras in the high school. I thought that the videos might give us some information that we could use if we should encounter an active shooter. So I asked the FBI special agent in charge if I could see the videos that the FBI was holding as evidence. He refused, telling me no one could see the videos. I tried to explain to him that I would assure him that the tapes would be used by the USMS only for training purposes. He refused with no reason.

I was outraged, so I went to the judge who had heard the case in Federal District Court. The judge agreed with me and said he would issue a court order ordering the FBI special agent in charge to allow me to view the tapes. I thanked the judge and told him I wanted to try one more avenue through United States Attorney Tom Heffelfinger. Tom and I had worked together and had a mutual respect for each other's responsibilities. Tom called me and said I could review the tapes in his office. I went there, reviewed the tapes, and discovered there was little we could use in our preparations.

There is more to this story. Steve Gilkerson and I were talking about the actions of the tribal police officers. These officers were heroes. They saved lives. However, they received no commendation. Sadly, we knew that, if officers from any other agencies performed like these officers did, there would be medals and media attention. I wanted to do something for them. I belonged to the International Association of Chiefs of Police (IACP). The IACP gives an award at their yearly convention called the Indian Country Officer of the Year. The special agent in charge of the Minneapolis Alcohol, Tobacco, and Firearms office, Mike Boxler, was a member of the Indian Country IACP Committee. Mike was enthusiastic to put forth the Red Lake officers for the award. It took a while but the officers were awarded the IACP Indian Country Law Enforcement Officer of the Year Award. I was honored to be one of the presenters. These heroes certainly had not sought the spotlight, but they were certainly proud to accept the award.

One of the saddest cases we worked on was the shooting murder of Michael Zebuhr. Michael was a graduate student who was visiting Minneapolis. At about 10 p.m. on March 18, 2006, Michael was walking with his mother and two others in the Uptown area of Minneapolis. Uptown is a very nice, artsy neighborhood. Suddenly they were accosted by a group of street robbers. Although Michael's mother gave up her purse without any resistance from any of the victims, one of the robbers shot Michael in the head killing him.

I learned of the killing from one of my deputies who was assigned to the MPDs Violent Crimes Apprehension Team (VCAT). Police Chief Bill McManus met with neighborhood residents and business owners in the Uptown area. Along with Bill was his homicide lieutenant, Lee Edwards. I decided to attend to show our support in the investigation. After the meeting, I told Lee Edwards that the USMS would help in any way. He thanked me.

Sgt. Al Kramer, who headed VCAT called me and told me how the investigation was going. Our two deputies and the VCAT officers worked nonstop and were able to find the mother's cell phone in a garbage can behind a residence in north Minneapolis. A fingerprint on the phone was identified. Al and I, along with most of VCAT, watched the residence for hours. Finally, we went in and talked to the residents.

Sometime later the killers were identified as Billy Ray Deshawn and Donte Jacobs. We also learned that a 1994 White Ford Taurus was used by the killers. That car was discovered torched in an apparent attempt to destroy evidence. The investigation led to Duluth where we believed the person who torched the car, Derrick Johnson, was living. Early one morning we met with Duluth police. I could see they were surprised to see Minneapolis police and USMS personnel working together on this case. We found Johnson and arrested him.

Sometime later VCAT arrested Billy Ray Johnson. The intensive hunt for Donte Jacobs, who was 17, ended when he surrendered to police in Arizona. Once more our partnership with VCAT and the MPD resulted in murderers being arrested and off the streets. We were doing exactly as I hoped we would—help make the streets safer for the people.

I took our responsibility to transport federal prisoners very seriously. The higher risk the prisoner was the more resources I devoted. One of the more noteworthy prisoners was Mohammed Abdullah Warsame. Warsame was sentenced in Federal Court in Minneapolis on July 9, 2009. He pled guilty to providing material support to al Qaeda. Because he has pled guilty, I can now share my thoughts and experiences about him.

Warsame does not look like a terrorist or what I thought a terrorist should look like. He is pudgy, mild-mannered, often smiled, and was congenial. Nevertheless, we took extraordinary precautions with him. I watched him during the period he was in our custody. Despite some unusual conditions, he never faltered. I saw in him a commitment that made me extremely careful. My commitment was carried out by our personnel who handled him. We never let our guard down. The attorney for Warsame tried to belittle our efforts to Federal Judge Jack Tunheim. To his credit, the Judge asked me many questions about our security precautions, but in the end told me that he had confidence in our efforts. I wish I could say more about the precautions, but I can't. Suffice it to say that once again I was proud of our team.

In July of 2005, USMS Director Ben Reyna resigned. Director Reyna was President Bush's choice. Ben Reyna was the former chief of police of the Brownsville, Texas, PD. He was not the typical bureaucrat. He was a very sociable person, easy to talk to, and very supportive of the efforts of the U.S. marshals. I got along well with him and I felt he appreciated my efforts.

Shortly thereafter, Deputy Director Don Gambatesa also left. I first met him when he interviewed me for the U.S. marshals position. Don was also not the typical bureaucrat. He was a retired secret service agent. I had many good conversations with him and he was always supportive.

Changes were coming to the USMS that were to influence my decision to retire. John Clark was appointed acting director and then director on March 17, 2006. Mr. Clark was very different from Ben Reyna and Don Gambatesa. Clark had risen through the ranks of the USMS. He worked within the bureaucracy and it was the way he knew. Things started to change quickly. It was apparent to me that he had great confidence in the long-time employees of the service and less confidence in the appointed U.S. marshals. Advisory boards that were tasked with shaping USMS policy were formed. Their membership was primarily career employees. The few times I had occasion to talk to Director Clark, my sense was that my offers to contribute on policy matters were disregarded. A new deputy director, Robert Trono, was appointed. He was employed by the U.S. Department of Justice since 1995. Again, my few encounters with him left me with negative vibes.

I think the fact is that, when you are appointed to head an agency where you have not previously served, you don't have any preconceived notions. You have no favorites and everyone has to prove themselves. On the other hand, when you have worked in an agency for a long time, you do have favorites and you naturally rely on those favorites. So, as 2006 went on, I began to think of retirement. Finally, my wife Kim and I decided that it was time to leave. I retired on December 31, 2006.

Some of my employees asked if I wanted a party. I declined. I had many parties over the years and now I just wanted to leave quietly. In fact, a reporter wrote that after 44 years of service, I simply quietly left.

Pat Mahaney and Al at Al's retirement

Looking Back

✦

I learned a lot about life from my New York City friends Pat and Phil Mahaney, Mike Marro, and Johnny Shea. From them I learned that common sense, physical courage, and hard work are more important than formal education.

Mom and Dad taught me a work ethic that stayed with me throughout my life. I remain proud of my dad who worked hard, loved a beer or two, and loved singing with his family as he played the piano. My dad's early death at 47 instilled in me a lifelong physical fitness ethic.

My mom was a survivor. She beat colon cancer in a time when all that was done was cut out the cancer and hope. After my dad died, she found a wonderful man, Stanley. They lived happily for 20 years until he died. She taught me that life is worth making comebacks from tragedies.

The FBI was as diverse a group as you can imagine. Agents were ex-military, former school teachers, lawyers, accountants, business people, and a smattering of any other type of professional you can think of. Personalities range from gentle to aggressive know-it-alls.

The working conditions are clean and sterile in most cases. Violence rarely occurs and, when it does, it has a profound impact. The FBI often promotes the wrong people. The agency calls its leaders managers and administrators.

The term leader is not used. So most of the time that's what they get, administrators, not leaders. There have been exceptions and leaders have developed from the ranks of the administrators.

Some of the noteworthy and exceptional leaders that I knew are Art Nehrbass, Jim Murphy, Milt Ahlerich, and Joe Martinolich from NYC. There were Charles Bates in San Francisco, and John Otto, Larry Lawler, Dick Blay, and Nick O'Hara, all of whom I met in Minneapolis.

The fact remains that most of the FBI's managers and administrators have little understanding of how to lead toward efficiency and effectiveness. A professional arrogance developed among the administrators. This arrogance spread to many of the agents. It was a battle for the agents who wanted to work as equals with police. I was one of those agents who felt like a salmon swimming upstream.

I was often told by my supervisors and by some agents that police were generally less competent than FBI agents. The same people said the police couldn't be trusted and were often brutal. I found just the opposite to be true, whether it was the NYPD, San Francisco PD, Rapid City PD, Grand Forks PD, Minneapolis PD, Champlin PD, and countless others.

In recent years, the FBI has greatly increased its resources devoted to white-collar crime and counter-terrorism. Resources devoted to fighting violent crime have decreased. The problem is that the FBI administrators won't admit this. As U.S. marshal I tried to organize a multi-agency fugitive task force. The FBI agent in charge refused to participate, telling me the FBI only participates in task forces when they are in charge. When I questioned the ability of the FBI to devote adequate resources to a fugitive task force, the SAC told me they don't give up anything.

Despite all of these shortcomings, many of the brightest, hardworking, law enforcement professionals I have had the pleasure of working with are FBI agents.

I will always have a special place in my heart and in my memory for the paramedics we worked with on the FBI SWAT team. All of these fine public servants had a relationship with us that went far beyond the call of duty. Mike Murphy volunteered to man a perimeter post with an M-16 rifle during the siege of the CSA compound in Arkansas. Nancy Larson taught me a lesson I will never forget. During a training exercise, she volunteered to play an armed criminal. We all knew she would be carrying some sort of dangerous weapon. As the scenario unfolded, other SWAT team members and I confronted this potentially armed and dangerous woman. It was my job to search her. Nancy is an attractive lady and I was reluctant to search her thoroughly, even though we thought she was armed. So I did a cursory search and as I was handcuffing her she pulled out a blank firing gun and shot me numerous times. From that day forward, when I had to search a woman, I did it thoroughly or I held her at gunpoint until a female officer arrived to do the search. Thanks Nancy.

After I left the FBI, I remember Nancy calling me one Saturday morning. She explained that the SWAT team was leaving for a mission out west and she was told that none of the medics could come. She couldn't understand why, after all they had done with the team; they would not be called to go. I tried to explain that it was likely the bureaucrats who run the FBI made this decision without knowing how valuable the medics were. She was in tears when she told me she couldn't live with herself if one of the members was injured or killed and their medics weren't there to help.

Paramedic Mike Peach was never in good physical condition. But he and all the medics participated fully in the strenuous physical training the SWAT team did. We trained in the Metrodome in Minneapolis. We used to run around the concourse during the winter. I can see Mike panting and really working hard to keep up with us. I don't know how he did it but he did.

These were without exception special people.

Recently, I received a DVD from one of the paramedics, Mike Murphy. You might remember Mike from earlier in the book. Mike was the former navy medic, who saw action in Vietnam, serving as a navy corpsman with the marines. Mike was with us in Arkansas during the siege at the Covenant, Sword and Arm of the Lord (CSA) compound. The DVD he sent me is a recording of the 2007 North Memorial Medical Center annual awards ceremony for public safety personnel. He gave the keynote address. In the address, Mike speaks of the importance of having heroes in our lives. Along with the video he sent a note that says in part:

> I wanted you to see this speech because it was written about you and the rest of the team that I am so very proud to have been a part of. . . . It is my tribute to you and the team and all the dedicated "soldiers" I have known.
>
> . . . I have learned from many people in my life, but inspired by only a handful. You can count yourself among those few. If I have earned your respect in return, I can do no better. Thank you, my friend.
>
> (signed)
>
> Mike

Yes, Mike, you have earned my respect and love.

The military has a saying: rank has its privilege (RHIP). Rank also has its responsibilities. There is another saying that I found true: the commander is responsible for all the troops do and fail to do.

The higher in an organization you are the greater the responsibility. As an army lieutenant and captain I was responsible to my commanding officer. As an FBI agent and supervisor I was responsible to my superior. In both cases, at the level I was, I was not responsible nor did I have to answer to civilian authorities, the media, or the citizens.

That all changed when I became police chief. Now I was responsible to the mayor, the city council, the city administrator, and the citizens. I was very visible. Whenever my cops did something noteworthy, whether it was good or bad, I was told and held responsible. Even if I wasn't present when the cops acted, I, the commanding officer was responsible for their actions. That was no problem to me. I accepted the responsibility enthusiastically. The buck stopped with me.

As chief I also had some privileges. My pay was the highest in the department. I drove a new police squad (car). I had the option of wearing a uniform or civilian clothes.

This is what my deputy chief, Al Bruns, wrote about working with me:

I was introduced to Al Garber when he became chief of police for the Champlin Police Department. Al had recently retired from the F.B.I., but wasn't ready to totally retire by any means. At the time, I was sergeant of investigation. I was not used to a chief wanting to know everything about every case the investigation unit handled. I found out in a hurry that Al Garber was very much hands on, more so than any other chief I had ever worked for.

Shortly after Al became chief, the captain of our department became ill and ultimately retired. I then became second in command and worked directly with Chief Garber.

Chief Garber is a law enforcement officer through and through. Whether as a federal agent or chief of police, he wanted to be on the street working directly with the officers. As Al Garber and I worked together, I developed a great respect for him. I am proud to have him as my friend.

Best wishes,

Allen (Al) Bruns, Chief of Police

Champlin Police Department, Retired

When I moved on the Minnesota Department of Natural Resources, I became accountable and responsible on a far greater scale. I held my staff responsible for the actions or inactions of the people who worked for them. However, it was me the media came after. It was me who the governor, the state senators, and the state representatives wanted answers from. Again, I enthusiastically accepted this responsibility. Where I wouldn't accept responsibility was when employees went to the media or to legislators to try to get something that benefited them or to give excuses for their actions. As DNR Commissioner I had some privileges. I was the highest paid employee in the DNR. I drove a new state car with a reserved parking space. I had a comfortable and private office.

I remember trying to explain RHIP to my assistant commissioner for operations, Brad Moore. Brad was a hard-working career employee. He did not have any military experience. Brad just could not understand why he deserved a reserved parking space. He couldn't understand why his employees should call him commissioner and not Brad. He believed he should not have any privileges his employees didn't have. Brad never realized the intangible benefits that the privileges of his position could bring to him. It is interesting that Brad later became the commissioner of the Minnesota Pollution Control Agency. I met with him not long ago and he said he has his own reserved parking space and requires his employees address him as commissioner. He finally got it.

On October 16, 2008, I spoke with Steven Bosacker, who was Governor Ventura's chief of staff. Steven was person who ran the day-to-day operations of the Ventura administration. Steven is blessed with the unusual skill of being able to see the big picture. He always amazed me with his ability to be knowledgeable in so many diverse areas. I asked Steven a number of questions that I hoped would prompt him to reflect on my service as DNR commissioner.

This is a summary of our conversation: I was selected to head DNR because I had impressed the governor during my interview for the position of commissioner of the Department of Public Safety. The governor was looking for people who simply wanted to serve.

However, he had promised the public safety job to Charley Weaver. When the DNR commissioner candidate was forced to remove his name from consideration, the governor chose me. I was chosen because of my enforcement and regulatory experience. The governor saw the DNR as a regulatory, enforcement agency overlaid on natural resources issues.

The governor saw my strengths as loyalty and principled leadership. Steven had some hesitation about me as DNR commissioner. He didn't know if I had an interest in natural resource issues. He was concerned about my ability to bridge the gaps between conservationists, hunters, environmentalists, and the DNR.

The fact that my name was kept secret until the formal announcement did not surprise Steven. He said the governor's team of advisers knew they had to have privacy to bounce around ideas. They knew they needed the room to brainstorm and to make mistakes. He added that Minnesotans in general respected Governor Ventura. They wanted to give him a chance to succeed.

Steven said that, even in the area of governmental branch relations where

I was weak, I was willing to learn about the relationship between the executive and legislative branches. The fact that I had no ties or partisanship gave me the strength to operate.

Since so many of the governor's cabinet was learning, Steven convinced the governor to attend all cabinet meetings. During these meetings, Steven was concerned that my strong personality would clash with other commissioners.

As he reflected on the Ventura years, he had no major concerns about me. He learned that I would always keep him advised of potentially explosive issues before they became public. He admired my ability to sit down with people from all sides and "manage from the center." He and the governor wanted "people who were not done learning." I lived this principle.

Steven told me the most significant accomplishment my administration made was to bring new forest management to Minnesota after my trip to Finland. He was proud that I "learned from the world."

His greatest disappointment was that he wished the DNR would have been more involved in water management issues, specifically the effects of chemical runoff from farm lands into the Mississippi River. The entire length of the river was ultimately affected. The governor was very concerned that our team was not coordinated. We did not balance the use of farmland in relation to its effect on water into the future. Perhaps if we'd had a second four-year term, we might have gotten our act together.

All things considered, Steven would still have chosen me for public safety commissioner. But he was really glad the governor gave me, a non-traditionalist, a chance to be in the natural resources arena.

For my part, I learned a lot from Steven. He was even-tempered and never spoke badly behind a person's back. He is an honorable man, and that is why the governor picked him as his right-hand man.

As I looked back, I called on a person I greatly respect, Jack Rajala, to reflect on my DNR administration. I wrote about Jack earlier. He and his family own about 35,000 acres of forest land. In the some 50 years he has been involved, over five million white pines have been planted on his land. I had not spoken with Jack since I left the DNR in 2002. I called him recently and asked if he would meet me to discuss my administration. He said, of course. This is a summary of his thoughts.

When he first heard that I was Governor Ventura's choice to be commissioner, he thought, who is he? He wondered if I was the governor's second choice since his first appointee quit after a few weeks.

Jack had no idea where the governor stood on natural resource issues. Now he appointed an unknown. Jack had an open mind toward me. He was looking for change and he hoped I would be approachable. He knew that the DNR was the driving force in forestry. The DNR really directed the public discussion. If the DNR has strong leadership, then forestry moves ahead. No one knew the governor or me or what our ideas about forestry were.

As time passed, Jack learned that I asked good questions. I didn't tell people when I didn't know. Everyone was interested in how I would deal with the imbedded DNR employees. He was also curious about whether I would come to northern Minnesota where forestry was most important.

Jack and I first met at a Minnesota Forest Industries Association meeting in Duluth. I listened and didn't talk much. He thought I took all the advice well and assimilated it. In one of my later speeches, I talked about change. He thought I had a sense of the importance of the forests to jobs and people overall. He saw that I related well and trusted the people involved in forestry. I asked what we can change to make things better.

Jack became a strong supporter of the Forestry Summit and the Demonstration Forest. The Demonstration Forest is a large landscape depiction of what is going on in forestry across the full spectrum of ownership, private, public, and non-profit. Jack saw me pushing for change and asking questions. The presence of the governor at the Summit really showed how important it was.

Although many people challenged my ideas, I had the backing of loggers, foresters, and industry to get rolling toward change. As a result of the Summit, my ideas were widely accepted by the Minnesota Forest Resources Council and the Minnesota Forest Resources Partnership. Both of these organizations put their strong support behind me. This led to a commitment on the part of landowners to support the Demonstration Forest. When I committed DNR lands, the counties and major industry followed. DNR staffed the forest with DNR Regional Forester Chuck Spodin in charge.

Jack said that without leadership from the top, the DNR would not be the Minnesota forestry leader.

To me, the most important thought that Jack had was why my book was so important. Walk-away forestry doesn't work. What you do today is only a beginning. You, and those who follow you, must be there for the life of the forest. My book is important because it will be a record so that all who are interested can stay connected to the initiatives we started. Continuing these initiatives is the only way they will amount to anything.

Jack gave an example of why the record is so important. During the administration of former Governor Perpich, some $35 million was appropriated from the federal government and from Minnesota for forest intensification. This money was a settlement for locking up 900,000 acres of state and federal forest land to make up the Boundary Waters Canoe Area (BWCA). Years later, no one can show what happened to the $35 million.

One of my decisions after the huge blowdown in the BWCA in 2000 impressed Jack. I ordered the DNR to survey state land that bordered the BWCA. Then the DNR set up salvage timber sales to reduce fire danger, get regeneration going, and bring some revenue to the state.

Jack and his associates felt that a new level of bi-lateral cooperation had been reached. I fought hard to get money for the new way of forest management. I largely answered the critics and tempered the ongoing debate. My administration had a mission and was moving on. The Demonstration Forest put a positive in place that trumped all the negatives.

Every acre that is to be harvested for timber must have a plan that will result in new life. If you end the life of the land, you must make a new life. This is epitomized by the fieve million white pine trees growing on Rajala land. The days of just cutting trees is done. Now land must be managed.

These thoughts by Jack Rajala made me again realize how fortunate I was to have the opportunity to meet and work with him.

As U.S. marshal, I had a free reign to use our resources as I saw fit. What I didn't realize until later in my term, was that there were officials in Washington who didn't agree with my way of doing business. They subtlety withdrew support and eventually made me feel quite alone. What I came to realize was that the new USMS administration would not tolerate a U.S. marshal who championed positive change. Status quo was the name of the game.

I have mentioned my dear friend and longtime partner, Steve Gilkerson often. When I asked Steve to write what it was like working with me he wrote:

> I first met Al in 1970 when he and I worked together on the FBI Truck Hijacking Squad in New York. Since that time I have worked for and with Al on the Minneapolis FBI Criminal Investigations Squad, FBI Minneapolis SWAT Team, The Minnesota Fugitive Task Force, the Champlin Police Department, and the U.S. Marshals Service. These working relationships encompass a period from 1970 to 2005. I can *say* without any reservation that as both an investigator and a supervisor I have NEVER met another person I would rate higher than Al in integrity, loyalty, dedication, intensity, capability, innovation, performance in achieving the goals, OF EVERY UNIT THAT HE AND I WORKED ON. These traits did not diminish one bit in the 35 years I worked with Al. They were recognized by others as well as me and, as a result, Al was assigned the most difficult and dangerous jobs on the Hijack Squad, the Criminal Squad, and the SWAT Team. They also were reasons Al became the SWAT Team Leader, FBI Supervisor, Police Chief, DNR Commissioner, and U.S. Marshal. I always considered Al to be the FBI equivalent of General George Patton, an American hero with many of the same traits.

After reading what Steve wrote I was overwhelmed. Throughout our long friendship we have never expressed our respect for each other. That's just the way it is. The people who are really close to me and with whom I have experienced life and death don't need to say how we felt. We express it through actions.

I asked Governor Ventura if he would consent to include his recollections in this book. He graciously and enthusiastically agreed. This what he said:

I am different than most chief executives in that I value a person's character more than the schools and the courses a person may have attended.

When filling executive posts, I also took an unorthodox approach. I wanted people who were not connected to the established lines of power. I wanted fresh faces that were not tied down to old connections.

I was fortunate to have met Al Garber when I needed a new commissioner of the Minnesota Department of Natural Resources. He had the qualities of diligence, honesty, and loyalty; the qualities that I valued most. That, of course, was in addition to his achievements as a U.S. Army Ranger, FBI agent of more than two decades, and police chief. In short, he was my kind of guy.

He was an independent voice with literally no extraneous loyalties.

I met Al when I interviewed him for the job of commissioner of the Minnesota department of public safety. Although I was mayor of Brooklyn Park, Minnesota, at the time when he was chief of police of neighboring Champlin Police Department, we had never met.

I was looking for a person who had the qualities of honesty and loyalty, and a work ethic second to none. It was really an interesting interview. We actually spoke more about our life experiences than we did about the job. Our military experiences made the rest of the interview something more than a job interview.

At the conclusion of the interview, I came to the conclusion that Al would be a welcome member of my team. However, based on advice I had been given, I decided that Charlie Weaver would be my Public Safety Commissioner. As time passed I regretted my decision not to give the public safety job to Al.

However, I asked Al if I could call on him in the future. He didn't hesitate for a moment when he answered yes.

It's funny how things work out. About two weeks later my candidate for commissioner of the Department of Natural Resources withdrew his name. I did some checking concerning Al Garber's background. One of the people I contacted was Don Glasser, an FBI agent. Don knew Al when both were FBI agents. Don told me Al was loyal, honest, and hard-working. My way of choosing people to work for me is to go to trusted sources.

I was not as interested in Al's knowledge of the DNR as I was interested in his personal qualities. In fact, I was looking for a new face who could manage an agency that had a generally bad reputation in terms of accepting new ideas and producing results. After I looked at his experience, I decided Al would be the type of person I needed to head the the DNR.

When he came to see me, I told him I needed his help and asked him to head the DNR. He told me he was honored to be offered the position, but that he didn't know much about the agency. I told him that he had spent his career so far protecting human life and now he would be protecting wildlife. He accepted.

What followed in the next two weeks was really astounding in government. We kept his name a secret until I made the public announcement. Given the fact that the media was normally all over the DNR, it was amazing that his name didn't leak out. This was a tribute to the type of people who were working for me. I had no leaks.

When I introduced Al to the media, they were shocked. How could I appoint a person who was not an insider? I guess it took them sometime to learn that being an insider was not important to me.

Al gained Senate confirmation quickly and without any trouble.

What I came to appreciate about Al was that he was always honest with me. I knew he would never tell me what he thought I wanted to hear if it was not the truth. I also liked the fact that he knew I had a busy schedule. When we met, he was thoroughly prepared to discuss the issue. He was not reluctant to bring one of his staff to the meetings, if he was not familiar with the issue.

I could depend on him to get me answers. He was not the kind of person who would beat around the bush. I remember an incident that illustrated his traits of honesty and candidness. A proposal had been made to me to release a group of inmates who were serving time for lesser drug offenses in state prisons. When he heard about the proposal, he came to talk to me. I think he knew that I was strongly in favor of the proposal. Nevertheless, he told me that many of these inmates had a history of violence and other major offenses. He asked me to consider each inmate's background before releasing them. I have to admit I had not considered Al's ideas. Of course there were other factors that I considered before I made my final decision, but I did appreciate his candid comments based on his experience.

Another quality that was valuable to me was that he was very selective in asking me to appear at DNR events. I came to learn that when he did ask there were very good reasons. When he announced his choices for deputy and assistant commissioner, he asked me to be there. I did attend.

One of the most significant events during his time as commissioner was the Forest Summit. He asked me to attend and give opening remarks. I did, and the conference was a resounding success.

Loyalty is a two-way street. There were times when people came to me seeking to circumvent the commissioner.

I always told them I had a DNR commissioner to deal with their issue. In return, Al was loyal to me without exception. I remember the time when my comments to Playboy magazine got me a lot of negative press. When I told my cabinet members that I was sorry for any negative effects my comments had on them, Al stood up and told me in front of my entire executive staff that he had not lost my loyalty. He said I earned his loyalty.

When Al contacted me to write an introduction for his book, I accepted without hesitation.

The day that the governor gave me his comments, we spent almost three hours talking about all sorts of things. Nothing has changed as far as I am concerned. The governor is a patriot and a rebel. He is deeply concerned about the future of our great country. His common sense approach to the most serious issues still amazes me. I don't think we have seen the last of Governor Jesse Ventura, at least I hope not.

One of persons who I was closest to is my ex-partner in the FBI, Tom Lagatol. I have told a lot about Tom earlier in the book. I asked Tom if he would write something for my book. This is what he wrote:

My Partner—Al Garber

I expect there are many ways to describe my dear friend Al, but I'll relate an event that had nothing to do with our working together. It, in my opinion, is more than representative or typical; it's what one comes to expect after knowing him as a friend for any length of time.

As the end of May 2003 was approaching, I had been planning a celebration in honor of my son. He was graduating from the United

States Military Academy at West Point and I wanted both friends and family to be with me as I honored and celebrated his accomplishment. It was going to be an affair to remember. Heck, I spent months planning it, assembling the guest list, having printed invitations, food, entertainment . . . you get the idea.

Well, as the time to send out invitations came, I wanted to give my good friend more than an impersonal, mailed invitation. I wanted to tell him about it personally; so I called him. I didn't really expect Al to come to the affair as we now live half a country apart. I simply wanted to tell him about it and my son. We exchanged the usual pleasantries and, when I told him that while I would be happy and proud to have him there, I truly understood and didn't really expect him to attend. I should have expected his response but to be honest it kind of choked me up a little. He said, I'll be there. You just tell me where and when. I'll be the second proudest father there. To, and for me, simply stated, that's Al Garber.

I could write more . . . pages more, probably a book's worth of the escapades we had together over some seven or eight years; but it really all boils down to a few words, a couple of sentences something like this: Men of honor live their lives in a way that most people don't remotely understand. They do what they do because it is right, not expecting favor or reward. Having Al as a friend is an honor, one that I will hold dear long after anyone will remember what I've written here.

Tom Lagatol
Special Agent FBI, Retired
1969–2002

What is remarkable to me is that after all of the difficulties I had in fitting the mold that the FBI wanted for me, two of my dearest friends are retired FBI agents. Go figure.

The Bucket
(Making a Difference)

✦

One of the things I've wondered about as I wrote this book is have I made a difference? I have long subscribed to the "bucket theory." The theory says that life is like a bucket of water. To see if you have made a difference you put your hand in a bucket of water and stir the water. Then you pull your hand out and wait a minute. At the end of a minute, look at the water and you will see no change.

The theory is supposed to equate to life. If you buy into the theory you have to conclude that you made no difference.

I guess I believed in the "bucket theory" until just the other day. I had an experience that convinced me that the theory is not so simple.

I was riding to the airport in a cab driven by Jim Thoreson. I know Jim because he is the commander of our local American Legion Post. We talked about the Legion and all that Jim does for the members. He really is the glue that holds the Legion Post together. He devotes countless volunteer hours.

Many of his clients that he drives as a taxicab driver are elderly and handicapped. They rely on Jim to take them shopping, be on time for doctors appointments, and otherwise be their lifeline for everyday activities.

He goes the extra mile, like carrying their groceries to the door, and making sure he leaves in time considering weather for their doctor's appointments.

Jim is considering moving from Minnesota to Alabama so he can be near his children. I remarked that the Legion and the elderly will miss him greatly. That's when he told me he believes in the "bucket theory." He concluded that he will not be missed and that others will take his place.

He really lit up a light bulb in my brain. I began to reflect on my life and whether I have made a difference. I concluded that there are two buckets. One is an organization bucket and the other is a people bucket.

If you put your hand in the organization bucket, it can be pretty discouraging. For Jim, the American Legion and the cab company will not change after he leaves.

For me, despite all I have tried to accomplish through hard work and dedication to duty, I have not changed any organization in a lasting way.

The U.S. Army, the FBI, the Champlin police, the Minnesota DNR, and the United States Marshals Service conduct business as usual. Al Garber made no lasting changes either good or bad.

However, the people bucket is where we have all made a difference. Those of us in the local Legion Post will not forget Commander Jim Thoreson and all he has done for us. The elderly whose groceries he carried; got them to their doctor's appointments on time; and came promptly when they called, will, I am certain, always cherish him.

My friend retired Minneapolis Sgt. Mike Quinn expressed the difference we have made:

> I got to know Al when he was looking for someone to teach chemical agents at his SWAT schools. I was the chemical agents trainer for the Minneapolis Police Emergency Response Unit at that time. I helped with a number of SWAT schools in Minnesota, North and South Dakota, and Iowa over a period of several years.
>
> What I remember about all these schools and the thousands of students was the officer survival tactics that Al and Steve Gilkerson brought to these schools. Most of those officers had never received that kind of training. I know there is no way to measure what hasn't

happened, but I know from my 30 years of experience in law enforcement that Al and Steve saved many lives; lives that would have been lost without that training. That training survives to this day as officers generations behind us continue to practice the techniques brought to Minnesota by Al Garber and Steve Gilkerson, two of the best trainers I have ever had the pleasure to know.

Those new officers will never know the difference that was made, but I do, and I will be eternally grateful to Al and Steve for the lives they saved.

Michael W. Quinn
Sergeant, Minneapolis Police (Retired)

For me Sgt. Roger Spradlin became a proud U.S. Army Ranger, in part as a result of my encouragement. I am forever sorry that he lost his life fighting in Vietnam. Lt. Michael V. Santo became a fine officer who served proudly in Vietnam. I believe his success started with whatever I was able to impart to him when he was a brand new officer. Although I haven't seen Mike in many years, his memory is fresh and clear in my mind.

Retired FBI agents Tom Lagatol and Steve Gilkerson have been forever influenced by our experiences. Needless to say, my life has been shaped by those same experiences.

There are two police officers, among the many Steve and I worked with, who will certainly never forget us. These two officers of the Winnipeg, Manitoba, Police Department told us how a tactic we taught them saved their lives. This tactic originated with the Israeli military. It is used when searching a building for armed adversaries. We taught them how to do the unexpected. About two weeks after the class, the Winnipeg officers were searching a supermarket for two armed "ass holes." When the officers came to a door, they did the unexpected. The "ass holes" shot where they expected the officers to be. This gave the officers a chance to end the gun battle.

Retired Minneapolis Police Sgt. Bob Schnickel told me that the highlight of his long police career was being a member of the only FBI/Police SWAT team ever, our team.

My wife, Kim, whom I first met when I was chief of the Champlin

Police, expressed very well how I touched her life forever, both positive and negative.

The current commissioner of the Minnesota Pollution Control Agency, Brad Moore, was my assistant commissioner when I was DNR commissioner. Brad told me he now understands that rank has its privileges along with its responsibilities. He is addressed as commissioner and has his own parking space. Brad also told me he will always remember that I told him there are very few life and death decisions we have to make. So in most cases be cool, take your time, and don't look back.

Sgt. Bill Palmer, Minneapolis PD, so eloquently wrote earlier in the book how important his participation in the only USMS/MPD SWAT team was to him.

When I called Governor Ventura to ask if he would contribute to my book, he said, "Yes, Commissioner, I would be glad to."

The writings of my son are so important. I did make a difference.

I was fortunate to put my hand in the bucket again in becoming a husband and a (step) father. My bucket has had ripples I never imagined. For all these years, I thought the ripples were about work first, and family and loved ones second. Now I realize my influence has been on family and loved ones first and career second.

I am immensely proud that I have made a lasting impression on the most important people in my life. I wish you the same.